Isle of Memories

Snapshots of a childhood on the
Isle of Wight in 1950s and 1960s

by
Jo Cooper

Isle of Memories by Jo Cooper
ISBN-13: 978-1539448532
ISNB-10: 1539448533

First Published in 2016 by Jo Cooper

Copyright © 2016 Jo Cooper

All rights reserved.

No part of this book may be reproduced or transmitted in any form or by any other means, electronic or mechanical, including photocopying and recording, or by any information storage and retrieval system, without written permission from the publisher.

All and any infringements will be pursued to the extent of current copyright legislation.

The photos in this book were mostly taken by my father and are owned by me. There are a few others taken by outside sources. Whilst every effort has been made to contact the copyright owners of some photographs and acknowledge them it was not possible in all cases. Copyright owners are invited to contact the author so that acknowledgements can be stated in any future edition.

**Dedicated to
Carolyn Mary Bennison,
my sister and my friend.**

Acknowledgement

I wish to record my thanks to Sue Court who helped me discover my ability to recall and write my story. I wish also to thank Yvonne Gilbert who proof read my manuscript and the many friends in Binstead and on the island whose stories I have included and who helped me uncover more childhood memories. Thanks also to Robert, my husband who has supported me throughout the writing of this book and to my children, grandchildren, nieces and brother in law who have patiently listened to me telling endless stories of my childhood.

CONTENTS

Map – Binstead in the early 1950s

Introduction

1	Falling Downstairs: My First Memories	1
2	Mother	9
3	Leys	22
4	Our Car called Anna	38
5	Safe and Secure	53
6	The Shelling of Scarborough	67
7	Play	75
8	Our Pets and Other Animals	86
9	Accidents & Injuries	92
10	Beaches	99
11	Shopping and Rationing	111
12	Celebrations	120
13	PNEU and Binstead School	132
14	May Days, Carnivals and Dressing Up	143
15	God and the Convent School	152
16	Holy Cross Church	165
17	Teenage Years	174
18	Whispers	182
19	The College and Leaving Home	189
20	Sad Days	195
21	Robert	204
	Postscript	212

Binstead in the 1950s

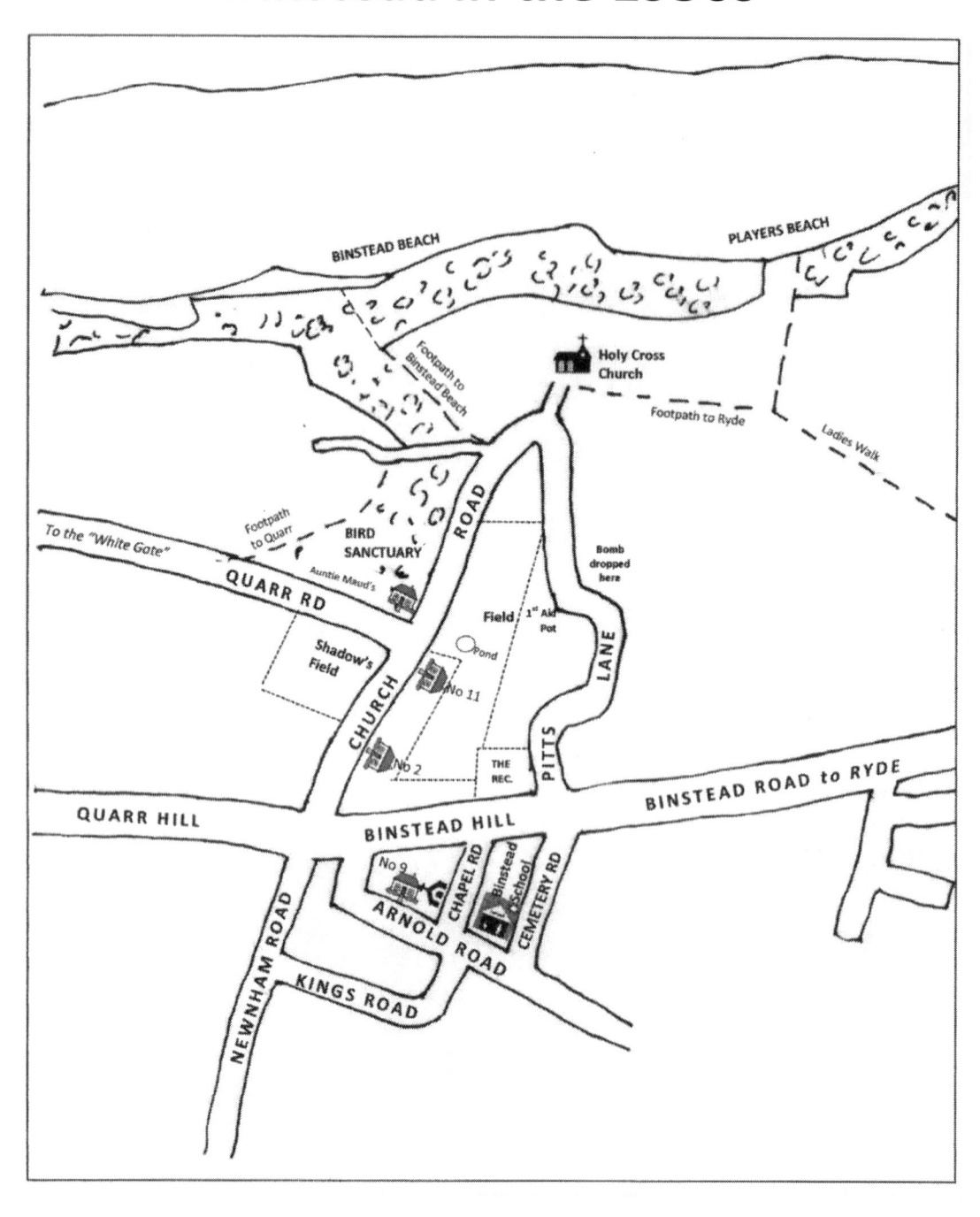

INTRODUCTION

Carolyn and I sat in the cottage in silence. 'There's a lot to sort out,' Carolyn said.

'I hate that job,' I replied.

'I know,' she said. 'It is never pleasant.'

It was October 2001 when Mother died. After a major operation on her spine she gradually became weaker and so she spent the last months of her life in a nursing home in Wootton.

She had a strong heart but her mind was going and she was not expected to return to the cottage. Her house had to be sold to pay for her care in the nursing home. My sister Carolyn and her husband David had always loved it and so they bought the cottage intending to live there when David retired. Carolyn and David had sorted out a lot of mother's possessions already.

'There's not a lot left to share out really,' Carolyn went on.

'I just want things to remind me of her,' I said, 'that's all. I have a house full of furniture I don't really need any more.'

Walking back from the Appley Beach, Mum and the author's son Philip stride along Ryde Esplanade. Their arms are around each other.

Carolyn sighed, 'So are there any items of furniture that you do want?'

I wandered around the room, 'I'd like to have Mummy's small desk as it was so personal to her. She kept all her special things in there.'

'And I'd like to have Daddy's desk if that's alright with you,' Carolyn replied. Daddy had died in January 1967 and Mum had kept his desk. It had an ornate bookcase top with glass doors. In this she had displayed her ceramics.

I opened Mum's desk and found a large envelope stuffed full of letters I had sent to her from Paris when I was 18. 'And look there are letters here from you too,' I said to Carolyn.

I cuddled the letters as they had meant a lot to her. 'I would like to have all Daddy's photos, please, if you don't mind. They will always be there for you to look at.'

'That's a good idea,' Carolyn said

Taken with Dad's automatic shutter release, the Drawbridge Family pose during a meal in the garden at Leys Church Road Binstead.

I picked up a large cardboard packing case and went to the bottom two drawers of Daddy's desk. There were albums and boxes of prints. I packed them into the box. Robert, my husband, put the box in the boot of the car and we returned home to Greenford in West London.

I couldn't face opening the box for a couple of months. When I did I realised that there was hardly any information written about the prints. The pictures in the albums were without any titles, dates or place names. I recognised most of the faces but that was all.

I started to file them under headings. There were lots of us at various beaches on the Island so that was my first title, "Beaches". Daddy loved taking pictures of the three of us as he was very proud of his family. There was another title: "The 3 of Us". I found pictures of endless views none of which I recognised. As I fingered each picture I sat and smiled as I remembered my childhood on the Isle of Wight. Every photo ignited a memory.

Suddenly I found a more recent picture. It was of Mum with my son Philip then aged 11 walking from the beach at Appley near Ryde. He had his arm around her as if to say 'I love you' and she had reciprocated and put her arm was around his shoulder. A little uncomfortably I thought. I put the picture down on the desk to keep safe and look at again.

Daddy loved his camera. He had a gift in creating pictures and then taking photos.

'Now you sit there and read a book.' he said. 'I want to take a photo.' He also loved developing the pictures in the loft at our house in Binstead.

One day Dad announced he had a new gadget to fasten to his camera. 'Look, I attach this to the camera, compose the picture, set the timer off and go back to my place and we can all be in the shot.'

Owing to deafness Daddy often didn't hear the click of the shutter. 'Has it clicked?' he asked Mum out of the corner of his mouth.

'I think so,' she said without moving her head.

He took one such picture of Mum and himself on Binstead Beach. They were sitting side by side in front of the tree we climbed. Mummy was sitting in an old deck metal chair. Behind Mummy's head was a wooden headboard which had been mended by Dad. Mummy was going to cover and pad this to make a comfortable head rest. It was a job that was never done. Always conscious of her appearance she had a scarf neatly around her neck. Her hair was tidy and smoothed back into a bun. Daddy looked relaxed and dressed for the beach. His hair was ruffled, his shirt open at the neck and he was wearing his sports jacket. Although not seen in the picture I imagine he was wearing his bathing trunks. He always did when going to the beach.

Carolyn and I used to get terribly embarrassed as he walked down to the beach from our house wearing his jacket, swimming trunks and brown lace up leather shoes. I stroked their faces as if doing so I could touch them again.

I longed to go back and have dinner with them. I wanted to lay the table with two knives, two forks, a spoon and a serviette each as mother had always insisted.

It struck me at that moment that when I die these photos will be handed on. What will my children do with them? They will not know what was happening in each picture and in some who the people were. I looked at the lovely photos lying on the floor all around me.

I decided that they must not remain as just black and white pictures of people and places without any story. I resolved to write about the pictures so that

Another photo taken with Dad's automatic shutter release, Mum and Dad enjoy an afternoon on Binstead Beach.

my children and grandchildren could understand my happy childhood in the 1950s and 1960s.

At first I threw these stories down on the computer randomly. I scanned the picture into the computer and put the picture at the top of the page and below it I typed my memories. I had no idea of how to do it. No idea of how I could write a story that my children would enjoy and would enhance a photo taken by Father. I wrote as if I was telling my family about the event surrounding the picture. It was an enjoyable task but daunting because there were so many photos. I started with a burst of enthusiasm, but as my work of running a swim school became more demanding I closed the box and left it until I had time. The box stayed shut for many years.

My husband, Bob retired in 2013 and we started to pack up as we had bought a house on the Isle of Wight. We already owned a holiday flat in the Strand in Ryde and planned to stay there until the renovations and extensions had been done to the house. The flat was furnished so we put our London furniture into store together with the box of photos.

'There is no room for unnecessary boxes at the flat,' Bob insisted. 'There just isn't any space.'

A year later we moved in and our possessions were delivered to our bungalow called "Shadowsfield". There was the box full of the photos just as I had left it. I reopened the file on my computer and decided I was going to put all my memories into one book. I reread what I had composed all those years ago and realised that they were not good enough.

In 2015 I met Sue Court at Holy Cross Church, Binstead, where I sing in the choir. She is an English Teacher and had written several books herself and is in the process of writing her own memoire. I asked her if she would help me to sort out how to write a book about my childhood that would be interesting for my children and grandchildren to read and maybe others too. Apart from the many grammar corrections, Sue taught me to imagine myself as a child again and write how I would have thought and what I would have said. This made the whole task much easier. I put myself back in the pictures and saw myself there in the sunshine again in my garden, on the beach and on the hills of the Isle of Wight.

As the words went down on the paper more memories came flooding back. I revelled in the discovery of my life and my family. I laughed as I wrote about my schools, the games we played and the places we went to.

I have loved writing this book and hope that reading it will give pleasure.

Jo Cooper November, 2016

1 FALLING DOWNSTAIRS: MY FIRST MEMORIES

I stood at the top of the stairs in my pyjamas. There was a gate, picket style. I couldn't climb over it, the way I climbed out of my cot. It was too spikey. I had to wait until Mummy came to open the gate and take me down.

'Mummy!' I called out. 'Downstairs!'

'Won't be a minute,' she called back

'Downstairs!' I tried again.

'I won't be a minute I said.' She was cross now.

She didn't come. The radio was on, and I could hear her working in the kitchen. I wanted to be there. I was impatient. I wanted to go downstairs. On the stair side of the gate was a latch which was a simple hook that locked into a loop. I leant on the gate and reached it easily. I fiddled with this and it lifted and the gate swung open, me with it. I held on for moment and then my little fingers let go and I rolled down, bump, bump, bump the fifteen steps.

I screamed as I hit the hall floor. Mother rushed to me from the kitchen to find me on the ground. Ever calm Mother said, 'Whoops a daisy, you have had a long tumble.' Next to me was the hall table on its side. On the floor were the remains of a beautiful blue glazed bowl of daffodils. They had spilled out over the lino, the compost scattered around mixed with pieces of bowl and bulbs with their green tops and exposed roots.

'Oh dear! You have knocked over the daffodils,' she said softly and sympathetically as she rocked me. 'Poor little daffodils. We will have re-plant them. Poor little daffodils.'

My cry was loud but not for myself or my arm which was hurting but for the daffodils.

'Poor little daffodils!' I cried repeatedly.

'Which bit hurts, darling?' Mum said

'Poor little daffodils!' I repeated through my tears

She took me to the scullery and sat me on the draining board. She ran her hands up and down to check I had not broken anything and found a graze on my elbow and so she put my arm under the cold tap. Again she squeezed my arm to see if it were broken. Her first aid training had confirmed that my arm was not broken and despite the fall I had survived relatively unhurt.

I continued to wail, 'Poor little daffodils!'

To pacify me a new bowl was found quickly for the poor little daffodils. It was a pudding basin and considerably plainer than the beautiful blue one. It had come from the kitchen and was usually used for steamed puddings.

'There, there we'll put them back in this bowl. They will be alright, I'm sure. There, they look fine,' she said sweetly as the bulbs were replanted and placed back on the hall table. As soon as the hall table and bulbs were settled and everything was back to normal, I stopped crying.

Later that evening the details of the event were relayed to Daddy.

'I think it is time, we taught our youngest to climb downstairs. If she can open the gate once she can do it again,' Mummy said.

'I'll remove it tomorrow. I don't hold out much hope for the daffodils. They haven't made any progress at all. Just how long have they been at this stage?'

'Ages and ages,' Mother sighed

The next day I was given a lesson on how to climb downstairs backwards.

'Both feet go first on to the next step down followed by your hands which go on the stair above,' Mother instructed.

A few days later there were changes in the bulbs. Buds started to appear within the daffodils' green leaves. Then the magic of the buds bursting out and the tall yellow daffodils appeared.

After climbing downstairs all by myself Mummy greeted me at the bottom. She scooped me up in her arms to show me.

'You must have frightened them so much when you knocked them on to the floor; that they decided to flower once they were replanted.'

They were beautiful and I was proud as I was told that the miracle of their flowering was down to me.

---oOo---

I am an Islander. I was born on St. George's day, the 23rd of April 1947 in a semi-detached house called "Gretton" in Arnold Road, Binstead on the Isle of Wight. My sister was two years older than me. She was born on the 2nd May 1945 which was just eight days before the end of World War 2 and Victory in Europe Day.

Daddy was not at home when I was born and my arrival was conveyed by letter. A phone call was impossible as my father was deaf. My sister's name was Carolyn Mary and I was called Jocelyn Maud, a name Mummy thought mirrored my sister's. Daddy had wanted a boy but was quite happy as he could abbreviate my name from Jocelyn and call me Jo.

I cannot qualify as a "Caulkhead" or those who, as well as being born on the Island have parents were also born here. My mother was born in Leamington Spa and my father in Yorkshire. My maternal grandparents came to the island to retire when my mother was 15 years old. My father's eventual move to the Island is a mystery to me; however his Aunt Maud lived in Binstead. I am therefore a humble "Islander".

My early years were spent in "Gretton". There was no electricity and everything was lit by candles and oil lamps. My grandfather was still alive then and living there but he was dying of cancer of the throat. Mummy had to go from nursing him and cleaning up projectile vomit to attending to me, the new baby and my two year old sister, Carolyn. The workload was massive. She had a table outside his room, on which there was water and a bottle of Dettol, a popular antiseptic of the day. Although she knew cancer was not catching she treated the situation as she would do if she were doing basic barrier nursing. She poured a neat solution of the disinfectant straight from the bottle on to her hands. She rubbed her hands together vigorously, using the fingers of one hand to clean between the fingers of the other. She rinsed them in the bowl of water and she dried them with the small towel. She put this into the dirty laundry basket and replaced it with a clean one. This routine took place every day after leaving him and before returning to us.

There was very little outside help in 1947. The National Health Service was yet to come into force in 1948. Mummy had been a Red Cross Nurse during the war and this training helped her deal with the workload. Eventually with the aid of the doctor who had recognised the strain she was under my Grandfather was admitted into hospital. Mother visited him regularly.

'I began to love him as I watched him slowly slipping away from this life,' she told me. 'Then one day during a visit I was talking to him. A nurse was also there and then when I had finished my sentence she said, "He has gone now."'

It was a relief as he had been in a lot of pain. He was buried in Binstead Cemetery in the same plot with my grandmother, Madgie Kate. Mummy found going to the grave very distressing and so, following advice from Father Heald, the Rector at Binstead, she did not go any more. There is no headstone for them.

After he had died Mother's first priority was to get electricity in the house. Her father had been so against this and his disapproval haunted her. In a dream she saw her father was coming at her angrily waving his fist.

There were also many potted Aspidistra in the house. Mother had watered these and wiped the leaves to keep them shiny as her father loved the plants during his life. They had been there ever since they moved to Binstead. Mother hated them but hadn't the heart just to throw them away. She watered them with salty soapy water until they died naturally. And then she threw them away.

The house had two reception rooms and a kitchen with scullery downstairs, three bedrooms and a bathroom upstairs. To make ends meet mother let the back sitting room out as a bedsit to a paying guest. This didn't work out. This guest was a very domineering woman who continually complained, often threatening to leave. After the last one of these threats mother accepted her resignation and she was gone.

This left the back sitting room free and a place to play in. There was a long hall leading up to the room and in it was a bed next to the window, the top of it just reached the window sill. Carolyn was five and I was three and we invented a game which involved running along the corridor and throwing ourselves onto the bed. This was great fun but got a bit boisterous. It was my turn and I threw myself at the bed and into the window and smashed it. Fortunately it stayed in one piece. Mother came running. We were removed and Mother mended the window with Sellotape across the endless cracks. It remained broken for some considerable time until money was put aside to fix it.

The front sitting room had an open fire. We spent the time in here listening to the radio. After lunch we tuned into the programme called "Listen with Mother", a 15 minute show with stories and nursery rhymes. This was a regular favourite of ours at 1.45 in the afternoon. When it finished we were sent for an afternoon nap, giving Mother some time to herself listening to "Woman's Hour". The programme was made up of items for the housewife of the 1950s all introduced by women speaking in clipped BBC accents. There were recipes, for example, "A new way to use tomatoes", fashion tips for the seasons and once there was an item about the beginning of the term from school children. There were visiting speakers; a Mary Richardson spoke about Emily Davidson, the suffragette, who died at Epsom trying to stop the King's horse.

A few days after the hairdresser game my father photographed the author and Carolyn for this picture outside our house in Arnold Road Binstead.

During teatime at five o'clock we tuned into "Children's Hour". This preceded our bath or wash and then bed.

---oOo---

Carolyn and I had great imaginations and in the front sitting room, we made up a game about being hairdressers. Carolyn got hold of scissors from Mummy's workbox. I was the first customer.

'Good morning madam,' Carolyn said to me. 'Do you want your hair cut?'

'Yes please,' I replied in play.

'Would you like to sit here? Would you like a magazine?'

I sat down and my sister made a good job of chopping off all my curls.

We had been quiet for some time and Mother thought it prudent to check on us. Fortunately for Carolyn this discovery was just in time to stop me being the hairdresser. I only managed to cut a small chunk of my sister's hair.

The following day we went to the real hairdressers.

'They were only playing at being barbers,' Mummy told Gerard at the shop. 'I should have realised that they were up to no good. They were too quiet for too long.'

My hair was in a mess as Carolyn had cut it quite short.

Gerard inspected the hair styles created by us. 'As Jo has done less damage on Carolyn's hair it will only require a small trim. However I'm afraid Jo's hair is going to be very short,' he said, 'Almost as short as a boy's!'

Mother looked embarrassed, concerned and upset.

He paused. 'It won't take long to grow though, I'm sure,' he said trying to reassure Mummy.

The author in Alderney with short hair dressed in a kilt and mistaken for a boy

It did take a while to regrow. During this time Mother had to relate the tale of Barber's shop game to the many people who asked. However it took very little time to dry on hair wash night.

I had been handed down a bright red tartan kilt. It wrapped around the waist and was done up with two leather buckles. There was a Scottish safety pin to hold the front of it in place.

'This is a real Scottish kilt and you are lucky to have the real pin that goes with it,' Mother said convincing me of the quality of this second hand skirt. 'This can be worn by boys or girls.'

Shortly after the hairdressing game we went on holiday to Alderney in the Channel Islands. It was October and I wore the kilt often as the weather was cold. With it I wore a short battle dress style woollen top, second hand of course, over my hand knitted jumper.

We stopped at a café in the main street. Mummy picked up the menu. 'Coffee?' she mouthed to Dad. 'Yes please,' he replied.

'Jo! Carolyn! What would you two like? I think orange squash is a good idea.'

'Would you like some cakes or biscuits with your drink?' asked the waiter.

He brought the drinks and gave me a glass of orange squash. Thirsty, I picked up the glass and bit it. I ended up with broken glass on my tongue. I presented my tongue to mother who quickly scraped it off.

'How on earth did you do that Jo?' asked Mother.

'I just bit it and it broke,' I replied.

The café owner was very concerned and apologetic about the incident.

'I do so apologise. Would the little boy like to choose a cake?' he said.

'Yes please,' I said, 'the pink one.' I was given a plate which had on it a fairy cake with pink icing.

'Thank you,' I said, 'I'm Jo and I'm a girl.'

---oOo---

When my Grandfather died Mummy and Daddy moved into the front bedroom. I came too in my cot. They had separate beds in this large double bedroom at the front. My cot in the corner had a screen around it.

Daddy used to snore. It was difficult to call him owing to his deafness. So Mummy used to lob her prayer book across the gap to land on his chest to make him wake up and roll over. The night they made the decision that my cot should be moved into another room was when Mummy was woken up not by Daddy's snoring but by me who was standing up in the cot and peering over the top of the screen and shouting. 'Throw something at him. Throw something at him.'

To make the move out of my parents' room more exciting I was given my own big bed. Mummy made up the bed in the room next to theirs and I watched.

'You are now a big girl,' Mother told me. 'You can climb out of bed by yourself now, but good girls stay in bed all night unless you want to use the potty. It's here under the bed.'

I didn't always abide by this rule as on light summer evenings I would climb out of bed and stand on the window sill and watch the activity outside.

One day I went to bed in the middle of the day. I didn't suspect anything unpleasant but I was allowed to get into Mummy's bed. Two men in white coats appeared. One was a dentist and the other was his assistant. I was told that I had some bad teeth that needed to come out. 'You will go to sleep and won't feel a thing,' Mummy reassured me.

Sure enough they were there at the foot of my bed and one man came up to me holding a mask which he brought forward towards my face. I jumped up and ran to Mummy clinging on to her neck as tight as I could. I was having none of this. Mummy calmed me, put me back into bed, sat on the edge and stroked my hair. She put the mask over my face. I remember the first breath of this horrid stuff. Chloroform had a nasty taste and smell. When I woke up the men had gone and Mummy was there. They had taken out some milk teeth.

The tooth fairy did not come for those bad teeth but all the others that had naturally dropped out were placed under our pillows to be replaced with a silver sixpenny piece.

Mother had to be inventive one day about the tooth fairy. It was evening time when I was busy consuming my favourite marmalade sandwiches which had been cut into triangles and called Grey Rabbit sandwiches after a character in the Alison Utley book.

'There was a crunchy bit in that sandwich,' I told Mummy. She had no answer as she couldn't understand it.

A few minutes later I shouted, 'My wiggly tooth has gone.'

Mother looked into my mouth. There was a gap where the tooth should have been. Then it dawned on her, 'You must have eaten it.'

She paused and we laughed. 'No harm done,' said mother.

'The tooth fairy, the tooth fairy, she won't know!' I cried.

'I'll tell her, don't worry. I suspect she already knows.'

The tooth fairy did know and a silver sixpence was under my pillow the next morning.

My sister got the measles and the doctor was called to verify that I also had it. There was a massive and very noisy thunder storm when the female doctor arrived. She came up to the Mummy's bedroom. Carolyn was in Daddy's bed and I was in Mummy's.

The storm was fierce and right overhead. Just as the doctor walked into the room I stood up on the bed, 'They have dropped the dan piano!' I shouted, not yet able to pronounce "gr".

Mother tried to explain to the doctor that she had told us not to be afraid of thunder it was only God moving his furniture.

'The removal men are not very good and they keep dropping tables, pianos and chairs!' she explained.

The Doctor sat on the bed and took out her stethoscope.

After another loud bang I jumped up and down and yelled, 'That must be the danfather clock!'.

I don't think the doctor had listened to Mother's explanation about the furniture removers as she announced, 'I think this child is delirious!'

She went away and left no firm confirmation that I had caught the measles from Carolyn, but a little concerned as to my mental state. It was a week later that Mummy decided that I didn't have the measles after all.

A bungalow became available to buy in Church Road just around the corner from my father's aunt, Auntie Maud. She was very elderly now and Mother made many visits to her to help out with household chores.

'When I die I am leaving the house to Bryan,' Auntie Maud told them. 'Buy the house with a mortgage and this can be repaid when my house is sold after my death.'

Leys, 11 Church Road was bought and we moved in November, 1952. We were very close now to Auntie Maud in Quarr Road and visiting was easy. These visits didn't last long as Auntie Maud died in January, 1953. My last memory of Auntie Maud was of her lying on the stretcher going out of her front door, I stood watching and said goodbye.

I was five years old.

2 MOTHER

Mum's reassuring smile greeted me at the end of every school day. One day I ran out of the door of Binstead School, saw her and waved. Passing through the gate I hurried down to her. There was a twinkle in her eye and then I spotted it.

'Whose dog is that?' I asked.

'Ours,' she said. Just then Carolyn joined us.

'Whose dog is that?' she asked.

'Ours!' Mum and I replied.

Willie Pickle had arrived in our family. He was a six month old pure bred dachshund puppy, a standard in size and black and tan in colour. We loved him from the outset.

Mother's unforgettable smile was always there at the right time. Whenever I was sick, my bed was tidied as I waited, the bottom sheet was pulled clear of folds.

'I've made sure all the ruckles are out,' she reassured me. Once in she tucked in the blankets and sheets tightly and gave me that lovely smile. There were other times when I tried her patience and I was smacked.

She loved being a mother. She was an expert at being a housewife, the job expected for women in the 1950s. This was a job she had done since her mother died when she was 23. She sewed and made clothes out of the rag bag. She altered the hand-me-down clothes so they fitted me. Her cooking skills matched those of Mrs. Beeton. She started learning how to cook and keep house when her mother became progressively ill.

Mother gardened: she grew fruit and vegetables for the table. She researched what to do in the garden from books left open in the house so when she returned to the garden she looked proficient at what she was doing.

She was proud; an emotion she said was a sin. She was always well groomed and so were we. There were never any buttons missing or tears in our clothes. There were 'mends'. She always hung her coat up on a coat hanger when she came in and then put it away in the tall boy in the hall. This sin of pride was drummed into us with the phrase, "Pride before a fall."

---oOo---

Mother, Betty Leigh was born in Leamington Spa on the 23rd March, 1912, a few weeks before the "Titantic" sank. She told me many times of the injustices of the tragedy and how there were not enough lifeboats and they were filled with the rich.

Mummy was 37 when her cousin on her father's side, Constance Wingrove suddenly said to her, 'Of course your parents were never married.'

'What?' Mother was astounded.

'Oh I thought you knew,' she continued.

'No I didn't Connie,' Mother was indignant. She was married and had two daughters. She knew nothing of this.

Connie continued, 'Madgie met Edward and fell in love. This developed and they decided they wanted to marry. However Edward was already married. They searched and searched but his first wife could not be found. She had gone to Australia with their daughter Harriet.'

Mother sat down, stunned.

'So sorry, Betty, I thought you knew all this,' Connie put her arm around her.

She thought of her mother and things started to fall into place. 'That is why there was never an engagement ring and I often wondered why Mummy never took communion. Why didn't she tell me before she died?'

'No,' said Connie, 'she felt so strongly about the sin of living together with Edward unmarried that she felt she shouldn't take communion again. She obviously never told you because of the same disgrace.'

Madgie regularly attended matins at Holy Cross Church in Binstead instead. Madgie and Edward's relationship was a true love match. Unable to declare his love by giving Madgie an engagement ring, Edward gave her a gold gate style bracelet to cement the relationship.

A studio photo arranged by "Nanny" of Betty Leigh taken in Leamington Spa when she was three. This was sent to Madgie, her mother.

This shame transferred to my mother and she kept the secret from me until I was 48.

'How brave of her,' I said to Mummy when she told me. 'How modern. No-one thinks twice about living together nowadays.' The bracelet was handed down to Betty. I wore it at my wedding and Mum gave it to me as a Christmas present before she died. I still have it.

'I promise I will hand this down to my daughter with the love story,' I told Mummy when I opened the present.

Madgie and Edward lived in a flat at the top of a house in Beaumont Crescent in West Kensington on the corner of North End Road in London. Her sisters referred to the flat as the "love nest". She had three sisters: Adela Frances, Louisa Fanny and Alice Harriet. Louisa and Alice changed their names when they went on the stage and joined the members of the D'Oyly

Carte Opera Company who mixed with the well-to-do society in London. Their stages names were Louie and Alice Rene. Louie was to be their principal contralto from 1894 to 1914.

When Madgie became pregnant she moved to Leamington Spa and had her baby there. She left her with a Nanny so Mother's early years were spent in Leamington Spa. Nanny had a teenage son called Jimmy. Mummy spoke highly of her Nanny who wrote to Madgie regularly, keeping her in touch with her daughter. In one letter she told of how Betty Leigh, who had a mind of her own, decided in church one day not to put her penny collection into the pocket that was passed along the pew. She smartly left her place and took it straight up to her friend the vicar and gave it to him. He thanked her and told her to go back to her seat. Nanny said that it looked as if she was giving him a tip.

Nanny's son went off to war. The weather was hot and sunny that June day that Jimmy left to go to fight. Holding tightly to his hand Betty walked down the lane to the corner. There he said quietly 'Go back to Nanny. I think she will need you now.' She skipped back to her Nanny who wiped her tears away before cuddling Betty.

Jimmy was blown to bits at the Battle of the Somme some time during the summer and autumn of 1916. There was no body to grieve over, no grave to visit and no understanding of when and how he died. He had just gone, disappeared. Nanny fell apart and Madgie collected her daughter, deciding that she was more important than the London society in which she mixed.

This situation hid Madgie's illegitimate daughter away from London society, so no-one knew about her.

Betty Leigh in her Sacred Heart Covent school uniform with her mother circa 1923

Owing to her illegitimacy Betty Leigh was never christened, it was forbidden by the church. Consequently when she was confirmed she had to be baptised first.

The sitting room of the love nest in Beaumont Crescent had two windows. One that looked around the Crescent and the other faced the North End Road, where she watched the locals going in and out of the shops.

During the autumn of 1916 there were heavy Zeppelin raids taking place over London. When there was a warning Betty and her mother sheltered down in the cellar. A rocking horse was stored there. Betty loved this and rocked happily during the raids. Others in the cellar may have been a little scared of what might happen but not Betty. She even added it to her prayers at night, 'God please let there be a raid tonight and then I can play on the rocking horse.'

After one of these raids, which killed many Londoners, Betty noticed from her window a group of people gathered in front of Mr. & Mrs. Holtz' General Grocery store. The store had been in the Holtz family for many years. Both Albert and Alice Holtz were English and were born in Fulham. However, the shop's name was too German sounding to avoid attention and the mob started to shout. A pot of paint was found to daub a message on the window and some barrels were over turned. Madgie stepped in and stood fully erect, her head high, between the store and the crowd. She calmed the group sticking up for the owner explaining the stupidity of attacking these two British people and stopped the trouble. There were apples and potatoes scattered across the pavement and Madgie helped Albert to pick them up. She then went in and comforted Alice.

The news from the Front was constantly bad but life went on as normally as possible for Betty. She was sent to school. She was reading to the teacher, a Miss Bonnet who had a ruler on the book.

The impatient teacher snapped at Betty 'Come on! What's the next word?' but the ruler covered the next line.

Betty was indignant. 'If you remove your ruler,' she said politely, 'I could then see the words and read them.'

Betty was hit with the ruler. Madgie removed her from that establishment and a more suitable school was found.

The family moved to Salisbury, where Edward Vigar became the station master of the Railway sidings. They lived in a large house that came with the station. Betty Leigh was sent to the Sacred Heart Catholic Convent a two mile walk from her home. This she did twice a day as she returned home for lunch. She loved this school and was an excellent pupil. The Reverend Mother gave her the pet name of 'Peggy'.

Despite being well mannered and hard-working, Betty was quite single minded and opinionated. A bishop was visiting the school and all the girls were told to kneel before him and kiss his ring. She knelt but did not kiss the ring. The Bishop snorted and said: 'How many more heretics do you have at this school, Reverend Mother?'

She did not reply but told "Peggy" to move on. Mother did not like bishops, calling them "religious tycoons" throughout her life.

At the age of 15 Betty passed her Matriculation which consisted of many subjects. She was all set to go on to do her Highers when her father Edward decided to retire and move to the

Isle of Wight. Betty's education was thought not to be important at all. In 1927 consideration of any woman's education was not valued; this was a year before women over 21 got the vote.

During the early part of the 20th Century the Suffragettes has been protesting and suffering to get votes for women. These brave women had committed crimes and were arrested. Although Madgie and her sisters did not take part in any of these activities, she was supportive.

When the law changed in 1928 she told her daughter, 'You must vote at every opportunity, even if you have no political leaning. Vote for the suffragettes and Emily Pankhurst. They fought and suffered for you to get the right to vote.' Mother passed on this same message on to me and I have repeated this to my daughter.

Madgie, Edward and Betty moved to "Gretton", 9 Arnold Road, Binstead. There was no question of Betty being allowed to continue her studies and do her highers. Although a school was found in Portsmouth Edward would not let her travel over the Solent every day. A small art school was found in Ryde but this did not work out at all so Betty then trained in shorthand and typing. She became very proficient at it, so proficient that she became a teacher.

A rare photo of my mother, with her parents, taken when they had moved to Binstead.

Betty adored her mother whose her health was not good. She developed diabetes which gradually got worse. In the beginning she was always thirsty but it was the fainting that prompted her to go to the doctors. The treatment of diabetes was in its infancy in the 1930s and the discovery of Insulin in the 1935 was too late for Madgie and the condition eventually took her life that year. Betty was 23.

She was left to look after her father as an unpaid housekeeper. Edward was a Victorian father. Betty was the dutiful daughter and looked after him. There was little love between them. Edward was strict. He expected his daughter to do as she was told. He kept her on a very tight rein or so he thought. Betty wanted to ride a horse. She was sure that her father would forbid it so she didn't ask. She regularly took her riding clothes and changed at her friend's Delia Mootham's house in Pellhurst Road before going to the stables nearby.

Mother is riding Cocky, a[...] between Delia on her ri[...] John the stable owner[...]

One day as she was riding a bus overtook the group.

Betty was very visible on her horse and my Grandfather was riding on the bus. He spotted her, his eyes wide open he watched her riding. It was obvious to Betty that her secret was out, so she sat up straight in the saddle and acknowledged her father by touching her hat with her riding crop. She thought she was in for a row when she returned home. All was quiet for a while until he remarked. 'I do not approve of your riding,' he casually said and then after a pause he added, 'Well I suppose you've got a good seat.'

Betty used to ride many horses but she often rode a grey called Cocky. He had a bit of a "hard mouth". He didn't respond very quickly as he had been badly treated by a previous owner. Betty was out riding Cocky when they approached a hedge which she was ready to jump. But Cocky had other ideas and refused. She was thrown over his head and over the hedge, brushing her chin and nose on the horse's cropped mane and landed on her neck. The horse then peered over as if to say:

'What are you doing down there?'

Betty was bleeding from her chin, nose and forehead. She stood up and carried on, remounting Cocky for the end of the hack, but her neck was injured slightly. She made no fuss, and no fuss was made of her. She went to the doctor and was given a collar to wear for a while.

Betty became a Red Cross Nurse during the war years. She was prevented from joining the services.

'I wanted to join the WRNs like my cousin Clare Woodward but I had my elderly father to look after, and I couldn't leave him.'

She was interviewed by a large elderly lady in a tight Red Cross uniform. 'Hello, I'm Miss ⁻owne with an "e",' she said as she shook Mother's hand. 'Sit down, sit down!' Her hair was ⁻d back severely into a bun without a wisp of hair out of place under her nurse's cap.

⁻ill have some basic training which starts next week,' she told mother, 'and owing to ⁻ituation on the Continent, there will be a major incident training taking place on ⁻ing all the emergencies services later in the month.'

⁻ared and confused. 'No need to worry Vigar,' she said without emotion. 'I ⁻'AD. With war a strong possibility, County branches of the Red Cross have ⁻ their own groups of volunteers called Voluntary Aid Detachments. This ⁻Members are known as VADs.'

⁻learn on the job Vigar when I arrived in France. Just work hard at ⁻on get the hang of it.' Mum felt she had joined a military

⁻the civil defence and the ambulance service will be there,' she ⁻oss. So there is no need to worry.'

'Yes ma'am,' Mum replied.

On Saturday 11th March 1939 the Air Raid Precautions (ARP) exercise took place. This covered an area between Ryde and Bembridge. Mother's group was sent to the Duver at Seaview. She did her best with her limited knowledge, but she found herself late in the evening at the end of the exercise with two casualties, one ambulance, the commandant and an ARP Observer glaring at her.

The first "casualty" she got to was John. He had a label tied to his wrist which stated that he had a broken leg. Mother went to the other "casualty" Rodney, whose label said that he was suffering as a result of a gas attack. The two "casualties" were just three yards away from each other. There was one ambulance, so she called for a further one. Mother comforted the gas victim and put him in a comfortable position to help his breathing. She then returned to John and dealt with his "broken leg".

There was a strong north wind blowing in from the sea and it was extremely cold. Miss Browne and ARP Observer were warmly dressed; John and Rodney were not.

Mother went backwards and forwards the short distance to them both. 'I am so cold,' John said. 'So am I,' said Rodney.

Charles Bryan and Betty Drawbridge on their wedding day. The photo was taken in Vonnie's front garden at 2 Church Road Binstead.

She had already covered them with the thin blankets that were available in the ambulance, but they were still very cold.

'I'm not sure how much more I can cope with this,' said Rodney.

'Neither can I,' echoed John.

'Right,' said mother now more concerned about Rodney and John than the "casualties" they portrayed.

'Rodney, put your arm around my shoulder, we are going to get into the ambulance.'

Once he was in and settled, trainee Red Cr[oss] nurse Betty Leigh Vigar asked the ambulance driv[er to] help her to move John onto the stretcher and l[ift him] into the vehicle.

The ARP Observer tutted. 'Doesn't sh[e know] what she had done!'

'Vigar!' Miss Browne roared. 'You ha[ve put a gas] attack victim in with a casualty with a br[oken leg. The] gas casualty will contaminate the othe[r...]

'Yes,' Vigar said firmly, 'but they are a matter of three yards away from each other. It's logical that if Rodney was in an area where there was gas, then so was John.'

There was silence. 'And,' my mother continued, 'they are both getting extremely cold and they need to warm up!'

Vigar travelled back in the ambulance to the hospital where she had left her bike. She rode home back to Binstead promising herself that she would wear extra underwear next time.

She worked at Ryde Hospital, where she did basic nursing duties when an old woman was brought in with an infected leg.

'The smell was awful! It had started to become gangrenous,' she recounted.

All of a sudden Mummy heard the staff nurse shout, 'Vigar! Get out!'

Betty had started to sway and was about to faint. She left the room and arrived in the sluice just in time to vomit in the sink. She took sips from a glass of water, because she was anxious to get back to work but was stopped by Mary another VAD who had a message from Sister. 'You are to remain here until you have completely recovered,' Mary said.

As part of her duties she was a member of the first aid team in Binstead. The first aid post was in a house in Pitts Lane. This large house, in which a room was given over to the Red Cross, was situated on a bend opposite a field. This field had been a stone quarry and there was a large dip in it. As soon as the air raid warning sounded she cycled round to the first aid post from her house in Arnold Road.

On her journey one day a low flying German plane was seen coming up Binstead Hill, firing his machine gun as he went. Betty got off her bike and stood transfixed not knowing what to do. Suddenly she was grabbed by an off duty soldier and thrown into a ditch. The soldier lay top of her protecting her from any bullets. The plane disappeared and they stood up.

'e you alright?' asked the soldier.

ng Betty replied, 'Yes thank you I am fine. What about you?'

the soldier replied.

herself down, thanked him again and they went their separate ways. Betty ike to the First Aid post.

d, the senior VAD of the group said 'You are late Vigar. And you've got

g down the situation and making humour she said, 'I'm so sorry I'm a ditch with a soldier.'

of all sorts of people who for one reason or another did not take as an older man, Mr. Atkins, who had been through the First ledge was invaluable especially in training when he described

'What's that pretty whistling sound?' Betty in her innocence said one day.

'It's a bloody bomb! Get down!' Mr. Atkins shouted.

The group hit the floor putting as much of themselves as possible under the beds that were ready for casualties. Fortunately for the group the bomb fell in the dip of the field opposite, its explosive power limited to that area only. Relieved they all stood up.

'That was close!' Betty said.

Mr. Atkins laughed 'We are all very fortunate. It was a fat lot of good going under the first aid beds. They are camp beds made of wood and canvas: they would not have protected you at all.'

When her mother Madgie died a close friend of the family, Yvonne Ashby, who was known as Vonnie made a promise to herself. She vowed that she would take Madgie's place until Betty got married. Vonnie had gone through a tragedy herself as her husband had died of consumption when she was pregnant. She had a daughter called Roma. It was Vonnie who was partly responsible for Betty meeting Charles Bryan Drawbridge.

I asked my mother one day in the 1990s 'Where did you meet Daddy?'

'I first became aware of your father at Puckpool. He was sitting on the steps in front of the huts. You should remember the steps as we had a beach hut there when you girls were in your teens. Daddy was gazing out to sea. His Aunt Maud, together with Vonnie, introduced your father to me one day at church. It was expected at that time that an introduction was the correct way to meet. Apparently he had been going to church to watch me, he told me later. 'Auntie Maud could not understand my sudden interest in religion.' Bryan said.

The war was in full flight and the Island was getting a battering. On our bikes we used to ride up onto the Downs at Brading and watch the dog fights happening overhead. Our outings together were not spectacular. It was war time; you grabbed what happiness you could get.

Auntie Vonnie is with my parents on their wedding day.

'Weren't you scared that you might get killed?' I asked.

'When war was declared on 3rd September 1939 I didn't care. I was 27, Mummy was dead and I was just an unpaid housekeeper for my overbearing father – that was what was expected of me. There was no electricity in the house, my father wouldn't allow it. I worked in Ryde at the Typing School. I came home at 12.30 every day to give him his lunch and then returned to work. In the evening I cooked his evening meal, cleared up and tidied up ready for another day. He was very stubborn, but then so was I.'

She paused to take a mouthful of tea and then continued with her revelations about my father. 'Your father kept proposing. And I kept refusing. My father would not allow it; we had nothing to live on, we had nowhere to live, he was deaf and had no career. There was too much against it.'

'One day there was an horrendous raid on Portsmouth where he was working as a fireman. I watched out of the back window at Gretton, Arnold Road and saw the red sky over the Portsmouth area and I immediately wrote to him, and said that if he was to ask "that silly question again" I might have a different answer.'

'Daddy wrote back immediately. He said that it was a good thing that he was not on the pneumatic drills that day as he was so happy he could have dug up half of Portsmouth. Daddy's letters to me during that time were in the loft at Leys and I lost them in the move to Wootton. I regret that, they were lovely letters and full of little drawings. He drew a pin man style donkey on each letter. He called the donkey "Hepzibar". He added two baskets slung across his back that were always lots of flowers for me.'

Bridesmaids, Roma Ashby and Elizabeth Ashe at my parents' wedding, are standing near the door of Holy Cross Church Binstead.

'Now we had to tell my father. Bryan could manage my father very well really and took charge here. Holding my hand and with his body erect he asked my father firmly for my hand in marriage. Before my father could voice any obstacles he pushed a ring on my engagement finger obviously, owing to his deafness, not hearing any comment from my father.'

'After he had gone there was a row. I had expected it.'

'You may have children and I don't want any noisy children living here!' he shouted. 'Well if you marry this man, you will have to leave. You won't have anywhere to live.'

'I stood tall and looked at him squarely in the face, 'I would rather live in a hovel with Bryan than stay at Gretton with you'. Then I walked out.'

'The next time Bryan came round the situation had changed. My father realised that his unpaid housekeeper would leave and he would be on his own with no-one to cook and clean for him.'

'So after we were married, Daddy came to live at Gretton. We were given the small back bedroom. When I did eventually have Carolyn my father looked into her crib and cried. 'She is Madgie come back to me.''

'The ring that he had pushed on my finger was a simple engagement ring with a small diamond that he had bought. When it was announced that we would marry, Betty Ashe, his sister said that his mother had put aside one of her rings for Bryan to have for his future wife. This was the wrong size and had to be altered. Now this sort of work was not allowed during wartime. However, a friend of the Drawbridges, a jeweller did the work and made the Drawbridge ring the right size. He then removed the stone from the original engagement ring to make a wedding ring. The jeweller took this small diamond from the bought ring, as payment for the work. There were no records then of money changing hands for a job that should not have been done.'

'Auntie Vonnie lived at the top of Church Road with her daughter Roma. I used to spend a lot of time there at Number 2 Church Road, and I looked after Roma sometimes. They had a dog called Bonnie. It was from here that I married.'

'In 1943 there was a feeling that the war had taken a turn for the better. The pride of the German Navy the "Bismark" was sunk in May. Bombs were still falling on the Island and Newport took a battering in April. However there was a feeling of more optimism.'

'Rationing was severe but people in the village were very generous. I was given clothing coupons for my dress. I went to London with Betty Ashe, my future sister in law, to get my wedding dress. There was never a question of me being married in white. That was a waste of coupons and money and I was far too sensible. The first dress I chose was in aqua marine. Betty Ashe was furious and put her foot down.

'My dear Betty, not green! You are marrying in war time, you have no money put by, Bryan is deaf and has no career. To marry in green was just too unlucky.'

'So I picked a soft pink dress and jacket. I teamed this with a brown hat and shoes. The dress doubled up as a going away outfit as well. I kept the dress for many years, wearing it for both of your christenings. I did have the zip fastener undone under the jacket.'

'I was also given coupons to help with the catering for

Taken by my father, this picture is of Mother taken on their honeymoon. She discovered she had sat on a snail when she stood up.

the reception. The cake was legendary. From various friends we collected the dried fruit. This was in very short supply and we topped up the amount quoted in the recipe with prunes. I couldn't get almonds so we used the inside of apple pips which, as you know, have a strong almond flavour. The cake was delicious.'

'From Auntie Vonnie's at number 2 Church Road, on the 19th June 1943, my father and I walked down to Holy Cross Church. Roma walked with her mother Yvonne, and Elizabeth with her mother walked from Woodlands, the bungalow at the top of Quarr Road, where they were living with Auntie Maud. The Isle of Wight was a restricted area and permission had to be sought for my mother's sisters, Adela, Alice and Louie to cross the Solent. They came down from Kingston in Surrey. Bryan's guests included his sister Betty without her husband. Uncle "Tat" William Drawbridge, Bryan and Betty's brother was also away in the Navy on active service.'

'I had two bridesmaids. Auntie Vonnie's daughter Roma Ashby was one and three year old Elizabeth Ashe, Betty's daughter and Bryan's niece was the other one. They had pink dresses with black ballet pumps. Your father very rarely sang throughout his life, not that he couldn't, it was because he couldn't hear other singers or the music accompaniment. But he sang on our wedding day, "Praise my soul the King of Heaven" at the top of his voice. My father, of course, gave me away. The reception was held at Auntie Vonnie's.'

Mother continued, 'Our honeymoon was at the Farringford Hotel in Freshwater. We had a lovely time, but through one thing or another, perhaps Daddy did not know enough, I returned home a virgin. I think it was the first time for your father as well. He was so scared of hurting me. Oh we cuddled all night and there was a lot of loving. On the first night home, it happened, Daddy was bit rough and well the rest is history. The next morning I went to the doctor's. Your father insisted as it was very painful and there was blood everywhere. The doctor's verdict was that before the previous night I had been "very aggressively a virgin".'

'There were lovely photos taken on the honeymoon. Your father got me to pose seated by a pond at the Hotel. It is a lovely picture, one of his favourites. When I got up I found that I had been sitting on a snail. There were lots of areas around Freshwater that were restricted and photos were not allowed to be taken. If the chemist who developed the film had discovered any suspicious pictures he could confiscate the whole film. So I was put in strategic places to hide various objects that would have given the identity of the place where the photo was taken.'

'We went back to live with my father at Gretton and life continued on. It was 1943, the war still on, with its problems. I wanted children but I felt that it was not the right time. However, it was Dr. Crampton who reminded me that I wasn't getting any younger and that if I wanted children then I should start thinking about it soon. It took a while, what with Daddy being away so much, and not being able to relax at home with my father there. Anyway Carolyn was born in May 1945 right at the end of the war. I remember lying in bed and listening to the celebrations for VE Day on the 8th May on the radio and outside. The war in Japan didn't finish until August.'

Mother did not talk openly about sex. Conversations about intimacy were not done in her day and age. I was surprised at her ignorance even later in her life. Obviously my father was not very adventurous. She continued, 'Your father during his preparation for confirmation at school was sent for by the head master. He knew this was THE talk regarding the birds and the bees. He was quite looking forward to it. Being deaf he had missed a lot of the stories and information chats in the playground. Unfortunately, the headmaster did not speak very clearly at all and spent most the conversation being embarrassed, turning away from your father so he missed out again.'

'We had a good marriage. He adored me and you two girls. He worked so hard to make enough money for us.'

I sat quietly absorbing her story and thought I had no doubt that they loved each other.

3 LEYS

'Why are you just watering the iris?' Carolyn asked Mummy during one very hot summer day. 'Why aren't you watering all the other plants in the garden as well?'

'I'm not watering the iris,' Mother said quietly. 'I am watering the soil under the iris.' Mummy pushed the end of the hose further down into the long spikey leaves and continued, 'In very hot weather the clay on which the house is built dries out and a large crack in the wall appears just here behind the iris. You can see more of them on the lawn over there.'

The back garden of Leys 11 Church Road, Binstead.

Carolyn and I turned to the brown stretch of grass where there were large cracks.

'That one is big enough to put my foot in.' I said.

'That's right,' Mummy continued. 'The same thing happens just here under the iris, but it has made a crack appear in the wall of the house. In winter when the weather is wet the clay moistens and the crack comes together and disappears. If I keep the soil wet the crack closes. It happens every year when the weather is very dry. Watering the soil under the wall does the trick.'

Mother kept an eye on the situation throughout the summer and watered the soil, iris and wall periodically. In winter the opposite would happen, our garden would become very squelchy.

The house that needed watering was Leys, 11 Church Road, Binstead. It was a detached chalet bungalow and was the place where I would spend my childhood from the age of five until I left home at 18 years old.

As I child when faced with something unpleasant Mother taught me to think about something nice.

'Take your mind to a place where you were smiling and enjoying yourself.'

I have taken this piece of advice. When I have something unpleasant to face up to or I have felt lonely, I go back to Leys. Despite the rows Carolyn and I had in that house and Mummy and Daddy's arguments, Leys was a place of calm, security and full of love.

Mummy confided in us, 'Half way through a row when I was trying to get my point across, Daddy would turn his hearing aid off.' I saw them one day. Daddy had his arms around Mummy as she pounded his chest.

Leys was the last of the identical bungalows in Church Road. When we first moved in there were fields to the left and in front of the house. Both fields had horses in them.

Mother was assured when she bought the house that there were no plans to build in the two fields. This was not the case and first to be built on was the field at the side. Later on Shadowsfield in front of us was turned over to houses.

We called the field Shadowsfield because of the horse that lived in the field called Black Shadow. She was a retired mare and we loved her.

'Shadow's there looking over the fence Mum,' I called out. 'Have you got anything I can give her.'

Mum was preparing a steak and kidney casserole for the evening. 'OK I think she'd like a carrot,' she said. Mum went to the larder and picked up a large carrot. 'Oh hang on a minute. Take that last apple from the bowl, it's bruised and going off.' I took the carrot and apple and rushed to the back door. Daddy picked up his camera and followed me.

The author, bare foot with Black Shadow in her field.

'Hold out your hand flat, so she will take the food and not accidently bite your fingers.' Mother said.

Shadow was often covered in flies, but I didn't care. I would have loved to learn to ride but there wasn't the money.

Daddy took a photo of me with Shadow. In it I am "dressed" in a pairs of shorts and an Airtex shirt. My collar is tucked in one side, my shorts are twisted and I have no shoes on. It is obvious that what was important to me on that day was to see my beloved horse.

In the autumn Carolyn and I used to go picking blackberries in the Shadowsfield. It was Shadow's field and despite our love of the animal we were a little in awe of her. She was more loved when she was one side of the fence and we were the other. Once in the field we had to avoid her. We made sure when we were walking to the next clump of brambles she was on the other side of the field. Sometimes we were caught unawares but we were never hurt.

When picking blackberries we had to make sure they came off the bramble easily.

'They are not ripe if they stick to the bush.' Mother said.

We brought our two plastic bowls full of blackberries and presented them to Mother.

'Lovely,' she said, 'haven't you got a lot today?'

She washed, cleaned and sorted them. She sprinkled them with sugar and put them in a shallow bowl in the larder. We had to wait for tea time to have a bowl of this lovely black fruit. Fresh blackberries are best served with cream. As that was not available Mother served them with the top of the milk. Milk was unpasteurised, delivered in bottles and at the top of the bottle was a small amount of cream. Mother shared out the top of the milk evenly between us and sprinkled on a little more sugar. Blackberries picked at just the right time were firm but soft enough to melt in the mouth. They were delicious. When we had finished the fruit we had the sugary cream flavoured with the blackberries at the bottom of the bowl to enjoy.

Carolyn, the author and Willie Pickle in the front garden in the snow at 11 Church Road Binstead.

The field at the side of us was large and hired by the Julie Upton Stables for their horses. They would arrive with the stable girls riding them bare back. This was impressive enough but often they would be holding the rein of a further horse. I once saw two girls come. The bare back rider was leading two horses and the other girl was on a bike leading a further horse. They delivered them to the field and then left. Both girls were on the one bike.

The grass was long in summer and with its wild flowers was very beautiful. There were oak trees near us. Under these the horses sheltered from the sun and rain.

There was a dip in the field next to us which in winter and spring became a pond which dried up in summer. In the spring I regularly climbed over the picket fence in my wellies at the side of our garage and paddled in the pond. A big oak tree hung over this, one long branch spread over the water. There were reeds on the far side. I was fascinated by this. I paddled and got tadpoles and newts, carefully carrying them back. I stored them in the garage in jam jars with the idea of watching their development. Mother, either taking pity on these creatures or perhaps deciding they were just too smelly, threw them away.

I used to go home with my treasures and with my Wellington boots full of water.

'Mum, my boots leak.' I announced.

'No they don't! Mum she goes in too deep and the water goes over the top,' my sister said, divulging the truth.

In the well-established oak trees in both fields there were red squirrels. Mother loved the fields and the trees and cried when they came to cut them down to clear the area for building. The workmen realising her distress gave her some bags of logs to burn. These made well needed fuel to keep us warm in winter.

When the builders filled in the pond to flatten the land the water dissipated and our garden became even more squelchy in winter. In parts it became almost like a bog garden. With the pond gone frogs were often found in our garden.

The houses that were built were small bungalows and I made friends with our neighbours, the Smiths. Mr. Smith worked for Hetty's the builders which was the construction company contracted to build these houses. Compared with our house, these were very small. Before the building started the ground had been flattened with a sort of clay like material on which we played cricket.

There was a narrow path left between our house and the new house so that access could be gained to the field at the bottom of the garden. In this field Julie Upton's riding school still put their horses. One night we were awakened by neighing and the sound of a horse's hooves. I thought someone was stealing the horses. I was scared that someone would take my Black Shadow.

Mother realised exactly what was happening. She came downstairs and got the telephone directory to find Julie Upton's number.

'Hello Miss Upton,' said Mother, 'your white stallion has jumped over the gate and has come up the narrow pathway at the side of our house and is trying to get to Black Shadow in the field opposite.' The call was quick. Julie obviously sprang into action.

Carolyn and I got out of bed and found Mother near the phone.

'What's going on? Is someone trying to steal the horses?' I asked.

'No, no, the white stallion is feeling a bit amorous. Go back to bed.'

Julie Upton arrived soon after and the stallion was rounded up and put back into the field.

The building of the houses did not distress to me at all but now I can understand my mother's sadness at the loss of such beautiful fields and trees. Black Shadow was in that field because she was retired. One day she disappeared and we saw no more of her. The field lay empty until more builders came.

"Leys" was a lovely shape, but not very well built. We accepted the cold in the house. Our bedrooms and the kitchen had their own electric convector heater which was turned on when it was needed and turned off when we left the room. These were modelled to look like a round cylindrical paraffin heater. The cold air entered at the bottom where there was the electrical element. This air travelled up the funnel and out of the top. There was no heating on when we slept. In cold weather we had a hot water bottle and lots blankets above and below us to keep us warm.

The long hallway had no heating at all and we would rush between rooms and fires on cold days and nights.

The hall had another use. It was a training area for Willie Pickle our dachshund to learn how, when it was too cold or wet to go outside, to retrieve. The bathroom was at the end of the hall and for this game the door was open to extend the length of the run and with our backs at the front door we would roll a ball along the floor. This would always end up on the back wall behind the toilet.

We held Willie tight and at Mother's command, 'Go fetch it,' we would let him go and he scuttled, scampered and slid along the floor, faithfully bringing the ball back.

'Good boy,' we all said as we gave him lots of pats and kisses.

Willie's retrieving skills were improving and we clapped and cheered when he got it right.

'Look he's brought back the toilet brush!' Carolyn shouted one day. We fell about laughing. From then on the game became known as "Lavatory Cricket".

Taking a bath in winter was difficult. There was no radiator in this bathroom at all and a convector heater was out of the question because it was run on electricity.

'Water and electricity don't mix. You must never touch an electric appliance with wet hands,' Mother instructed us.

The bath water was heated by an immersion heater situated in the kitchen. We only had one tank full for a bath. This filled up to about seven inches from the bottom.

'Stop moaning! We were only allowed five inches in war time,' Mother pointed out.

Whilst the bath was filling I sat on the edge carefully feeling for the water from the hot tap to become cooler telling me that the supply of hot water was finished. I had to turn it off quickly. In very cold weather the bath water soon cooled and there was no need to turn on the cold tap to cool it down.

I quickly and very bravely took off my clothes, got in the bath and sank into the water. I soon got used to it so I began to relax and enjoy it. I did not vigorously wash as the more movement I made with the water, the quicker it got cold. I lazed back with eyes closed and disappeared into an imaginary world.

'Hurry up in their Jo,' shouted Carolyn, 'I want the toilet.'

I did not answer. 'Bother!' I thought.

'What are you doing in there?' she went on.

'Soaking off the dirt,' I shouted back.

Mother joined in, 'Jo can you please hurry up, we are all waiting.'

The water was now cooler, making getting out of the bath far worse than getting in. When wet the cold air made me feel colder. I wrapped a towel around me and covered it up with a dressing gown.

Carolyn was banging on the door now. 'Alright, alright! I'm coming.' I shouted.

I rushed out and Carolyn rushed in. I went straight into my bedroom and stood over the fire.

'Don't touch the fire with wet hands,' Mother shouted from the kitchen.

The bathroom was the room to which I ran to find sanctuary when I lost my temper with my sister and needed to sulk. I would run in there, slam and then bolt the door. This caused difficulties as the best way to calm me down was to leave me. This was not possible when someone in the family wanted to use the toilet and I had locked the door.

We wore dressing gowns around the house when we were ready for bed. When we took them off these were placed over our feet while we slept. Tucked up tight in our beds we were warm and cosy however cold it was outside in the room.

One morning in January Mummy woke me up for school. She came into my bedroom singing and flung back the curtains.

'"Oh what a beautiful morning!"' she sang loudly 'There is a heavy frost today.'

From my bed, I looked at the windows which were covered inside with beautiful white patterns made by the ice.

'Nature has been using her paintbrush last night and made beautiful patterns,' Mum shouted.

Towards the bottom of the window there were long strips of ice. I got out of bed, put my dressing gown on and went to the windows.

'Mum there is ice on the inside of the windows,' I said. The temptation was too much as I picked off the solid pieces of ice and dropped them on the floor.

'Yes I know it is very very cold,' Mummy called back from the kitchen. 'And Jo, don't drop the ice on the floor please. Put it in a bucket.' Without seeing, my mother always knew.

'Bring your clothes into the kitchen and you can dress in here,' she went on.

We went to the kitchen where it was warm as the large convector heater was on. Mummy had made Daddy's breakfast before he went to work.

---oOo---

Carolyn and I loved helping Mother make cakes. We would help measure out the ingredients. My favourite was a Victoria Sandwich.

'We need two eggs, and four ounces of castor sugar and the same of self-raising flour,' she reminded us.

In the corner of the kitchen was the larder. This was four foot from the floor and stretched back just as far. Underneath this was the coal hole which was accessed from outside.

Mummy went to the cupboard she reached in. 'This really is a stupid design,' said Mummy often. 'How tall did the designer of this house think we are to be able to reach into this cupboard? It's ridiculous! The back of the shelves are never used. I would have to climb into the cupboard to get there.'

I giggled at the thought of mother climbing inside the larder.

She reached the large round tin flour bin which was put on the table and took out the self raising flour. I stood on a chair and with a desert spoon in my hand I dug deep into the packet and took a spoonful and slowly and carefully put it on the scales. I checked the measure. The dial had hardly moved. I repeated the process one spoonful at a time onto the scale and I checked the dial each time. 'Have I got there yet Mummy?' I asked.

'No not quite you need another two ounces, the same amount as you have already put on the scales.'

Carolyn sighed, 'Mummy how long is she going to take to do a simple job?'

'Now Carolyn! that's enough,' Mummy said.

It did take some time until the four ounces were reached. 'There,' Mummy said breathing a sigh of relief, 'and you didn't spill any. Well done! I'll put it on this saucer as we don't need it just yet.'

Mummy weighed the sugar. 'It is a little more difficult to do,' she said. She measured the margarine too as this needed a knife to cut through the block. 'I don't want you using knives until you are older.'

'Who would like to help me grease and flour the tins?' she asked.

We both took a sandwich tin each. Covering our fingers with margarine we greased the bottoms and sides of the tins.

'Make sure you cover it all, especially that bit between the bottom and the sides. We don't want the cake to stick when it's cooked.'

Mother finished off the greasing as we wiped our hands.

'Can I put in the teaspoon of flour for you to shake around the bottom of the tin?' I shouted.

'Not too much now,' Mother said

I carefully scooped up a teaspoon of flour and dropped them into each of the two cake tins. Keeping them flat Mummy shook each tin around until the flour stuck evenly to the fat. She blew off the excess into the sink. I thought this was magical.

'There, they are ready now,' she sighed.

Mother took a dishcloth and then wrung it out firmly. She laid this on the table and placed the bowl on it. 'This will stop it from slipping.,' she said. Then she took a large wooden spoon and creamed the castor sugar into the margarine.

She was quite exhausted when she had finished but the mixture was a now a pale creamy colour and was light and fluffy. 'The trick here is not to use the margarine straight from the fridge as it would be solid and more difficult to cream!'

'Now we must add the eggs and flour,' she said. 'The eggs can curdle at this point so you add a little flour. Jo will you use your teaspoon to add a little flour.'

I added the flour and she gently folded it in.

'Each egg has to be checked for freshness before adding it to the mixture,' Mum instructed.

Carolyn broke an egg into the cup. She sniffed it and looked at it closely. 'Is this alright Mum?' she asked.

Mum peered into the cup. 'Yes that's fine. We would certainly know if it was off as the smell would be awful!'

Carolyn continued to check each egg individually before adding them to the lovely creamy concoction.

When the flour and eggs were evenly distributed she put the mixture into the greased cake tins which she put on to a baking tray. 'I'll put them in the oven as it is very hot.'

Now Carolyn and I were in front of the mixing bowl. We lined up with our teaspoons. 'Can we clean the bowl out?' we asked.

'Yes but no arguments.'

We took it in turns to take some of the raw cake mix from the bowl and scraped the wooden spoon. There was enough as Mummy had left a little in the bottom of the bowl. We didn't row over this as we knew Mummy would take the bowl away and wash it.

Carolyn and I made sure that the doors and windows were shut when 25 minutes later Mummy checked the cakes. She carefully opened the door.

'Keep still girls. We don't want to make a draught as the cakes will sink if they get suddenly cold.' She pressed the top of the cake to see if it sprung back up again.

'Yes they are done. Mind! Stay out of the way now the cake tins are very hot.' She turned the cake tins over separately, laying them on the wire tray. She stopped, looked up and crossed her fingers.

'Let's hope they haven't stuck to the bottom of the tins.' They hadn't and after cooling Mother added strawberry jam and put the two halves together.

In the kitchen there was a Belfast style sink with taps that came out of the wall; a Belling electric stove; a fridge and an old fashioned sideboard more suited to a formal dining room. The kitchen table had an enamel top and two drawers at the side, where cooking utensils were kept.

The kitchen was where we mostly gathered together. At the weekend and on holidays we always ate our breakfast there. Daddy would read his newspaper and Mummy, Carolyn and I would chat. Mother would teach us table manners. I stood up one day and stretched over the table, and over the cups full of tea, the saucers and butter to reach the marmalade jar.

Mummy looked sternly at me. '"Would you please pass me the marmalade?" Is what you should have said and certainly you must not just reach over the table. That is not the way to behave. We'll have no boarding house stretches here at this table.'

I started to take the jar from Mummy's hand but she would not let it go. 'And what do you say now?' she said.

'Thank you,' I said meekly.

'Would you pass me the butter please Mummy,' Carolyn smugly asked.

'Goody two shoes.' I thought.

When cleaned and thoroughly wiped the table was used by Mother for dress making. She laid the material out first on which she pinned the pattern. She whistled quietly while she did this as she was concentrating very hard. Carolyn and I learnt this was not the place to be as a mistake could be costly. Her Singer Sewing machine came out and mother stitched the pieces together. This machine was worked by hand and had only a straight stitch.

---oOo---

The bungalow had four bedrooms: three downstairs and one upstairs. I slept in all three of the downstairs rooms at some time during my life there from the age of five until I was 18.

First room on the left was a bedroom that was originally described as a dining room. I thought this silly as it was a long way from the kitchen.

'The food will have got cold before it reaches the dining room.' I said. We never used it to eat in at all.

I had this as my bedroom for a while. As I loved tinkering on the piano this was put in the same room along the inside wall. 'It is an expensive piano, a Bechstein upright, and it must not get damp by being on an outside wall,' Mother insisted.

There was a fireplace in this room across a corner. I placed my bed in front of this. I thought it looked very modern and unusual. Across the picture rail in the opposite corner

Daddy had built a wardrobe. It was simply a wooden frame attached to the picture rail on which a curtain was fixed. The rail for the clothes was fixed to this.

One night I was woken up by a gnawing sound coming from the opposite corner. I was cross being disturbed from my sleep. At the side of my bed were my slippers. I picked one up and threw it at the hanging wardrobe.

'Shut up, whoever you are. I want to sleep,' I shouted.

The next night I made a pile of shoes at my bedside ready to attack the noise in the corner.

'Shut up! Go to sleep! This is my bedroom! Go away!' I shouted as I threw each shoe at the curtain. This happened a lot during the night, the gnawer was persistent.

In the morning the pile of shoes by my bed was no more but there was a pile in the opposite corner high enough to cover the base of the curtain. I had been woken several times by the noise.

'Are you having nightmares?' Mummy asked me the next morning.

'No there is a gnawing sound that wakes me up a lot,' I replied.

'I think you've got a mouse,' she said. 'I'll get a trap from Wood and Wilkins when I go into Ryde. I'll set it behind the piano.'

The next night the gnawing started again. There was a short silence and finally a snap. After that there was silence.

In the morning the pile of shoes was by my bed and Mother checked the trap. There lying dead was a tiny mouse.

'It was only a tiny field mouse,' she said sympathetically.

'But he had big noisy teeth though!' I replied.

The next bedroom, in the middle of the house was the first one I slept in when we arrived at Leys. To add a little more money to the housekeeping Mother took in paying guests. They were scientists who worked at the Old Needles Battery above Alum Bay. They stayed for the week but went home at the weekend.

She also let the rooms for holidays and the house was turned upside down. My old bedroom at the front was their sitting room and the room next to the bathroom was their bedroom.

The day before Mr. and Mrs. Bevan were due to come to stay, Carolyn and I were feeling a little unwell. The day after they arrived Carolyn and I were covered in spots.

Mother told the Bevans we had chicken pox, but we had to be kept out of the way. The first few days we stayed in bed under Dr O'Brien's order. As we recovered and were feeling better we wanted to get up and play but still had to stay in the room while the guests were in the house. Covered in calamine lotion to stop us scratching we must have looked pretty awful.

Mother cooked the meals, made the beds, tidied the rooms and was the perfect hostess. At the same time she nursed the sick and did her best to keep us amused. This went on for two weeks. When they finally left we could leave the room and have the full run of the house again.

---oOo---

The master bedroom was the largest and at the end of the hall. It was the coldest as it had two outside walls. I spent my teenage years in here and remained there until I was 18 and left home. My piano was moved into this room and placed against the inside wall.

'Can we decorate my new bedroom please?' I meekly asked at breakfast one day.

'Yes it is a bit dull in there. A fresh coat of paint would brighten it up,' Mum said. She pulled down Dad's newspaper that he was reading and conveyed the request to him.

'Right you are,' he said. He shook his newspaper back into shape and continued reading it.

'We'll choose the paint,' Mum said. She was now working at Pack and Cullifords. 'I'll get a paint chart from Wood and Wilkins when I go out for coffee."

The next evening two paint charts lay on the kitchen table. There was star near the primrose yellow in the emulsion paint chart, and further star near the mushroom colour gloss paint.

'Do you like the primrose yellow?' she asked me. It was such a small square of colour that I really couldn't see it on my walls.

'It's a lovely bright spring colour don't you think?' Mum went on

'Yes it's lovely,' I replied. 'I'm sure it will be very nice.'

'Now as regards the gloss paint there is this new idea.' Mum said excitedly. 'To help me get the exact colour I want it is sold with a small paint pot of intense colour. We then mix it to get the exact colour we want and put it on the door, window frame, skirting board and picture rail.'

I looked at Mum's choice. It was alright I suppose I didn't really mind. Mum put the two colours together. 'What do you think?'

'That's fine,' I said.

'Hmm yes very nice,' said Carolyn butting in over my shoulder.

The paint arrived and the furniture was pushed into the middle of the room. There were two tins of primrose yellow emulsion, a tin of creamy coloured gloss paint with a small tin of intense brown paint.

'I'll start with the door and woodwork,' Daddy said. He was of course a professional in the building trade so I was sure he knew what he was doing.

Daddy opened the tin of gloss paint and gave it a stir. 'Are you sure this is the colour you want? Isn't it a bit pale?'

'Daddy you have missed the point,' I said.

Mummy took over and explained as she opened the small pot of intense brown. 'You mix it in to get the exact colour,' she said adding the brown to the pale paint. Daddy stirred it in. 'Is this enough?' Mummy said. We gazed at the pot of paint now slightly darker.

'Add a bit more,' I suggested.

'O.K.,' she said.

Daddy stirred it thoroughly until he thought it was all mixed. 'I'll start with the door and work my way around the room clockwise,' he said.

An hour later Daddy came into the kitchen with paint brush in his hand. 'Come and see this,' he said and we followed him back to my bedroom. 'Is it my imagination or is the colour getting paler?' Daddy commented as he reached the picture rail at the side of the window. We went to the door and inspected it. Then we went to the picture rail near the window and looked closely at that.

'I think you are right,' Mummy said. We stood for a while in silence not knowing what to do.

The Mummy announced, 'The paint has cost a lot of money so give it an extra stir Bryan and press on.' The door where we started was a darker shade of mushroom than the skirting board and picture rail on its left hand side that butted onto it.

'No-one will notice,' Mummy assured me. 'It is such a small detail.' The primrose yellow emulsion went on the walls without a hitch.

Once finished I had a unique style of decoration. It made little difference to my room as I covered up the walls and some of picture rails with pretty colour wrapping paper that I was collecting. On top of those I added pictures of Cliff Richard and then when he went out of fashion, the Beatles.

I did all my homework in this room to the accompaniment of music from my Dansette Record Player. I daydreamed to the music by the Beatles but I did my homework better to the sound of the classics. Tchaikovsky's "Swan Lake" was my favourite which I played and played.

'You'll wear a hole in that record if you keep playing it,' Mum teased.

'Will I? Really?' I then realised she was teasing me.

The author and her mother in the sitting room with the Adam fireplace behind.

I had a large collection of records and I would sing along with them or lie on my bed and dream. I created harmonies to some of the songs and recorded myself singing with the record on my reel to reel to tape recorder. I wanted to be a pop singer, have a number one hit and meet all the famous stars.

I picked out the tune on the piano and played along with the record. The piano unfortunately was a half tone lower than it should have been. My extra accompaniment with the record was pretty awful.

I changed my bedroom around during the following winter so that the head was against the bathroom wall. I discovered then that I was warmer than I had been before when it was against the outside wall.

One of the treats we got when Mummy went to work full time was to get a television set. This was a Sobell and rented from "Radio Rentals" in the High Street in Ryde. Every Saturday morning we went into the shop to pay the six shillings and six pence rental. This was marked in a paying in book. The rental covered breakdowns...This was a good deal as early TV sets had a tendency to fail.

'The television won't turn on,' I called out to Carolyn. 'It's Saturday and "The Lone Ranger" is on at five o'clock. I'll just die if I miss that.'

Carolyn took some change and ran down to the telephone box which was outside the Post Office at the bottom of Binstead Hill.

The TV repair man came very quickly. We let him in and he went straight to the electrical plug and took it out of the wall. 'Look! The wire has come undone,' he said

We felt very foolish. That was a job that Daddy could have fixed.

'Oh,' I said. 'Would you like a cup of tea?'

The repair man fixed the wire, drank his tea and left in good time for us to watch "The Lone Ranger".

This large TV set sat in the corner of the sitting room. It had a lovely shiny varnished top. The on and off switch and other controls were at the side. There were two channels to watch the BBC or ITV. We watched a lot of ITV as this showed the American Programmes. I loved the Westerns. "Wagon Train" was my favourite with Flint McCullough the Scout played by Robert Horton. This ran stories about the pioneers who travelled across America. Ward Bond played the Wagon Master Major Seth Adams who at the end of the episode always shouted. 'Wagons Roll!'

Carolyn loved "Rawhide" starring Clint Eastwood as Rowdy Yates. He was the young impetuous cattle drover. He was kept under control by Gil Favour the trail boss played by Eric Fleming, the star of the show. Cattle were driven across the plains of America to get to market to be sold and various stories were created around this theme. Gil Favour finished the show with the cry, 'Hit 'em up, move 'em out.'

Both stories had problems with the Native Americans which in the 1950s and 60s were referred to as "Indians". All problems were overcome within the hour long shows. The Indians were often the baddies. It was rare that the native Indians were portrayed as friendly.

Mummy was very proud of her Adams Fireplace. I realised that this must be something special as on this she displayed her favourite china ornaments and special photographs. We had a coal fire in winter but used an electric fire when mother was too busy to light one.

We had a large garden full of flowers to cut. In my teenage years I picked these and arranged them in a vase and placed it on top of the shiny top of the television. I never considered that the water in the vase if spilt would be dangerous in contact with the electricity of the TV Set.

Once the television came, the kitchen table was abandoned for eating our evening meals, we ate in the sitting room. We each had our chairs and there were two low coffee tables on which we put our plates. Mum sat in the corner near the fire place; I was next; then Carolyn and finally Daddy. I shared a table with Mummy and Carolyn with Daddy.

Mummy and Daddy's bedroom was in the loft. There was a basic staircase to get up there. This was very simple in design. There were long straight planks going from top to bottom, on this were horizontal treads which were covered with a red stair carpet. They were very narrow but we got used to it.

This room was very hot in summer and freezing cold in winter. It was a long room with an alcove which took two twin beds for Mum and Dad. Opposite the beds was the window through which Mummy could see the oak tree on which red squirrels ran up and down its branches.

There was a door at the end of this room which led into the loft, a large storage area. Daddy with his love of photography created a dark room in here in which he developed the photos he had taken.

When it was meal times and Daddy was in his dark room, we had to run upstairs and bang hard on the door to attract his attention.

'Daddy! Daddy! It's lunch time.' I shouted as I continued to hammer on the door.

'Right you are,' Daddy said.

'That's enough banging,' Mummy shouted from downstairs.

When photos were always black and white Daddy took the film from the camera and processed this into negatives. This was done in the sink in the kitchen. The tap would be running through this container for a considerable time. Daddy's white clock was set for 30 minutes and continued to tick until the time was up. Then the negatives were pegged out to dry on a line above the sink.

This was exciting. 'What can you see Carolyn?' I said and we both squinted at the negatives not daring to touch them. 'Isn't that a picture of us on the beach?'

'Yes,' Carolyn answered, 'it's us at Compton Chine. Oh look. There's Willie Pickle.'

'No touching,' Daddy reminded us. 'Once they are dry I'll take them up to the darkroom and make pictures.'

'Can I come and watch you making the pictures?' I asked.

'Yes alright then.' said Dad.

'You mustn't touch anything,' Mother chipped in. 'Daddy uses chemicals and they can be dangerous.'

'I won't touch anything, I promise,' I said.

Mum touched Daddy's arm, 'Don't let her put her hand in the chemicals will you Bryan?' Mum was serious and spoke, mouthing the words clearly.

'She'll be alright, stop worrying,' said Dad.

With my hands firmly behind my back in case I forgot and touched something, I watched Daddy get three trays out. He filled two with chemicals and the third with water he had in a bottle.

'Poo!' I said. 'That's horrid! Doesn't that smell awful?'

Dad didn't answer but turned to the tall contraption and slipped a negative into a slot. 'This is called an "Enlarger". Look it has a light at the top,' he said. He clipped it shut and adjusted the height of the light at the top of the enlarger.

'Turn the light out please, Jo,' Dad asked.

He turned on a red light. 'Why do you need a red light?' I asked.

'Because I am going to expose the light through the negative onto the light sensitive paper,' he explained.

Unlike Mummy, Daddy was using words I didn't understand.

He took out a piece of paper which had been wrapped in thick plastic with a black lining. 'This is special paper and sensitive to light,' he explained. 'When I expose it to the light in the enlarger, it will react to black, grey and white of the negative.' When he had put the paper in the frame securely under the light he turned it on.

'Oh,' I said. 'But where is the picture.'

'Sssh!' he said as he watched his timer for 10 seconds. 'Be patient! Wait and see.'

I didn't understand, but Dad was concentrating so I was quiet.

He took the paper and using wooden tongs he placed it in the first of the three trays. 'This is the developer, I must leave it in here for 1 minute 30 seconds.' he said. Again he watched the clock.

I stared at the paper and very gradually the picture came into view.

'Look!' I squealed. 'There's Carolyn, Mummy and me at Compton Chine!'

'And Willie Pickle,' Daddy corrected me. 'Don't forget Willie Pickle.'

Again using the wooden tongs Daddy picked up the photo and placed it in the next tray. 'This is water, it washes off the developer.' he said.

'Oh Daddy it's magic!' I smiled as I looked at the photo.

He picked it up and placed it in the third tray. 'This is the fixer,' he said, 'It makes the image permanent so that the paper is not light sensitive anymore. This must stay in this one for four minutes.

'I'll look for another negative and you can watch it all over again.'

After four minutes he carefully picked up the photo and laid it on a muslin tray to dry flat.

'Don't touch! Leave them there until they are dry. They are still very wet.'

I tucked my hands behind my back again just in case I forgot.

I watched the process a couple of times before Carolyn came banging on the door. 'It's supper time,' she called.

'Right you are,' Daddy said.

Daddy was a member of a photographic club in Ryde and took pictures of models at the meeting place. He also took pictures of views. Neither of these two subjects interested me. I wanted to see pictures of us and of Willie Pickle, our dachshund, and Tigger the cat.

On January 7th 1967 Daddy died and with Carolyn and me now living in London, "Leys" was far too big and too expensive for Mummy to keep and she decided to move to a cottage in Wootton. I was so sad to leave my childhood home. Christmas 1967 was the last at "Leys". With Daddy gone there were no photos taken that day. The cottage was much smaller than the house so a lot of furniture had to be left behind including my piano.

I shed a tear as I left "Leys" after that last Christmas. The house had meant so much to me. I knew it had to happen. I knew Mummy didn't want to leave either but she put on a brave face as she said her good byes. 'Next time I see you I will be in the new house in Wootton. That'll be fun won't it?'

'Yes Mum it will.' I lied. That was not how I felt.

4 OUR CAR CALLED ANNA

'How long is Mummy going to be?' I asked Carolyn as we stood at the gate. 'She's been ages!' I sighed loudly to make my words have more meaning. 'Just ages and ages!'

'No she hasn't! No longer than her usual driving lesson,' Carolyn answered.

I sighed again and walked out into the middle of the road to look around the bend as if peering around the corner would make her come quicker.

'Come back into the garden!' Carolyn snapped. 'She'll be here as soon as she is finished.'

We waited. It seemed like for ever. Mummy was taking her driving test in our car.

She explained before she went out, 'I've had lots of lessons and Mr. Campaign, my driving instructor thinks I am ready for my driving test. He says that as I have had more lessons than any of his other pupils that I should be ready to pass. It doesn't seem fair, Daddy never took a test as he was driving when he was 20. He had been driving for eight years before the law changed in 1935 and tests were made compulsory.'

The author standing by Anna the car on holiday in King's Lynn, Norfolk.

'If I come home with a sad face in the car with "L" plates on you are to say nothing!' Mummy instructed us. 'Promise?'

'Alright we promise,' we said in unison.

It was a lovely day. My skipping rope lay on the ground waiting for me to pick it up and skip but I couldn't think about anything else except Mummy and the driving test. I put my foot on to one of the swirls on the closed wrought iron gate and climbed up.

'You'll get your foot stuck like you did the other day if you do that,' Carolyn said, 'and you will cry.'

'I won't! so there!' I retorted. I did but managed to pull it out before Carolyn saw. 'How long is she going to be? She has been ages!'

'If you had learnt how to tell the time you would know that she has not been gone that long.'

Around the corner of the Church Road Mummy came driving without the "L" plates. 'She's passed!' we yelled. 'She's passed!'

Mummy got out of the car beaming her "L" plates in her hand. 'These can go in the dustbin now,' she proudly announced.

Carolyn took them out of Mummy's hand, 'I'll do it! Well done Mummy.'

'Oh Mummy how lovely,' I said as I put my arms around her.

Mr. Campaign got out of the passenger seat and smiled at us cuddling Mummy.

'She got slower and slower as she drove,' Mr. Campaign told us, 'but the examiner thought her good enough to pass.'

'What fun we will have now I can drive,' Mummy announced, 'We can go anywhere we like without worrying about the bus.'

When Auntie Maud died Daddy was left the house which was sold and the mortgage on Leys was paid off. There was some money left over and Daddy bought a car. It was a grey Standard 8 and the registration number 68 AMK.

"Daddy's here with the car!" I shouted to Carolyn and Mummy.

Daddy had parked the shiny new car in the driveway. I walked around it. It was grey and had four doors. There were two bits that stuck out, one at the front and one at the back.

Daddy poses for the camera in Anna, our car.

'Look! Come here girls,' said Dad as he lifted a lid at the front. 'This is the engine.'

I looked in and saw pipes and bit of metal.

'Beautiful isn't it?' said Dad.

'Yes dear. If you say so,' said Mum

I walked around the car and looked at the bulge at the back. 'What's this for? Is there another engine in here?' I asked.

'No, no, no,' chuckled Dad. 'That's the boot.'

I stared at it still not understanding what a boot was. I had a pair of Wellington boots.

'How do you open it?' I asked.

'You don't.' Dad said as he opened up one of the back doors. 'You get into the boot through the car. The back seats lie flat so you can slot suitcases in.'

'Jump in girls,' said Mum and try out your seats.

'The back seat is designed for two people but three children could fit in easily,' Dad said.

I shifted myself over to the middle and discovered that there was bar hidden under the red tartan seat covers. It was quite uncomfortable to sit on.

Daddy continued to show us the features of the car. He sat in the driver's seat, pressed a button which turned the engine on. He twisted the knob on the dashboard. This made two little yellow indicator arms stick out of the car in between the front and back doors.

'Oh let me see, let me see, please do it again,' I said as I jumped out of the car.

The little arms lit up when they popped out of the side.

'Well! Do you like it?' asked Dad.

'Oh yes,' we all said.

'Jump inside again and get a feel of it.

'There are locks on every door.'

'That's good,' said Mum. 'You must always lock the doors when we are travelling. I don't want you falling out of the car.'

'Now,' said Dad 'to open the windows you slide them sideways.'

We were all was thrilled with the car, 'Shall we give our car a name?' Mummy said.

We used to play a game of making a word up with the registration number plates. As all cars registered on the Isle of Wight had a letter and then DL there were lots of "PDLs MDLs CDLs which became puddles, muddles and cuddles". This game, as we drove around the island, could get rather boring with the same words.

'Buddles,' I shouted one day having spotted a BDL.

Carolyn sighed like an exasperated teacher, 'There's no such word!'

'There could be,' I said.

Ever the diplomat Mummy joined in, 'I think you are thinking of "bubbles" darling. It's very similar, but "bubbles" has got two Bs not Ds'.

Our car was not registered on the island and AMK did not make up a word that we could use for a name.

'It could have been "America" if "America" was spelt with a "k" at the end,' said Carolyn.

'It's not, unfortunately. Shall we make up a name with the initials? How about calling her Anna Maria Kate?' suggested Mum

So our grey Standard 8 became Anna.

There was an open hole called a glove compartment in front of the passenger seat, and my clever Daddy fashioned a tray made out of wood that snugly fit in and made a surface for winter picnics.

The car opened up the Island to us. We discovered its secrets. There were new beaches to explore. The Downs were now within easy reach with places for us to run and play.

During Anna's first winter it snowed and roads became very icy. Daddy took the car into Ryde where they put chains over the tyres to prevent her from skidding. This made a horrid noise and a bumpy ride. Anna was only used for essentials in snowy weather. A dry day in winter did not stop us from going out. The temperature was very low but the sun was shining making a bright day in March when Mother announced, 'We'll take two Thermoses of tomato soup and cheese rolls today. We are going up on the Downs to get some fresh air.'

'Make sure you are wrapped up warm,' she called out.

The wrought iron gates were open and Daddy backed out of our driveway into Church Road. Carolyn shut the gates and got back into her seat behind Daddy. Mummy was in the front passenger seat and I sat behind her. Willie Pickle, our black and tan dachshund, was on the floor in the front between Mummy's ankles.

'Lock your doors, please, girls,' Mummy said. We dutifully slide along the little silver coloured metal strip across to the lock position on the door. 'I don't want the door opening and you falling out.'

'All set?' said Daddy. 'Then off we go.'

Our destination that day was Brading Down. We parked on the grass looking over the south of the Island. There was an area of short grass for parking. It was very uneven to drive on and Daddy drove very slowly and parked.

'What's happened to the grass there!' Carolyn asked as she spotted a neat patch where the grass was missing, leaving the bare earth. 'Look there's another one.'

'Someone has been taking turf again for their gardens!' Daddy remarked. 'I wish they wouldn't do that. It leaves such a scar.'

'Let's go over the road and down the hill and walk along the bridle path,' Mummy suggested. 'Take care how we cross the road.'

We got out of the car. Daddy checked every door to make sure Anna was locked tight and Mummy held firmly to Willie Pickle's lead. We crossed the road carefully and walked down to the bridle path which was lower down the hill. The path went through the woods. It was bracing but Carolyn and I ran around hiding, chasing and shouting at each other.

'I think it is safe to let Willie Pickle off the lead here, what do you think Bryan?' Mummy asked.

'What dear? What was that?' he replied.

'Let Willie off the lead.'

'Right you are,' he said and lent down and unclipped the lead to let Willie free. He chased after us and joined in the fun, in between smelling every tree and lifting his leg on them.

'Why does he do that? Why can't he just go to the toilet in one go?' I asked.

'He is leaving his mark for other dogs to find,' Mum explained.

We threw sticks for Willie to retrieve and for us to throw again. He was slow to get to the stick and quite often he would come back with a different stick but that added to the fun.

'Oh Willie Pickle. You are not the brightest of dogs!' Mum said.

Carolyn and I ran around the woods and found some primroses to pick for Mummy.

'They are lovely,' she said, 'they have such a beautiful smell.' I buried my nose in the yellow flowers and sniffed loudly.

'Yes lovely,' I agreed.

'I'm getting a little cold now,' said Mum. 'Let's turn around and go back to the car and have our picnic.'

With rosy cheeks and puffed out we climbed back up the hill, crossed the road carefully, got back into our places in the car. Daddy's wooden tray was fixed into the open glove compartment for Mummy to lay out the picnic. Four cups were put on the sturdy shelf and the hot soup was poured into them equally.

Mummy touched Daddy's arm 'This shelf is so useful, Bryan,' she said clearly mouthing the words carefully. Daddy smiled.

'We will have the soup first,' Mummy said, 'then the rolls afterwards.'

Warming our hands on the cups we sipped our soups which were just the right temperature. Then we munched through crusty rolls. Mum sighed as she looked at the view over the south of the Island.

'I love this view,' she said. 'You can see the monument on the top of Culver Cliff quite clearly. The sea at Yaverland is so blue today and quite calm.'

'I wish we could go bathing,' I said.

'No it's far too cold, it's only March, the sea hasn't warmed up yet.' Mum replied. 'Can you see the boating lake at Sandown?' I looked over Mum's shoulder at this small circle of water near the shore.

'That won't open until May or June at the earliest.' Mum said.

'What are those houses that go along the shore?' asked Carolyn

'They are mostly hotels and guest houses. Their owners are probably busy getting ready for the summer season when all the holidaymakers come to the Island.

'Look there is the train going into Sandown,' Carolyn shouted.

We watched the train chuffing along, its smoke billowing out, extending behind over the carriages.

'Daddy and I used to cycle up here when we were courting,' Mum said.

'What's courting?' I asked.

'It's the time we spent together before we got married.'

'What was it like then?' I asked.

'The view was very similar but you couldn't get on the beach because there was barbed wire, put there to prevent the Germans from landing. Daddy had to be very careful when taking photos. It was forbidden to take pictures that would help the enemy and there is an airport over there. It was shut during the war and obstructions were put on the runway, but once cleared it would be a good place for the enemy to land.'

Mum paused and finished her roll. 'Down there is the Roman Villa,' she said pointing down just below us. 'The Romans also invaded England a very long time ago. They were highly educated and built strong houses and taught the English Anglo-Saxons a great many skills. Down there are the remnants of one of their villas. A "villa" is a very substantial house.' I looked down and saw a shed! I decided I would finish my roll.

'In the far distance,' Mum continued, 'on the other side of that hill is Ventnor.'

We finished our picnic and Mum tidied away the cups and sandwich box and Daddy drove us home. He turned to the gates and Carolyn got out and opened them for him and when the car was in she shut them.

Later that same year, in August, the weather changed from being a dull day and now there was brilliant sunshine. 'There's no time to pack a picnic. Let's just get in the car and go for a drive up to Brading,' Mother suggested.

Carolyn and I changed into sun dresses and put on our sandals. We raced out to the car which Daddy had already reversed out of the garage and into the road.

We clambered in and were ready to go in no time. We locked our doors.

'Lock your doors girls, Mum said.

'We know you don't want us falling out,' Carolyn said. 'We have already done it.'

There were lots of cars on the top of Brading Down. 'As it is getting late,' Mummy said, 'let's not go down to the bridle path across the road. Let's walk down the hill towards Sandown.'

'Not all the way there?' Carolyn questioned.

'No, no not that far.'

The grass further down was long. unlike the grass at the top where it was short and regularly stolen for turf. We walked steadily down the hill.

'Not too far,' Mum repeated, 'Remember we have to climb back up again and it's a hot day.'

I took a step forward behind a bush and I heard a rustle. Suddenly Mummy grabbed me from behind around my waist. An adder snake had been sunning himself and I had trodden on his tail. He turned and with mouth open lunged forward and hissed at me. Holding me tightly Mummy started to walk back up the hill.

'Bryan! Bryan!' she shouted, 'Carolyn tell Daddy there are snakes! Jo has just disturbed one.'

Daddy fortunately was not far away, turned and understood quickly. He was wearing long trousers but Carolyn and I were without socks and were in sandals. Daddy picked Carolyn up and carefully climbed the hill back to the short grass.

'Watch where you walk!' Mummy instructed. 'We don't want to find any more.'

We arrived back at the car and Mummy was shaking! Carolyn and I didn't understand.

'Why were you scared of a grass snake? I've seen lots of them in the compost heap in the garden,' Carolyn said.

'It wasn't a grass snake. It was an Adder. They are the only snake in the British Isles whose bite is poisonous. You can tell the difference because it has a zig zag pattern all the way down its back.'

I was beginning to understand just what danger I had been in. 'What if it had bitten me? Would I have died?'

'No, darling. We would have got into the car and driven to Ryde Hospital where they have some special medicine and you would have been alright. But you weren't bitten so all is well.'

We drove home that day in silence. I was so glad we had Anna our car.

'It would have saved my life if I had been bitten by the Adder, wouldn't it Mummy?'

---oOo---

Going on holiday with the car was a new venture for the Drawbridge family. We had been to Barton on Sea when I was very small. The landlady, Mrs. Gardiner, was awful! There was still rationing in force and she used this as an excuse to serve us poor meals. We were hungry all the time. Half way through the stay Mummy had had enough and told Daddy in their room her feelings at the top of her voice. Mother made sure the door was open and that there was a reference to misuse of rationing. She was sure the landlady heard as Mrs. Gardiner was somewhat changed when they next saw her and the quantity of food improved. The family did not go there again.

Daddy organised a memorable trip to Alderney in October 1950. We flew there in a very small plane and I was sick. The weather on the island was poor and we were very cold all the time. We stayed in Fort Clonque which was situated at the end of a peninsula west of the island.

The causeway between the fort and the land flooded and we were cut off when the tide was in. Mummy didn't like that at all. Cooking was difficult. She could never get the stove to light. It had to be pumped and even Daddy found it difficult but he was the only one able to get it going.

Owning a car opened up new adventures. We were invited to stay with Uncle Leslie and Auntie Grace in Norfolk. He was a vicar who had worked on the Island where Mummy and Grace had made friends. They did not have any children of their own. Willie Pickle was not invited and was sent for his holiday to kennels.

They lived in a vicarage in King's Lynn. Arrangements were made and Daddy bought the ferry tickets. We were to travel by car. There was a new experience for Daddy and Anna the car as she was to be driven on to the ferry in Cowes and cross the Solent to Southampton.

Mummy packed the suitcases which in the 1950s were square and solid. Daddy had the job of sliding them into the boot of the car behind the back seats. He slid them in and then took them out and tried another way. He pushed and shoved them trying to squash them so they would go in.

Daddy took this photo of Carolyn, the author and Mother on the Red Funnel Ferry on their way to Southampton and to our holiday in Kings Lynn in Norfolk.

'Betty they just won't fit!' Daddy said.

'Each suitcase is packed really tight we must take it all. We are there for a fortnight! I don't know what washing arrangements I can have at the vicarage. We must take them all.'

'I can get them in if one suitcase is put on the back seat between the girls.'

'Will it be a small one?'

'Yes of course it will!' Daddy was getting angry now.

The car was packed tight, Carolyn and I had been to the toilet. Daddy had locked the house and Mummy had checked each window and door.

To start with I liked the suitcase between us on the back seat. It meant I had my secret spot which was safe and secure from my sister.

Mummy turned around and looked at us. She was about to speak when….

'We have locked the doors, we are not going to fall out of the car.' Carolyn said.

Daddy drove us to Cowes. 'Here we are!' he said as he drove through the small arch.

I looked up and there in front of us was the ship to take us across the Solent.

'I'll go and check in with the tickets,' Daddy said.

As soon as he returned to the car we were ushered forward to drive up the wide gangway and onto the ship at the side. We were the first car. Once on board we turned sharply left and were directed to the back.

'A little further forward sir,' said the deck hand.

'Forward!' Mummy said clearly translating the information to Daddy.

'Now go back towards me,' said the deck hand.

'Backwards!' Mummy said. 'Go towards the deck hand.'

'Left hand down a bit.'

After a few more 'Backwards, forwards Sir and left hand then right hand down a bit', we parked.

Finally the deck hand was satisfied and he said. 'Thank you Sir; that's fine.' He then smartly gave his attention to another car directing it into its place with the same phrases.

'We are in the stern of the ship,' Daddy said. 'That's what they call the back of a boat or ship.'

We waited in the car until the other cars were loaded and it was safe for us to get out. When we got out of the car it was cold and grey. I shivered.

'Wait there I am going to go upstairs and take a photo from that deck up there.'

'Can't we go inside now, I'm cold,' I moaned.

'Just wait a minute until Daddy has taken the photo,' Mummy said.

'Look there he is!' said Carolyn.

'Smile at Daddy this is the first day of our holiday!' Mum enthused.

I was cold and a little fed up. I was leaving my friends behind. I would be quite happy playing in and around my house. Why did I need to go on holiday? I did not smile. It was my first time of being on a car ferry and this was a whole new venture for me.

The photo taken we made our way inside where I could sit and sulk in peace.

'Leave her alone,' Mummy told Carolyn. 'She'll come round soon.'

Driving off at Southampton was easier as there was a large ramp on to the quayside. Mummy was ready with a map on her lap.

'Our first objective is to get out of Southampton and make our way to Winchester and then to Basingstoke,' she said.

The excitement of a new adventure soon wore off and it became a long and tedious journey. The suitcase between us was irritating as it had changed from being a nice little secret place into a wall that restricted my movement. Mummy navigated giving Daddy instructions. 'We turn left at the next junction and take the road to Reading.'

'Are we nearly there yet?' I asked.

'No darling not nearly at all.' Mummy replied. 'We are going to stop for a picnic lunch at Epping which is approximately half way there. That'll be nice won't it?'

I sighed, 'Yes I suppose so.'

Sometime later I moaned again 'Are we nearly at the picnic place yet? I'm hungry!'

'No you are not,' Carolyn said, 'I'm not and we both had breakfast at the same time so you can't be. And you had extra toast and marmalade. You are just greedy!'

'No I'm not!' I snapped back

'Oh yes you are.'

'No I'm not. I was hungry! Mummy I'm not greedy am I?'

'Girls that's enough! That is enough!! Bryan you need to keep on this road at the next junction. Look there is a sign to Windsor, we are on the right road. Now girls we have a long way to go. You have just got to learn how to be patient.'

It started to rain. 'Oh dear that is a shame,' Mummy said. 'Let's play the car registration game.'

Carolyn was good at this. She was two years older and quite bright. I was two years younger and quite lazy. Carolyn got all the words much faster than me despite Mummy trying to allow me to have a go. 'Ah here's one for Jo. Look KNG. What do you think Jo?'

'King!' Carolyn blurted out.

'Carolyn! That wasn't your turn that was not fair,' Mummy said.

'Well she's too slow!'

'Oh no I'm not!'

'Oh yes you are!'

'Not!' I snarled back over the suitcase barrier.

'Are!' Carolyn shouted back.

'Girls you sound like Cinderella's ugly sisters. Behave yourselves now!' Mother shouted over the noise and then she changed her tone of voice and said 'Bryan at the T next junction we have a right turn I think. Oh yes look at the road sign it says St. Albans.'

'Right you are,' said Daddy.

'Look we are nearly at Epping. Bryan can you find a place to stop and we can have our picnic lunch?'

Daddy kept to the route but nothing suitable was found. 'We'll just have to stop at the side of the road,' he said. Aware of his two irritable daughters he stopped in the middle of a long road. 'We will just stop here.'

On my left there was a ditch with running water. I couldn't get out of the car without stepping into this.

'I'm afraid there is nowhere for us to get out to stretch our legs.' Mum said.

The rain increased and it thundered down on the roof of the car. Other cars and lorries zoomed past spraying water all over us.

Mother had to raise her voice above the sound of the storm, 'We'll find a place to stop later on and you can get out and stretch then. This is only a passing shower!!'

She opened up the blue lid of the metal sandwich box and gave us each a cheese sandwich. 'I've got some squash in a bottle for you to have when you have finished your sandwich.'

Mum and Dad had tea. 'It never tastes the same from a Thermos does it?' Mum commented. 'But I needed that.'

'Thanks,' Dad said, 'Is there any more?' Mum emptied the Thermos into Daddy's cup.

'Now my darlings, you'll have to be careful and drink out of the bottle I can't find the cups.'

'That's OK!' I said confidently I was good at that. I took a long drink and then passed it to Carolyn. 'Look no drips on the front of my dress!'

'She's taken too much and hasn't left much for me! It's not fair!' Carolyn moaned.

Mother did not reply but turned and looked at Carolyn. 'Well she has.'

I was pleased when I saw that Carolyn had dribbled some orange onto the front of her dress.

We drove on through a few more towns. At each town I asked 'Are we nearly there yet?'

'No but we are going to stop and use the public toilet.' Daddy pulled in as close as he could to conveniences. It had stopped raining. 'We must be quick now,' Mum said, 'and mind the puddles!'

A little more refreshed we returned to our places in the car.

'We had got on the ferry at eight o'clock and now it was half past one and we still have a long way to go.' Mum said.

Daddy referred to the map. 'But we are over half way there. We have broken the back of the journey.'

The second half of the journey didn't seem to be as long as the first half. I longed to be able stretch out on the back seat. I felt sleepy but the suitcase was in the way of getting comfortable.

After numerous moans of 'Are we nearly there yet?' the rain had stopped and the sun had appeared. Following Mummy's instructions Daddy turned left instead of right and the wrong turning took us 20 miles out of our way. We stopped and Daddy referred to the map. We turned around and went back.

Finally Mum spotted the sign and shouted 'Look Kings Lynn!' She got Auntie Grace's letter out of her handbag and read out the instructions of how to get to the vicarage.

We turned into the drive way and we saw a great three storey Victorian house. There was a large lawn on the left in front of the building. A beautiful tree shaded a part of the lawn. Through the tree the church could be seen. Carolyn and I escaped from the car and ran, jumped and danced. All petty arguments were forgotten.

We were tired that night and excited so we slept soundly. Mummy woke us up as we were to go to church. She supervised and got out our best dresses and brushed our hair. 'You must look respectable. You must look your best.'

'We will sit in my reserved pew,' Auntie Grace informed us. 'Now you must behave properly in church.'

'Yes we will,' we replied. That's a bit silly I thought as we go to church anyway we know how to behave.

We had a big Sunday lunch of roast beef. 'Lovely Yorkshire Pudding,' Mummy commented as she looked at us sternly. 'It's truly lovely.'

I was a little confused as in front of us in this metal dish lay a flat half burnt offering. 'It looks awful,' I thought, 'and not nearly as good as Mummy's.

'Now Darlings would you like some Yorkshire pudding?' We humbly said 'Yes please.'

'You have such a lot on your plate I will give you just a little.'

We munched away through our dinners. I ate my food in order of preference. Firstly the burnt Yorkshire pudding then the soggy greens then the boiled potatoes and finally the meat. For pudding there was apple pie with custard. The apples were a bit sour but I could disguise that if I ate each spoonful with the custard.

Carolyn and I were early risers. The next day at seven o'clock we tiptoed into Mum and asked her if we could get up. 'Yes, of course you can. It's a lovely day. Go and find something sensible to play with. Stay close to the house.'

'Yes we will,' we said.

We dressed quickly, Carolyn put on a pretty dress and I found a pair of shorts and an Airtex shirt. In the bag with our clothes was my skipping rope. 'Let's do some skipping. That's sensible isn't it?'

'Yes of course!' said Carolyn

We went downstairs to the front door and opened it, the sun streamed in. Outside the front door was gravel.

'We can't skip here the rope will get caught on the stones.' I said.

'What about the grass?' Carolyn suggested.

I ran to the lawn. 'It's covered with dew we will get our shoes wet.'

The floor in the large porch by the open front door was made of large slabs of paving stones.

'Perfect!' said Carolyn.

'Let's see who can do the most before we make a mistake.'

I got up to fifteen and Carolyn almost matched me with fourteen.

We then turned to the rhymes we knew.

One potato two potato three potato four

Five potato, six potato, seven potato more.

Joyously we skipped taking it in turns shouting out the rhymes getting louder and louder. We were yelling when it came to:

Jelly on a plate

Jelly on a plate

Wibble Wobble

Wibble Wobble

Jelly on a plate.

We laughed raucously when we got to the line 'Wibble Wobble'.

'That's like Mrs. Fisher from the fish shop. She wibble wobbles when she walks doesn't she?' Carolyn said. We thought this was hilarious.

We were half way through a further rendition of "Jelly on a Plate" for the fifth time when a very angry Auntie Grace appeared wearing her dressing gown with her hair dishevelled.

'What on earth is all this noise? Don't you know your poor mama is having a lie in bed this morning?'

'But we asked her,' Carolyn said.

Auntie Grace put one hand on her hip and shaking a finger at us, she shouted, 'but she didn't tell you that you could make all that noise! Don't you know what time it is?'

'It's seven thirty,' Carolyn said meekly.

'Far too early! Far too early!' Auntie Grace muttered.

'But we always get up at this time,' I said.

Auntie Grace chose not to continue the discussion.

'Put down your skipping rope, wash your hands, come to the kitchen and I will give you some breakfast.'

We did as we were told and humbly went to the kitchen, sat down at the table and waited. Auntie Grace appeared shortly. She was dressed now.

'Because you have been so naughty,' she said like a school teacher, 'I am not going to give you a cherry on the top of your grapefruit!'

We looked at each other and I whispered to my sister. 'I don't like grapefruit!'

'I know,' she whispered back. 'Neither do I.'

Carolyn and I sat meekly eating our sour grapefruits without the cherries.

'Now I want you to go and apologise to your poor Mama.'

We escaped from the kitchen and ran upstairs to Mummy's room.

'Sorry we made such a noise playing skipping,' we said parrot fashion.

'We had to eat a grapefruit without a cherry! I don't like grapefruit!' I wailed.

Mummy laughed.

'What's funny?' I asked.

'Firstly I didn't mind a bit about the skipping rhymes. It was lovely to listen to you having fun. I think you woke up Auntie Grace though. You will have to think of something else to play tomorrow morning which is a little quieter. Secondly well done for eating the grapefruit despite you not liking it.'

'And without a cherry!' I chipped in.

'And without a cherry!' she repeated. Then she laughed again and went and told Daddy.

We could hear Daddy's loud laugh as we went downstairs and outside to explore in the sunshine.

Uncle Lesley was more fun and he arranged a drive out to the Wash. I thought we were going to see the sea where I could paddle and bathe. But the tide was so far out and the water too far away to paddle in.

We drove out to parks and visited country houses each day returning to the vicarage for supper. Carolyn and I were so hungry we quickly got used to Auntie Grace's unusual cooking.

There were ducks and geese in the back garden and we helped to feed them. One morning I was offered a duck egg for breakfast. Luckily Mummy was there and she refused for me.

'No thank you, Grace,' she said, 'They are very rich and the girls have such delicate stomachs.'

I was so glad she was there and that I didn't have to eat it like the sour grapefruit without the cherry.

On the last day Carolyn and I were playing with a ball on the lawn in the front garden.

'I bet you,' Daddy said 'I can throw this ball over the house.'

'It's a very tall house.' I said.

'I know, but I bet I could do it.'

He stood back on the lawn and launched the tennis ball up and over the roof.

Carolyn and I ran around the back and searched and searched. We looked in the run where the geese and ducks were but we found no ball.

'Daddy!' we snapped. 'You have lost our ball! It's not there.'

'Sorry,' said Daddy. 'We'll have to get another one.'

'I liked that ball!' I said my bottom lip protruding forward.

Mummy came to Daddy's rescue and ushered us all into the car for our journey back to the Island.

The drive home did not seem as long. Mummy was able to navigate better as she recognised landmarks we had passed on the way up.

'Ah, now I remember that war memorial and that dilapidated cottage. We are on right road. That's funny. Remember I said that it must be derelict and no-one could possibly live there. I have just seen an old lady and gentleman come out of the house with a shopping bag!'

The suitcase between us was still in the way but with my rolled up cardigan I was able to rest on it to sleep.

The trip to the Cotswolds was the last holiday we took in Anna during which we visited country houses, parks and towns. We stayed in a farmhouse in Evesham. Also there was Clare, Mummy's cousin and Daddy's sister and her family.

With his automatic shutter release Daddy, standing at the back, took this posed photo of our last holiday with Anna, our car. My cousin Elizabeth stands next to her mother, Betty Ashe. Next to her, holding Willie Pickle, is Mummy, her cousin Clare holding Texi her dachshund. Carolyn is next to her and the author is seated.

Anna's demise came quite suddenly for me. One day it was there in the garage and the next day two bikes replaced it.

'It's costing us too much now,' Mummy told us, 'and I'm not sure but I think the garage is over charging me for the repairs. You both have bikes now to ride and have fun with.'

We did have fun on the bikes riding around Binstead and I used to ride to school sometimes.

Although gone from our lives it wasn't the last we saw of Anna. When I first went to London in 1966 I stayed in a YWCA Youth Hostel in South Kensington, an area full of lovely four storey houses made into flats. Across the road Carolyn and I saw Anna, looking just the same, she was clean and well cared for. 'I'm glad she is giving pleasure to someone else all these years later,' Carolyn said.

5 SAFE AND SECURE

'Gosh what a choice of flavours,' I said to the girl in the Appley Café as I gazed into the display fridge. 'In my day I had a choice of Vanilla, Strawberry or Chocolate.'

'We still do those flavours but we have a few more now.' She listed them for me. I stopped her when I spotted the Peppermint and Chocolate ice cream. 'I'll have the Peppermint and Chocolate one please.'

'Do you want a large one or small?' she continued. '£1.00 or £1.50p'

I took a small one. In the 1950s I would have paid six old pence (two and half new pence).

I dawdled out into the sunshine and found a place to sit down on the wall. The bright sun was just like the sun ever was when I came to this beach in my childhood. However, there was more soft sand now. It reached the wall and was just a metre from the top. I slipped my shoes off and felt the sand between my toes. In the 1950s at high tide the sea came right up to wall. When the tide was out there was about a 10 foot drop from the top of the sea wall to the hard sand. The ladder had 14 steps then and now there were just four. The tide was in and there was a 25 metre walk over the sand shingle to get to the water.

I licked my ice cream and leaned back shutting my eyes to enjoy the sun's rays.

How different it all was. Children were playing the same sort of games as I did. I built sandcastles with my metal bucket and spade with a wooden handle. Today the children were playing with brightly coloured beach toys that were made out of plastic. With my sister Carolyn I used to throw a blow up beach ball. Today there was an exciting game of catch with a flat dinner plate sized piece of plastic called a Frisbee.

'Is that you?' a voice disturbed me from behind.

I turned and the bright sun blocked my vision of her face.

'Yes,' I said tentatively, still not knowing who it was.

She moved and I saw her face.

'Hello Jo. It is you.'

I recognised her immediately. 'Hello Liane. How are you?'

'Whatever are you doing here?' she said

'We've just bought a holiday flat in the Strand. Not far from where you used to live.'

She too had an ice cream and sat down beside me.

Our mothers had worked together in Pack and Culliford in Ryde. We had been close friends as children but had gone our separate ways when we left school. At Christmas we briefly passed on news every year when we exchanged cards. We hadn't seen each other since my mother's funeral.

Our conversation turned to our youth. We laughed and giggled at the fun we had; we squirmed at our stupidity; we marvelled at our escapes from the dangers we had created. We had both loved playing tennis. We laughed at our misplaced dedication to the sport. Dressed totally in white, as they did at Wimbledon, we caught the Seaview Service bus and went to Puckpool Park to pay five shillings for an hour on the tennis court there.

'We did have fun didn't we?' we both agreed.

Following a silence when we seemed to draw breath at the same time Liane asked me,

'If you had to write down two words about your childhood what would those words be?'

Without hesitation I said, 'Safe' and 'Secure'. I paused and then added, 'Although my Dad used to say that my guardian angel must have to work overtime to look after me!'

We fixed a date to have a meal together and parted.

My childhood took place in the 1950s. The war with the bombs falling on the Island, the reports of deaths and all its uncertainty had gone. We were safe. Although rationing was still in force, the shops were filling up with more goods and busy again, but the underlying fear of the future that was experienced by the previous generation was gone.

There were no inoculations, so Carolyn and I went through every illness. As well as the usual coughs, colds and sickness bugs, we had mumps, whooping cough and chickenpox together. I escaped the measles when my sister got it aged six, but I contracted this at the age of ten and I was quite ill.

Illness was something Mummy knew how to deal with. In the war she had worked at Ryde hospital as a Red Cross Nurse. Our beds were always made with 'hospital corners'. When we had been sick, a towel was folded over the top sheet and a bowl placed on a chair at the side within easy reach in case we were sick again. When we were both ill at the same time the middle bedroom resembled a hospital ward. With efficiency Mummy nursed us back to full health in the safety and security of Leys, 11 Church Road.

There was a major outbreak of Polio in 1956. Every mother was frightened for her children as was Mummy. Theatres and other meeting places were shut to attempt to stop the spread of the disease.

'They have closed the Lakeside swimming pool in Wootton,' said Carolyn to me with a voice of authority.

'No they haven't, you are just making it up!' I replied.

'No I am not lying. You can ask Mummy if you like.'

'How do you know?'

'Shirley told me. Her father who knows the maintenance man at the Lakeside dance hall told him.'

'That's not fair. Why have they shut it?' I asked.

'Because the water from the creek which feeds the pool could be contaminated with Polio,' Carolyn's voice was even more officious.

'I hope they open it again. I like swimming in the pool. There are no stones or clay there.'

Mother decided that this threat was not going to stop her carrying on with life as normally as possible. Following the general advice she installed a strict regime of cleanliness.

'Wash your hands when you have finished going to the toilet,' she told us again and again. When we came out of the bathroom at home she checked our hands to make sure we had.

When we went shopping in Ryde we walked around the shops as normal. We went to the butcher's, the greengrocer's and the grocer's shops but Carolyn and I waited outside every time away from other children. Finally we went into Betti's Café half way down Union Street. Mother had coffee which was served by the waitress at the table in two large pots.

'Half and half madam?' asked the waitress.

'Yes please and I would like three Danish Pastries and two glasses of orange squash.'

'Can I have a sugar lump dipped in your coffee Mummy please?' Carolyn and I asked separately.

Mother picked up a sugar lump and held it in her coffee until it was soaked and placed it in my mouth. She repeated the process for Carolyn.

We had come early that day to avoid the crowds so we didn't have long to wait for the waitress to return with our pastries and drinks. After we had finished Mother got out a penny for the toilet. We followed her to the Ladies room in the corner of the shop.

'Wait there,' Mummy said, 'I'm just going to make sure everything is clean.'

From her basket Mother took out a metal sandwich box. She put the penny in the slot and opened the toilet door and then took from the box a cloth and bottle of Dettol disinfectant. She cleaned the seat of the toilet and the chain and its handle. She also wiped the door handles both inside and out.

"In you go!' she said.

We both squeezed into the one cubicle. Mother was not going to pay another penny for use of another toilet. When we had finished we came out and found Mother cleaning the sink and the taps with neat Dettol before turning them on, filling the basin for us to wash our hands. Out of the box she produced a bar of soap.

'Use the soap please and make sure you rub the soap between your fingers.'

'I think it would be a good idea if we walked home today,' she said. 'The buses can get very crowded at this time.'

The Red Cross had taught Mother scrupulous cleaning routine that she carried out until the scare was over. Carolyn and I did not get polio.

This training came into force when one day in summer, we heard a loud noise.

'What was that bang?' Mum said leaning out of the kitchen window.

We stood silently and listened. Faintly we heard someone crying out.

'I think there has been an accident. Wait there, I'll go and look.'

Mother ran down the alley between the house and the garage and looked over the gate. She returned to the kitchen, and, without looking at us she put a bowl under the tap and started filling it with water. She looked serious and was frowning. She went to the cupboard behind her and took out her first aid box. She ran to fetch our blue stripy beach rug and a towel. She came back, turned off the tap, and with the rug and towel over her arm she picked up the first aid box and she ran out of the house to Quarr Road. 'Wait there,' she said to us as she left.

We followed her. There was a motor bike on its side and a young man was lying in the black gravel on the road. A car with damage to its door was on the other side of the road. Mum went straight over and knelt beside motorcyclist. 'Hello, young man. What has happened to you?'

He took a breath and mumbled, 'I turned the corner, hit the car and skidded.'

'You're alright,' Mum said as a small group of people joined the scene. 'Has anyone phoned for an ambulance?'

'Yes I have,' said our neighbour, Miss Cox.

'What's your name?' asked Mum.

'Ken,' he replied as he pushed himself up on his elbows.

'No, Ken, you stay perfectly still. She folded up the towel to make a pillow. 'An ambulance has been called, they will be here soon. Here's a rug to keep you warm.'

Using the warm water and cotton wool Mother gently wiped the dirt and stones from his face. 'Will you two girls go home please? There is nothing to stare at here.'

Carolyn and I did not obey her. We stayed transfixed with what we saw. Our blue stripy rug was covering Ken and lying out flat on the filthy gravel. Mother was nursing someone other than us.

She talked gently to Ken until the ambulance arrived wiping his face gently as if he were one of her children. The ambulance's bell heralded their arrival. Mother spoke to the driver as his colleague went straight to Ken. Mum's rug was handed to her, she shook and folded it. Ken cried in pain as he was transferred to a stretcher. 'It's alright Ken, it won't hurt for long.' Mum called out.

As the ambulance disappeared up Church Road, Mum picked up the towel.

'I'll carry that,' said Carolyn.

'Thank you, darling.' She scooped out the blood and dirt covered cotton wool pieces and squeezed them out. She tipped the remains of water out of the bowl.

'Why didn't you go home like I told you to?' Mum said sternly

We were silent we had no answer.

'Sorry,' I whispered.

'Yes sorry,' Carolyn repeated.

We walked back to the house proudly with our capable Mum who in our eyes was perfect.

This halo of perfection slipped a bit when she caused our safety to be compromised. It was a particularly hot Easter Monday, Carolyn, Daddy and I were in the garage. He was showing us what a lathe did. Suddenly Mummy's worried face appeared at the window in front of us.

She looked anxious, but spoke clearly enunciating every word so Daddy could read her lips.

'I've set fire to the hedge!'

The spruce hedge surrounded our house and back garden. It was eight foot high and three foot deep and was very dense. The fire was on the left hand side of the garden. The hedge extended up towards the house. There was a large Prunus tree which hung over the hedge and house. The situation was serious. Everything was very dry as we had not had rain for weeks. The fire could have easily have spread and taken the whole hedge then the tree and reach the house.

'Oh my God!' Daddy said as he went into action. Unperturbed, he acted swiftly. He picked up the ladder from the garage and leant it up against the hedge just to the left of fire. He was now in between the fire and the house. He knew that all evergreens are oily and, unchecked, the fire would quickly spread along the hedge. Carolyn was sent to phone the fire brigade. The fire raged ferociously. A whole section of the hedge was full of smoke. As I watched there was a gentle puff of wind which cleared the smoke and I saw a strong red fire burning fiercely. The pampas grass in front of the hedge was also engulfed with red flames. I loved staring into a warm friendly fire in the sitting room in winter time. This was an angry fire. I went indoors out of the way. Mummy got three buckets, and filling one while the other bucket was left to fill by itself in the kitchen sink, she ran down the garden carrying the precious water to Daddy.

Carolyn came into the garden. She looked apprehensive. She relayed a message from the fire brigade to Mummy. She spoke clearly:

'The fire brigade are busy with a heath fire at Brading and ask if we can manage?' Carolyn had proudly told them that her Daddy had been a fireman in the war.

I watched from the safety of the sitting room. Daddy was up the ladder emptying the water onto the source of the fire, while Mummy ran up and down the garden carrying buckets of water.

At one stage I went to my bedroom and on my knees prayed to God for help. The firefighting went on for a while and then the tempo slackened as the fire died down and eventually was out. My professional firefighting Daddy, still up the top of the ladder, damped down the remains of the hedge.

'It's such a hot day. The air is very dry and it might ignite again,' he explained. 'But all is well. Carolyn, will you tell the fire brigade please?'

Carolyn returned to the phone:

'My Daddy has put out the fire and he said to tell you that all is well.'

A while later the family came together at the site of incident. Daddy had his arms around Mummy who had black smudges on her cheeks and nose. I looked at the new hole in the hedge. All that was left were blackened branches on two trunks. The hedge was still green on either side of the damaged hole and through this gap there was now a clear view of the field on the other side.

One of Daddy's clever shots. Carolyn and the author walk down along Ladies Walk from Ryde to Binstead.

'We're just going down to the church,' Carolyn announced and we wandered out of the garden. This visit was nothing to do with thanking God for our deliverance; it was to simply play on the tombstones.

I took for granted that Daddy was able to put out the fire. I was frightened when it was burning but as Daddy put it out, all was well. He had been the hero. Mummy did not panic and, with Daddy, made up the team to put out the fire. Mummy knew how to keep her calm.

---oOo---

We did a lot of walking in my childhood. Often we abandoned the bus and strolled to Ryde via Ladies Walk and Spencer Road. In early June the countryside was full of new green leaves on every tree. The hedgerows were full of foliage preventing anyone from seeing through. We went down Church Road, where next to our house there were fields in which the riding school's horses grazed. The field was full of wild flowers. There were a few large majestic oaks, one very near the road. Just past this point there was the "squelchy" field. It always had a muddy patch behind the five bar gate. I never saw anyone in the field.

One day as we walked with Mum she suddenly stood very still. 'Stop! Listen!' she whispered.

I was expecting a noisy tractor, a car to come around the corner or some horses.

'Listen to the thrush,' Mum went on. 'Isn't that a beautiful sound? He must be in the woods.'

From Quarr Road to the entrance to Binstead Beach opposite the fields there was a copse described on the old weather beaten notice board, as a bird sanctuary. Carolyn and I left the thrush and ran on stopping at the bend to wait for Mum.

'Stay near to the side of the road when you go around the bends!' Mum called out.

In single file, Carolyn leading, we walked close to the wall, past the entrance to the large house called "The Keys" and the pretty thatched cottage. Holy Cross church stood proudly bathed in sunshine surrounded by endless tombstones.

'There must be a lot of bodies buried there,' Carolyn said.

'That's right. One headstone equals one body,' Mum said.

Mum and Dad were married there. We went to services there and so it was familiar to us.

'There is one famous tomb. It belongs to a Thomas Sivell, a smuggler.' Mum continued.

There were no cars to worry about now, so from our slow walk Carolyn and I exploded and ran on past the line of cottages. We stopped at the tree which heralded the beginning of Ladies Walk. I looked back for Mum and the cottages; these reminded me of a jigsaw I had at home that I loved. My jigsaw had Hollyhocks in the picture and I wondered why the owners hadn't grown them too.

We descended the steep hill down to the brook which ran into the sea at Players Beach. We didn't run as it was far too steep. There was a game of golf taking place on the course on our left. The woods opposite hid a house near the sea shore.

'How do they manage to play golf on such a steep hill? Won't the ball just roll down the hill?' I asked.

'I have no idea, I have never played golf,' Mum replied.

We crossed the bridge over the brook and climbed the hill. The golf course was on both sides of the pathway. Towards the top of the hill there was a gate which was the point where the tall proud elms formed a tunnel for us to walk through.

This route was popular. We met many people along the route; then we had to stop and say 'Good morning.' Mother repeatedly said, 'Lovely day isn't it?'

Once in Ryde we went to the different food shops that were at the top of the hill. Mother collected her shopping and we finished at Betti's café half way down Union Street for our usual elevenses. Carolyn and I ran down Union Street to the toy shop called Mainstones towards the bottom of the hill. It had two large window displays full of lots of lovely toys.

With our faces up to the windows I announced, 'I want that,' as I pointed to the doll that could walk and talk.

'You have that and I'll have box of paints and a drawing book,' Carolyn replied.

Mummy caught us up.

'Come on. If we hurry we could catch the 11.30 bus.'

One lovely day Mother decided we would walk home using the same route. Along Ladies Walk there was a bank at the side about two feet higher than the track. On it was a well-trodden path. I loved walking on this as I was higher up and in line with Mummy who had to hold my hand in case I fell.

We walked down the hill and at the bottom running alongside the brook was a path which led to Players Beach. This was straight, and there was a single line of paving stones which ran the full length to the beach.

'Can we go along the path and look at the sea?' Carolyn asked.

'Don't go out of sight will you?' said Mum ever cautious.

We ran along the paving stones towards the beach. Mummy stood and waited watching us all the time. We were right at the end when suddenly a man appeared from behind a bush and cut us off from her. She called us calmly and we came to her.

'Who was that man?' Carolyn asked.

'Had he just been to the toilet?' I added, 'I think he was doing up his trousers.'

'He is not a nice man,' Mummy said quietly. 'He does that a lot especially in front of Mummies and their children.'

Ladies Walk was busy that day and we met a couple we knew from Church who were walking the same route. With them we continued our journey home. This incident had frightened Mother so she reported it to the police.

---oOo---

This man had also been exposing himself to Mummy and other women in the village. He had been in our garden looking through the windows. Daddy was concerned.

'I've made you a truncheon,' Dad said, as he presented Mum with a long and fat round pole with a string attached through a hole at the top. She thanked Dad graciously and put it aside.

Later on after Daddy had returned to his job on the mainland, Mummy picked up the long heavy truncheon. 'I don't know what your father expects me to do with this,' she said.

One dull but dry summer day, Mummy said, 'Let's take your toys and go and have a picnic on the Binstead beach.'

She packed a small picnic, a Thermos of tea, a bottle of orange squash for us, and a sandwich. I took a small red suitcase, made of strong cardboard into which I had put my doll and her clothes. Carolyn took a drawing book and pencils. The path to the beach was dry and we ran ahead anxious to be the first one to get to the beach.

At the large oak tree at the end of the path we jumped down on to the beach. It was deserted. The sea was grey, still and uninviting. I shivered. I was glad of my cardigan.

We walked along to the end where the flat rocks were, where I laid out my dolls. Mummy put the rug down, we ate our picnic and my sister picked up her drawing book and started to scribble.

Just then this man arrived and walked up the beach setting his place about ten yards away from us. Carolyn looked up from her drawing.

'Isn't that the man we saw the other day at the other beach?' Carolyn remarked.

'Yes darling,' Mum said. 'He has been making a nuisance of himself.'

There was no indication in her voice that told me that she felt unsafe. She was alone on the beach with two small children far away from any houses. If she called for help, no-one could hear.

That day on Binstead beach we were the only people there. Mother sat quietly and still watching her two daughters playing. He was by his presence, cutting us off from our only exit. We could go no further towards Ryde as the tide was in and cut off the access to the next bay. There were woods behind us belonging to the Keys, but the grounds were extensive and too overgrown for us to run away from this man.

Cut off we were alone. Suddenly the man then took off all his clothes and lay face down on his towel.

'That's odd', I thought. 'He was sunbathing when there is no sun. It is cool and cloudy. This is not the normal thing to do. You change under your towel you do not show your body on the beach.' Without dressing the man got up and swam straight out to sea.

Mummy had seen her opportunity and she said in a casual manner.

'Carolyn! Jo! Pack up your things at once please.'

I complained 'We have only just got here,' totally unaware of the potential danger in which we found ourselves.

'Pack up your things!' Carolyn snapped at me. 'Do as you're told!'

Mummy turned and calmly helped me pack.

'Look dolly will be comfy in there,' Mummy said to me laying my doll on her dresses in the suitcase.'

She then turned to my sister, 'Everything is alright Carolyn.'

She helped us gather our bits and pieces and we walked smartly along the beach to the exit. But he had spotted us! He was suddenly there in front of us. Fully dressed, he cut us off at the fork in the path. We took the well-trodden route but he pushed himself through the brambles of the old and disused track. He stood there and looked at Mummy.

'Oh hello,' Mummy said to the man. 'Not the nicest day to be on the beach.'

Her tone of voice was calm, firm and polite as if she were speaking to an acquaintance she slightly knew. We started the long walk up the wooded path. Carolyn, who had sensed the danger we were in, was ahead beckoning me to move faster.

'Come on, come on!' she said.

I dawdled: 'Why? I want to stay on the beach.'

He was behind Mummy.

Suddenly she started singing at the top of her beautiful voice.

> "All things bright and beautiful,
> All creatures great and small.
> All things wise and wonderful
> The lord God made them all."

She knew all the words to the hymn and sang them confidently. She sang every verse and chorus. Her loud and lovely singing voice carried through the woods. It was a still day so anyone could have heard her for miles.

I was with my Mummy who was singing and I was safe. I was totally unaware of any danger at all.

We reached the top of the path and then went straight across the road to the house opposite and the police were called.

Two policemen came and we walked back to our house together. I did not want to leave Mummy's side. I was fascinated. One policeman was tall and the other shorter and blond. They already had a report on this man. There had now been three incidents relating to him involving Mummy, Carolyn and me. He was in our garden, he cut us off at Players Beach, but this incident was far more serious and frightening.

The taller policeman tried to discuss our visit to the beach with Mummy but they left. They were finding it hard to talk about this with me in the room.

The man eventually went to court, and Mummy was called as a witness. There was another woman to whom he had exposed himself. She also gave evidence.

He had apparently been a prisoner of war in Poland and had suffered at the hands of the Nazis and both Mummy and this other witness spoke charitably suggesting that he be put into a mental hospital where he would get treatment as opposed to jail. He was detained and we

A photo taken by the Author of her father the day we saw the prisoners getting off the boat.

never saw him again. Mother showed great sympathy for the man who had terrified her. She showed us how to put in practice the words 'Love your neighbour, do good to those who hurt you.' I never heard her ever say anything unkind about anyone.

---oOo---

'It's chilly today, put on your duffle coats', Mummy said. 'We're going to see Daddy off to work from the end of the pier.' He often worked on the Mainland as there were more jobs there. It was rare for him to find a decent job on the Island.

Daddy put his bag in the car, drove into Ryde and down the pier. The cars went on the walkway with the foot passengers. That cold day not many people were walking. There were planks all the way down made of very thick seasoned wood. Half way down there was an extension out into the sea with seats at the side for people to rest on. This area was also used by fishermen, the lines from their long rods dropping into the sea at high tide. Parallel to this was the green tramline, next to that the train line which carried the trains from all over the Island.

We saw the tram chugging along at the side of us.

'Go faster Daddy! Get there first. We can beat the tram.' I shouted. The tram was full. People were standing holding on to the straps and filling up the middle of the carriages. They were also crammed into both of the open ends of the tram where the exits were.

The boat had not arrived. It was cold and the icy wind made it colder. We were glad of our duffle coats and woolly hats. After being told 'Not to go too far', Carolyn and I wandered about looking for something to amuse us. Daddy and Mummy were making their farewells and giving each other their last minute instructions, at the same time as keeping an eye on us.

The paddle steamer arrived and I was fascinated by the man who was dealing with the ropes. He tied a small thin rope with a special knot, to a large rope which had a loop. I knew about knots because I was a Brownie but I didn't recognise this one.

The man on the pier then coiled up the small rope and threw it accurately to the deck hand on the boat. The deck hand pulled on the small rope which in turned moved the large rope which dropped for a minute into the sea. When he had hold of the big rope he took this and put it around this circular fixture which I leant from Daddy was called a capstan. As he pulled on the rope, the boat hit the side of the pier. It squeaked and groaned as if it were hurt. The man secured more of the rope by looping it in a figure of eight over two large brown metals objects. The boat rose and fell with the waves.

Working as a team the men hauled up the passenger ramps and secured them. These were green with ridges on the ramps to prevent people from slipping. I had walked on these many times but had not watched them being put into place before. The tide was quite high that day, and the boat was very high above the quayside, so the angle of the ramp was steep and the haul much harder.

I watched the passengers navigate the narrow ramps in single file, some holding their suitcases and bags in front of them, but some held them over the hand rail. I was scared that they might drop their valuable suitcases into the sea.

I became aware of a group of men standing in a line handcuffed together in pairs. The scene was all very drab. They were uniformly dressed in grey and their faces were grey as well. They looked scruffy as their battle dress style outfits did not fit and looked untidy. I wondered who they were. The first pair had their heads down. Behind them, the next two were laughing. One of the men pointed to the ramp where a young lady was trying to get on to the gangway wearing a very tight skirt and high heels. The step up to the ramp was quite high and as she bent her knee, lifting her foot up, her tight skirt rose and there was a glimpse of her stocking top and a suspender. I didn't hear the man's comment. She carried a clutch bag and had a suitcase. The deck hand spoke to her and took the suitcase. He threw it to a man on the pier.

My gaze turned back to the men lined up. One at the back caught sight of me looking at him. He gave me a lovely smile so I smiled back.

There were two men in charge of the group, one at the front and one at the back. At a command they all walked forward and in tight formation single file, together they negotiated the ramps. One hand was in front the other handcuffed to the man behind.

'Don't stare!' Mummy said. 'They are just old lags. They are going to the Prison. Feel sorry for them Darling.'

'What's an old lag?' I asked.

'An habitual criminal.' She said and then quickly corrected herself giving an answer that I would understand.

The front door of Leys. The window the author regularly burgled is on the left of the front door, hidden by roses.

'Those men keep stealing and cheating people. They're not dangerous they are just old lags.'

I didn't think the man who smiled would hurt me.

The next few moments we were involved in making our goodbyes to Daddy. He kissed me and his moustache pricked into my face. I loved him dearly but did not like his moustache. I was used to him being away so it wasn't a sad occasion at all. It was normal. I knew he would be back soon, he always was.

Before they cast off, Daddy found his camera and took a photo of us on the quayside, and I took a picture of him with my Box Brownie Camera.

---oOo---

Leys was our castle. We were safe there. At night time Mother always double checked that she had locked both the front and back doors. Breakouts from the prison were not uncommon. If we had had a warning Mother was then extra vigilant. I knew they were "old lags" so that didn't worry me.

Mother regularly opened the top window of my bedroom early on a school day to wake me up.

"Time to get up Jo! it's a lovely day!' she shouted. This window was on the left hand side of the front door. Mum lifted the window and fixed it with the bar. This had two jobs: to hold the window open and to fix down firmly across the frame to prevent it being opened from the outside. This did not fit tightly. The window frame had warped and the bar was difficult to secure.

I was not a "latch key" kid. I was a "break in" kid. Mummy had the only key to fit the deadlock of the front door. After school Carolyn walked down to the Pack and Culliford to collect the key from Mummy. I was too lazy to do that. I just got on the bus and went home. I tried the front door. It was locked. Carolyn was not home yet. After dumping my bag beside the window I went to the unlocked garage to collect the "T" shaped set square. Without difficulty I wiggled the top window open. I put the set square through the small gap and hooked it under the bar that opened the large window. Equally the bar that should have secured the large window was also wobbly. I opened the window, threw my school bag in and went back to the garage to put away the set square ready for tomorrow. I climbed in the window went to the kitchen and had a bowl of cornflakes.

Half an hour later Carolyn arrived home and unlocked the front door. I was lounging on my bed. 'You climbed in the window again didn't you,' she said.

'Yep! that's what I did.' I replied. She sighed, 'Put your bowl away in the kitchen please. Don't leave it lying on the floor! It won't get washed up there!'

We were taught rules of behaviour based on good etiquette and thought for other people. If we breached one of those rules we were told and punished.

Mother sewed and made a lot of our clothes. She knitted, crocheted and cooked. She had one skill above all others, she could teach. As well as teaching me all those household skills, she taught me to read. She never praised herself for her skills, she had to show humility, she must never show pride.

'I'm a jack of all trades and a master of none,' she often said.

Being the recipient of beautiful home-made clothes, eating her lovely meals and cakes, and my basic education, I recognise now how much she contributed to my safe and secure upbringing.

6 THE SHELLING OF SCARBOROUGH

At eight o'clock in the morning on Wednesday 16th December, 1914 my father, Bryan and his sister, Betty Drawbridge, then aged seven and three, were told to go upstairs to get dressed as Bryan had to go to school. It was nine days before Christmas. The war that was raging far away on the Continent was hardly affecting the Drawbridge family.

'Go upstairs and see if there are any fishing trawlers in the bay,' said their Nanny.

Bryan scrambled up the stairs ahead of little Betty. Once in the front bedroom he ran over and knelt on the blanket box in front of the large bay window. He liked counting the ships for Betty. She climbed up on to the box beside her brother. The two children were in the bedroom on the first floor at the front of their house at 69 Esplanade, Scarborough. The town was known as "The Queen of Watering Places" and tourists came to the area to take the waters and breathe the fresh air.

The two children gazed out to sea. There were three large ships in the bay that morning. Bryan counted them for Betty who repeated Bryan's words.

'One, two, three,' she said.

A studio photo taken of Betty Drawbridge on the left with her brother, the author's father Charles Bryan Drawbridge, circa 1914.

Betty liked dressing in this room so she could look at herself in the long swing Cheval mirror that stood at the side of the window.

'Look Betty! There are two very big ships and one smaller.'

Nanny came in carrying their clothes over her arm, and called the children to come away from the window and get dressed.

Bryan clambered on to the bed and stood up, Betty followed.

The ships fascinated Bryan, and he was watching intently when he saw flashes coming from them and then heard loud bangs. This was all new to him. He had never seen anything like this before.

Suddenly there was a loud thump, followed by the sound of breaking glass and masonry falling. The Cheval mirror smashed into thousands of pieces all over Bryan. The force had pushed him on to his back, where he lay stunned and silent. One large shard of glass hit the side of his head just below his ear.

Nanny rushed forward towards the bed. Terrified, she froze for a moment. Hearing the noise, the ladies' maid, Mary, ran upstairs and joined Nanny picking off the pieces of glass from Bryan who was bleeding copiously from the endless cuts.

Mary took out a pile of handkerchiefs from the large chest of drawers. These were too small for Nanny and Mary to cover the wounds to stop them the bleeding. Hilda, the children's mother, came in. She had been finishing her breakfast downstairs on the ground floor.

'What's happened?' she said. 'What on earth has happened?' She stood silent and still, surveying the scene.

'I'll get some bed sheets, to use as bandages,' said Mary.

Using her teeth to start the tear, Mary ripped the sheets into strips. It seemed that however many bandages they applied the blood still seeped through. The scullery maid, Sarah, joined them and helped make bandages out of the sheets.

'I've got some scissors here. I'll cut the sheets and they'll tear easier,' she said.

From the servants' hall in the basement, other staff hurried up the stairs.

'I'll get a doctor.' said the butler, Mr. Richards.

Scarborough was in chaos. People were running from their homes trying to get out of the town. Somehow Richards found a doctor who came and took over and managed to stop the bleeding.

'That cut by his ear is the deepest,' the doctor told Nanny. 'I want you keep an eye on that for me. If it starts bleeding again send someone to fetch me.' There was no question at that time that this cut might have damaged his hearing.

There were many injured that day in Scarborough, and the doctor left to help with others in the town.

This treasured letter from my father is the last one he sent to me when I had just left to go to work in London. He died eight months later.

68

For 35 minutes the three German battle ships, the "Derfflinger", the "Von der Tann", and a light cruiser the "Kolbert", shelled the town. A missile from one of the ships had gone through the window of the next door house, had ricocheted off their wall, and with its last vestige of energy had pushed through the bedroom wall of number 69.

Scarborough was unprotected. Records now show that the Germans knew this. 18 people died and there were more than 200 injured. 46 streets were damaged with homes and businesses destroyed.

There was outrage. At the Inquest the Coroner said:

"Our enemies had thought proper, in their wisdom, and their own interest, they supposed, for some reason or other to make an unusual attack which was contrary to the rules of all civilised nations on a defenceless and helpless community on a town which was not a fortified place in any shape whatever."

Part of the Drawbridge family photographed in their car, circa 1912. My grandmother, Hilda sits in the front passenger seat, my father, Charles Bryan looks out away from the camera, his older brother Tat stands proudly and their Nanny sits with her back to the camera.

The horror that people throughout the town and country felt was not the main priority for the Drawbridge family. Their concern was for Bryan.

---oOo---

The shelling of Scarborough was to change the life of Charles Bryan Drawbridge who was to become my father.

Shock set in. Clinical and emotional shock was not fully understood at that time. He was treated for his cuts but he remained silent. Bryan was ill for a year. The cuts eventually healed but he was severely traumatised. During that time he did not grow, nor did his hair or even his nails.

There is no mention of his injuries in any of the local papers of the time. There are lists of the dead and injured but his name is not included. The house next door that had received the direct hit is mentioned but nothing is written about the Drawbridge house.

Upon recovery my father was sent to Temple Grove Prep School in Seaford, Sussex. He was quiet, generous and hardworking, but he was severely persecuted at school. He was small for his age as he had not grown any taller since the shelling. He had missed a lot of schooling during the year he was ill. Consequently he was put in a class with children younger than himself. The severe injury had caused damage to his left ear. With his increasing deafness he became a target for bullies. One of his tormenters was two years younger than him. This tyrant grew up eventually to become a hero, being decorated for flying Spitfires in the Battle of Britain in the Second World War.

It was during this time at school that his loss of hearing became more and more obvious. No-one was concerned about his hearing before he went to the school. He had not complained about it. The scar on his neck had healed well.

A disability such as deafness was an embarrassment to his overbearing mother. Her wealth helped her to get Bryan to see various doctors and hearing specialists. He was subjected to drops with various oils being put in his ears. During one treatment his ears were washed with salt solutions and other mineral products. The most successful of the treatment was with electric shocks. This was effective and he was able to have a conversation on a telephone immediately and for a few days afterwards. However, this wore off and he was back where he started.

Hilda was a formidable lady and her primary objective was trying to find a cure for my father. He went along with this and didn't consider getting a training that would enable him to be independent. His mother died in 1937. Bryan was 30 and was free to concentrate on getting training and work. He moved to the Isle of Wight to be near his family and lived in digs in Ryde. His Aunt Maud lived in Binstead, his older brother William known at "Tat" was in the Navy and stationed in Portsmouth, as was his brother-in-law Percy who was his sister Betty's husband. Betty and their baby daughter Elizabeth lived with Aunt Maud in Quarr Road in Binstead.

In 1939 the Second World War started and Bryan, unable to be accepted into any of the services because of his deafness, joined the Auxiliary Fire Service in Ryde. He showed such bravery, going into dangerous situations, as he was not able to hear his colleagues calling if he needed to get out in a hurry. He was seconded to Portsmouth to fight fires and be part of the rescue squad. His duties included digging out casualties from the bombed buildings. He spoke very little about his war service either to me or to Mum. He once confided to my mother that the worst part of his job was finding bits of body, especially if they belonged to a child.

'They shouldn't have been there,' he said.

When he first joined the fire service the bullying, however, continued and he was called "Old Deafy". This ceased as the hostilities intensified. In 1943 he married Betty Leigh Vigar, my mother.

Following the war he found work on building sites. So many houses had been destroyed by bombing and needed to be rebuilt. He first worked as a labourer and then an opportunity came up to work in Alderney in the Channel Islands. The work was diverse and he received a City and Guilds qualification for carpentry when he completed the job.

He was an excellent carpenter but he was a bit slow. There were times when he would travel to a job on the Mainland, lugging his heavy tool box as well as his luggage. He would work there a week and then get his cards on the Friday. That must have been heart breaking. He accepted this. He never questioned whether this was because of his deafness or because he was slower than the other workers.

Being deaf had its advantages as he missed the taunts that were made behind his back. Mother hated the name of "Charlie", which was the name he was taunted with in a derogatory manner. My father showed strength and courage throughout his life. He was a gentleman in every sense of the word. He was strong, faithful and loyal. He loved his family and was proud of his two daughters. He never spoke unkindly about anyone and even in his last letter when he divulged to me the secret of his overbearing mother, it wasn't with malice or regret.

He wrote, *'I had to stay at home with my mother until I was 30! Only my mother's death (she was a cardiac case) and the war gave me independence.'*

He just stated facts.

---oOo---

Daddy was home for the weekend. When he went into the kitchen he found Mum on her knees with her head in a cupboard. 'I want to pop into Ryde and get some more nails for the fence. I'll go to Wood and Wilkins.'

'OK dear,' Mum replied. 'This dresser is filthy. The shelves need scrubbing and relining. Are the girls with you?'

'No, I left them in the sitting room playing.'

'Bryan! Carolyn is six and Jo is four. They could get up such mischief if left too long on their own.'

'Right you are.' Dad left the room and found us in the sitting room playing quietly. 'They are alright.'

There was a silence. Daddy waited and Mum continued to scrub the shelves. She wiped them with a cloth and emerged from the cupboard, red faced and with a wisp of hair over her eyes. She squeezed the wet cloth into the bowl of very dirty water at the side of her.

'I could take the girls with me,' he suggested.

'Oh darling would you, that would be wonderful, thank you,' she replied.

A peaceful two hours to clean out the sideboard, a job which had been put off for so long was an offer not to refuse. 'Could you get a couple of things for me,' she mouthed to Daddy.

Equipped with a wicker shopping basket, a string bag, a list and two small girls Daddy set off. We caught the ten past ten bus at the top of Binstead Hill. Carolyn took charge of buying the tickets. 'One and two halves to John Street please,' she said. Daddy handed over the money and I took the ticket.

We got off the bus and holding my sister's hand we walked along the road to the High Street. First we went to Barnet's the butchers. We stood in the queue which extended the whole length of the shop.

'Good morning Mr. Drawbridge, I see you've got the girls today,' said the butcher. 'I bet they are a handful?' As he spoke, he turned away but shouted louder.

'Pardon,' said Daddy cupping his hand around his ear.

'A handful,' he shouted. 'The girls?'

Carolyn touched Daddy's arm and mouthed the words clearly as she spoke. 'He wants to know if we are a handful.'

'Oh no, not at all,' he quickly replied. 'I would like four pork sausages and half a pound of streaky bacon please.' He handed over the ration book.

With the goods wrapped and placed in the basket we left the shop.

In the greengrocer's the assistant greeted us. 'Good morning Mr. Drawbridge, I see you have got the girls with you. What can I get you?'

'Two pounds of old potatoes please,' asked Daddy.

'Do you want your usual or the King Edwards?' she shouted.

Carolyn touched Daddy's arm and repeated the question.

'I think we should stick with the usual ones please,' he replied. Daddy held out the shopping bag and the grubby potatoes were poured in.

Daddy bought some tomatoes which were put in a brown paper bag.

'I won't put 'em in just yet,' said the young girl who was serving us, 'I see you have more to buy and they might get squashed.'

'Pardon,' Daddy said.

Carolyn touched his arm and repeated the information. I stood still and looked at the grapes. I was about to ask if we could have some, when Carolyn stopped me.

'Here let me have the list, I know what Mrs. Drawbridge likes. You just wait there.' She took the piece of paper.

'Not ill I 'ope,' the shop girl asked. 'Mrs. Drawbridge I mean.'

'Pardon,' said Daddy cupping his ear.

Carolyn answered her. 'No not at all, she is very well thank you. She is spring cleaning.' Carolyn then mouthed what was said to Daddy.

The assistant dashed about the shop filling the basket with a cabbage, four apples, some carrots, and a pound of grapes. These and the tomatoes were placed carefully on top.

'Now girls,' said Daddy, I must go into Wood and Wilkins to get some nails so I can finish mending the fence.'

We followed Daddy who turned right into Cross Street and walked into the shop. The nails and screws were at the back down a dark corridor. The man behind the counter was used to his deafness and they talked freely to each other. The nails were weighed out, put into a bag then into the basket and we left the shop.

Daddy referred to the list. 'Now,' Daddy said, 'a reel of white cotton.'

'We need to go to Fowlers Daddy,' Carolyn said, striding off. 'Follow me.'

After crossing the road opposite Pack and Culliford's we carried on down to Fowlers. We walked through all the rolls of materials stacked up each side to the back of the shop.

'Good morning Mr. Drawbridge, I see you have got the girls with you.' The shop assistant spoke quietly.

Carolyn took over, 'Mummy would like a reel of white cotton, please.'

The assistant collected the thread from the other side of the shop. 'I'll put it in a bag as it is going in with the vegetables and your mother won't like it dirty will she?' Payment was made, the reel of cotton in its bag was tucked firmly down in the basket.

'We'll get the bus from the Esplanade,' Dad said. Briskly Daddy walked down Union Street. Carolyn could keep up easily. I had to run.

We passed Shaplands. 'Wait a minute,' Dad called out. 'Would you like some iced buns?'

'Oh Yes please,' we chanted.

'Morning Mr. Drawbridge,' said the baker, 'Mrs. Drawbridge not with you, I see you have got the girls to help.'

Carolyn didn't wait for Daddy to understand and reply, she touched Daddy's arm and relayed what was said.

'Yes, I've got the girls. I would like four iced buns please and a large loaf.'

Carolyn found the string bag which was in the basket. The bread was wrapped in tissue paper and the four iced buns were put into a cardboard cake box. The box would not fit into the string bag. Carolyn took charge and sorted it out, so that the box lay flat on the top of the goods in the wicker basket.

'That's everything. Now to the bus girls,' he said and we strode off again down the road. We stopped at Mainstones as we always did and gazed at the toys. Daddy agreed, 'Yes they are all lovely, but there is no money to buy anything like that today.'

We got on the number 1A bus at the pier and sat downstairs. Carolyn and I sat together, Daddy was behind with the shopping.

'One and two halves to the top of Binstead Hill please,' Daddy said to the bus conductress.

'I bet those girls keep you busy!' the conductress shouted as she handed him the ticket.

'Pardon,' said Daddy cupping his hand to his ear again.

'The girls, do they keep you busy?' she said slowly looking straight at Daddy.

'No not at all he replied. They are no trouble.'

The bus stopped at the top of Binstead Hill and following Daddy, Carolyn stepped off the bus and I jumped. As I did so my kilt fell down to the pavement, the leather straps had come undone and it had fallen off.

Daddy sighed, put the baskets down on the bench, and picked up the skirt. He turned it this way and that. 'How on earth does this go on? How do I do it up?' He muttered to himself. I stood still in my short jacket and a pair of navy blue knickers.

Carolyn took charge again. She took the skirt and folded it. 'Jo!' she snapped, 'Carry that over your arm, Mummy will put it on when we get home.'

Our little family paraded home, Daddy carrying two bags, Carolyn holding Daddy's hand, and me walking in front in a pair of knickers, a kilt over my arm.

7 PLAY

'Can we go out and play Mum?' we asked whenever the weather was fine. We would never consider staying in on a sunny day.

Post war play was imaginative, creative and fun. Bedrooms were tidier than they are today as toys were harder to find. There were clockwork and early automaton toys which were very limited in their movement. Children were more active and used their imagination in play. A box could be a place to hide in, a doll's house or a garage. Often we did not use the toys how the toy maker thought we would play with them. The creators of the "Walkie Talkie" doll had not considered little girls like six year old Jo. To walk the doll, it had to be upright and then rocked from side to side. The legs moved forward individually extremely slowly. My imagination was far faster than that. To make it into any kind of the reality in my imaginary game, I would have had to hold Dolly's hand and rock her as we walked. I was too tall and had to stoop to hold her hand. I hadn't the patience to wait for Dolly to move each leg really slowly. If in my game Dolly was going somewhere, she would either be in her pram, carried by me, or I would bounce her along, her two legs hitting the floor at the same time. That was far faster and more real in my mind.

The doll said "Mamma" when it was turned over and turned back. In my game Dolly called "Mamma" when she woke up. She was obviously lying down. I did not go to her bed, turn her over and back again just to hear a weak "Mamma". She didn't have to say anything at all as I put all her conversation into her mouth. 'I want some dinner,' I said for Dolly. 'Please may I have some dinner is what you should have said Dolly.' I replied. 'Sorry,' said Dolly. 'That's alright. Just remember next time.'

The author being pulled along by Carolyn as part of her imaginative game of being a Mummy

Children were much more active than they are today. Television in Great Britain was in its infancy. Very few families had a set at the beginning of the 50s and there few programmes to watch. There was no day time TV. We only stayed indoors if we were ill or the weather was wet or bitterly cold. Our play was active and outdoors.

Carolyn and I played together a lot. We were a good team to create a story in which we could play the characters. Conversely we could row over the smallest things. One wet day I found Carolyn at the sitting room table drawing.

'That's my pencil!' I shouted.

'No it's not, I had it first!'

'Mummy gave it to me!' I yelled as I snatched the pencil and went to my bedroom and slammed the door.

Carolyn went to the kitchen, 'Mummy! Jo has taken my pencil!'

'Now now Carolyn,' said Mum, 'is a pencil worth all this shouting? I'll find you another one.'

A pencil was found and Mother sharpened it with the carving knife. 'There you are. It's nice and sharp.'

Carolyn was two years older than me. When I was born Carolyn became the older sister and started to talk to me as Mummy did. Mum was her role model. As I got older I rebelled against this and did not like being talked down to.

Carolyn thought it right to tick me off for minor misdemeanours. I often went to the garden and stole green runner beans from the vegetable patch and eat them raw.

'You shouldn't be doing that,' Carolyn said. 'That's stealing! Mummy will be cross with you. Stop it at once!'

'You are not my Mummy!' I snarled, 'I'll do what I want until she tells me not to.'

Invariably Carolyn went and told Mum and she would come and sort out the problem.

'You two are like the "Ugly Sisters" in Cinderella. That is enough! Stop this noise at once. Jo please don't steal all the beans we need them for Sunday Lunch.'

'I only took one or two,' I said humbly. 'I like them raw.'

I could be cross with Carolyn over anything. Carolyn was five and I was three when we took a bath together in the big roll top bath upstairs at Gretton in Arnold Road. Mummy's back was turned when I slipped sideways and went underwater the water. Carolyn pulled me up by my hair. I screamed and cried. I was furious and vented all my feelings on my sister, who in my eyes was at fault for pulling my hair!

Mum was used to us quarrelling. She never came down in favour of either of us. She was a diplomat and sat on the fence. This often made us angrier than ever.

In the 1950s we played with such freedom. Our games and activities extended into the roads and woods around our house without the worries that haunt parents today.

Michael lived in the bungalow around the corner and he had a playground in his back garden to be envied. I knew this garden as the house used to belong to my Great Aunt Maud. I knew the copse at the bottom of the garden and in this Michael's father had created a small adventure playground. There was a large oak tree at the end and from a strong branch hung a long stout rope. In front of this was a dip which in my imagination could have been a river, a swamp, or something equally dangerous, that if I fell would certainly lead to an unpleasant end for me. A local gang developed once this playground had been created and we would queue up to swing on this rope. Opposite was a rough and ready style platform. My objective was to be able to touch this with my foot as I swung across the dip.

---oOo---

Our house, Leys, was half way down a hill. It was a gentle incline, exhausting enough when running up to get the bus, but enjoyable when I rode down on my bike. Michael made a trolley of planks of wood and old pram wheels to ride down the hill. Somehow Carolyn, our friend Angela, from number 7 Church Road, and I persuaded Michael to let us all have a go. He agreed as long as he was in charge of the driving. His feet were placed on a wooden cross bar which was articulated with a large bolt through the bar at the centre, thus creating with the aid of two ropes and his feet the trolley's ability to be steered. Michael instructed us where to sit.

'Carolyn, you sit behind me, then Angela and finally Jo you sit at the back,' he said. We climbed on. 'Keep your feet on the trolley we will be going really fast.'

We walked back up the hill to have another go and patiently we waited for Michael to tell us to get on again. What joy it was to speed down the hill where the tarmac had no potholes. The short journey made the ride smooth. The wind was on our faces and our hair flew back. As the fame of this trolley and its location spread more children turned up to have a go. Michael extended the trolley with more wheels and wood and more of us got on and rode down the hill together.

There was a seating arrangement but no seats. Michael was at the front, of course, as he was the driver; I was at the back and always underneath someone else. I did not want anyone telling me I was too heavy to sit on someone else's lap. I was not overweight but I was taller than my friends. Carolyn sat in front of me with other children on her lap. Michael pushed on the ground with his foot and off we went. As we sped down the hill we sang the pop song of the day,

"*Last train to San Fernando,*
Last Train to San Fernando,
If you miss this one you'll never get another one.
Biddy Biddy Bum Bum to San Fernando".

We did not sing any more of the song as that was enough for us to get from the top to the bottom of the hill. When it had stopped we got off and walked back up the hill to have another go and to repeat the song again. During one of the refurbishments to the trolley, Michael added a brake. A piece of wood was attached to the trolley by a screw in the middle which when swivelled, hit a wheel and slowed us down. What joy! No-one fell off. There were no accidents and there were no cars on the road to get in our way.

'Carolyn!' I called, 'Michael has added another extension to the trolley.'

'That means there can be more of us on it,' she said. 'Wait for me! I'll get my shoes on!'

We walked up the hill to the top. Michael had added a further set of wheels and another plank. It was this very long trolley. With just six of us on board, we rode down the hill comfortably singing our song a few times. We loved this.

More friends arrived. 'Can we join in?' Angela asked for herself and her other four friends.

'Yeah, OK, but I shall be at the front;' Michael insisted. 'It's my trolley and I am the driver.'

'Of course it is your trolley.' We all agreed.

'Let's get on then!' said Angela.

There were a total of 11 passengers that piled on to the vehicle.

'I'll sit behind Michael,' said Rosemary. 'You sit behind me Angela.'

Carolyn was next behind her. 'Squash up there are more to get on,' she instructed.

'I'll sit at the back,' I said. 'Mary you sit on my lap.'

The author on the swing in Binstead "Rec".

'Are you all ready?' Michael shouted.

'Yes!' we yelled.

We started to sing the song, Michael took off the brake but the trolley was stationary. The volume of our singing died off.

We sat in silence. He tried again to get it moving by pushing off with his foot on the tarmac. Nothing happened. It just didn't move.

Michael said nothing. We all got off at the top of the hill and walked away. Alone Michael rode the trolley down the hill turned the corner into Quarr Road. We never saw the trolley again.

---oOo---

Carolyn and I had an enormous playground because we had very little restriction as to where we could go. We did not cross Binstead Hill which was the main road and had all the traffic from Newport and East Cowes to Ryde. We had a free run of the north side of the hill. I was allowed to wander or ride my bike all the way down Quarr Road as far as the White Gate which wasn't white. Mummy was happy to let us go down to Binstead Beach and as far as the church. I was not, however. permitted to go to Players Beach which is past the church.

When we first moved to Church Road in 1953 opposite and to the side of our house were fields. There were woods just past our house which spread down to the beach. We could get into these woods anywhere along Quarr Road. There was also a way in from the public footpath which ran from the entrance to Binstead Beach and came out in Quarr Road opposite the red post box. A notice which stated "Trespassers will be prosecuted" was nailed to a board on a tree. It specified that it was a bird sanctuary. This notice was very old, covered in mould, the words were almost illegible and as there were no barriers to entry we didn't think it was meant for us. From the woods we gathered flowers in spring time and hazel nuts in autumn.

These woods covered the old stone pits. They weren't very deep but provided an ideal place to play "Kick the Can". Someone was "it" and sat on the upturned can at the top of a quarry. As "it" counted to a 100 we all ran away and hid. The object of the game was to get back unseen to the can and kick it down the slope. "It" had to guard this. If we were seen and caught we were out. But there was a tremendous joy of kicking the can. The pleasure of seeing it flying through the air and down to the bottom of the hill was wonderful.

We played in the churchyard. There were many flat graves on which we could climb. When I was older and in the choir the open church was a great place where we could play "Murder in the Dark" as we waited on Friday nights for the others to turn up for practice. This game stopped when we realised that lights could be seen from the outside.

In the 1950s we regarded Binstead as our playground. We had no fears and we had great freedom. There was a recreation ground locally known as "the Rec" at the bottom of Binstead Hill in which were fixed play things.

My favourites were the two swings. They were simply constructed out of two chains and a wooden seat attached to a simple frame. Next to these was the seesaw which was equally simple in design. There was a central unit on which the plank was secured. One end was longer and consequently it would rest on the ground at that end. This worked a hole in the ground which filled with water in wet weather. When someone leapt off the short end in a hurry, the long end with the child on it would splash into the puddle. Many a forceful game was played on this. As I was often bounced high in the air I learnt to hold on tight to the metal bars on the plank. There were three bars, inviting three children at each end to play. There was also a contraption consisting of two uprights and a bar. This did nothing and I did nothing with it.

To get to the "Rec" from our house we had to walk up Church Road and down Binstead Hill finally squeezing through a hole the hedge opposite the Post Office. However, the shortest route home was through the field next to the "Rec". This was the same field which backed on to my house where there was a pond in the spring in which I fished for tadpoles. The hedge separating the Rec from the field was reinforced with barbed wire. There was a space under the hedge in the corner behind the bar which did nothing. When it was lunch time or Mother needed us home she would stand in the garden and sing our names out over the field. Her voice carried and we heard her easily.

Being lazy and not wanting to climb the hill I once crawled through the hedge to take a short cut through the field. I tore my jumper on the barbed wire. The grass was long and I crawled along unseen or so I thought. I was stopped in my tracks when all of a sudden I heard.

'Get out of here you little ruffian!' A large but well dressed woman shouted. 'Go on clear off! Don't you dare come back here again! Do you hear me?'

I didn't reply. I ran back the way I came under the barbed wire and through the hedge. I went home the long way with dirty knees, filthy hands and a torn jumper. Mother was not pleased.

On rainy days we played indoors.

'Can we build a tent in the sitting room Mum?' we asked.

'Yes I can't see why not. Don't break anything will you. Take care of the Rose and Clop on the mantelpiece.'

'We will,' we chanted back.

Rose and Clop were two porcelain figures that Daddy had given Mummy when they were courting. Rose was a lovely lady dressed in a crinoline pink dress and Clop was a horse. Daddy had paid a little less for him as he was a second as he had a wobble.

We pushed the furniture back and used chairs and our candlewick bed covers to build.

'They keep sliding off the chairs,' Carolyn said.

'What about clothes pegs?' I suggested.

'Yes good idea. Go and ask Mum.'

I returned with a bag of clothes pegs. This did the trick and we managed to get a roof on our tent.

With more chairs and a wooden clothes drier our tent extended. Carolyn stood back and observed at our construction, 'We need some more covers!' she decided.

'I'll go and ask Mum,' I said

I returned with a pile of curtains and blankets. 'This should be enough.'

We continued to build until the tent was now large enough to involve the pushed back sitting room furniture as well. To fix the curtains onto these we used heavy books.

'Lunch time,' called Mummy from the kitchen

We stood back to admire our creation. It had a skylight, a bedroom and sitting area. 'We'll play in it after lunch,' we agreed.

When we had finished eating we returned to the sitting room but the magic had worn off. It was more fun to build than to play in and it was certainly more fun than taking it down.

'Can you please fold up all the blankets and curtains? Return your bedspreads to your beds,' Mummy said. 'The pegs need to be put back in the bag and hung up in the porch outside the back door.'

Folding large heavy curtains was difficult for little hands and Mummy came in to help.

---oOo---

There was a roller skating rink in Ryde to the left of the pier entrance. I longed to be able to skate. Reluctantly Mummy gave us roller skates for our birthdays. These skates were fixed to our shoes with a leather top which went over the toes. There was a strap to go around the ankle to fix each skate firmly.

The kitchen was chosen for us to practise as it had a wooden floor. We pushed back the kitchen table and chairs. One chair was on the table. This left a small area for us to try and learn to skate. The longest run we could get was a matter of four yards from the corner near the door to the hall and over to the fridge. Neither of us were natural skaters and we only managed to skate the four yards a few times without falling over.

Mother was relieved when we gave this up. 'Well you tried didn't you? I'd rather you found out now than break your leg at the rink!'

---oOo---

From quite an early age I loved playing with water. We had a large Belfast sink in the kitchen and I enjoyed pouring from one jug, bowl or cup into another. There was a hole at the end of the sink under the taps. I tried to fill it up with water but each time it flowed away.

'What's this for?' I asked.

'It's an overflow system,' Mummy explained. 'If I were to put the plug in the sink and then leave the taps running the water would go into the overflow and not on the kitchen floor'. I had to try this. Fortunately for Mummy and the kitchen floor it worked.

Mummy's cousin and friend Clare Woodward came for Christmas in 1954: consequently there was a glut of Schweppes tonic bottles. Clare's favourite drink was a gin and tonic and she stayed for seven days. Mummy showed me how to blow over the top of a bottle to make the sound like a fog horn. I discovered that if I put some water in the bottle the note it made would be higher. I chose eight of these. I poured the water in and blew over the top. I checked the note by blowing over the previous bottle and ended up with a tonic scale. I could then play a very basic tune. It was quite exhausting but fun. Mother was full of praise and said how clever I was. I didn't take the glory of the praise as I felt that as it was so simple to do praise was not deserved.

The bottles with their different amounts of water in them remained on the side for a considerable time until they went putrid.

'Jo, can I throw these away now please? They're awfully smelly!' Mum asked.

I had moved on to another game by then. I agreed.

---oOo---

I was 10 when I met Liane. Her mother, Auntie Lillian, as I called her worked with Mummy in the children's department at Pack and Culliford in Ryde on the ground floor. They sold rather expensive children's clothes and the school uniforms. Among these were the brown tunics, berets, shirts and ties for the convent. The shirts were in very pale cream, called "gold" according to the school song.

We sang

"Alma mater, let the flag unfold,

Stand brave, stand true under the brown and gold."

We thought we were so clever to replace word "mater" and sing Alma Cogan instead. She was a popular singer of the day.

Liane and I became firm friends. We made plans at school as to whether Liane would cycle to me at Church Road Binstead or I would cycle into Ryde to her flat in St. Thomas's Street. My house had a large garden in which we could play tennis, but her flat was near the sea where we could change and go down to the beach with our towels and have a bathe. We didn't have to walk far as there was a gap between the houses full of sand that led us to the sea.

There was a shed at the side of house. We decided one day to use this as our meeting place. It was situated outside the back door and down a slight slope. We cleaned this of all the garden detritus that tightly filled the space.

It was very old; oblong with one window, and a small door. Inside were two long shelves, one under the window was shaped with curves and the other opposite. The shed leaked but that wasn't important at the beginning as we started the project in summer. Anna our car had been sold as it was costing too much to run; consequently there was a large empty area in the garage available for all of the garden tools.

We had two lawn mowers. They were very heavy to use and move. They had a rotary cutter at the front, a heavy roller attached at the back and a metal container at the front to collect the cuttings. I often volunteered to mow the lawn. The front and back gardens were on a slope. It was too heavy for me to use properly but by pressing down on the handles I lifted the cutter from the grass. I ran as fast as I could pushing only the roller. Using the momentum I had gained from the run I then dropped the cutter down onto the lawn for the last half to be mowed. I left off the grass collector as this only added weight to the machine. Mowing the lawn for me was lengthy and tiring, but I preferred this to washing up or tidying my bedroom.

Liane and I beavered away taking the spades, shovels, large garden forks, trugs, trowels and small forks to the garage. We also moved the terracotta flower pots and packets of seeds which were in the small cabinet on the shelf opposite the window. During the life of the shed each item brought back into it had with it some soil which had dried, fell off and remained on the floor. There were beach deck chairs and two upright seats which now have the over glamorous title of being called "directors chairs".

We swept the dried mud from the floor, cleaned the window and removed all the cobwebs and spiders. Once we had got this cleaned out and Mummy realised that we were quite serious in our venture, Daddy was asked to recover the roof.

He stood in the shed his head close to the ridge and lifted up his arms. He put his hands on the roof, and moved his arms sideways. The whole of our precious shelter moved with it. 'There's not a lot of life left in this shed,' he warned.

'Don't do that!' Liane and I shouted.

'It'll fall down,' I yelled.

'Alright, alright,' he said 'I'll put new felt on the roof.'

We breathed a sigh of relief.

Daddy looking at the two shelves on the walls said, 'I could make a table out of this lot,'

He was on our side now. We looked at each other.

'How?' asked Liane.

'Wait and see,' he teased.

He took down both shelves and cut the one with the curved edges in half and put the straight edges together. He sawed two strips off the other shelf and put them across the join and hammered them in place. From a narrow shelf it was now a table top with curved edges.

'It's got no legs,' I thought.

Using more wood from the garage a leg was fashioned.

'One leg,' I pondered 'where are the other three?'

Daddy went back to the garage and we were left trying to understand what he was going to do to make this a table. He returned with various pieces of wood and more screws and nails.

'Where do you want this table?' Daddy asked.

We hadn't thought about that at all.

'I suggest that you have it in the corner here at the back,' Daddy continued 'What do you think?' he paused.

Liane and I hadn't a clue.

'Then you can put your chairs around it and still have space at the front.' Daddy went on.

We both agreed and the table was fixed securely to the wall. He leant on it to test its strength. It was fine.

'There! That's going nowhere,' he announced.

'Thanks Dad,' I said.

'Yes thanks Uncle Bryan,' repeated Liane.

'Now where do you want this old cabinet fixed to the wall?' Daddy picked up the small cupboard that had housed the seeds. He screwed this to the side of the shed in the middle opposite the window.

We filled the now clean shed with the two director's chairs around the table, and put the two deck chairs up against the side ready to be made into "beds". Mum had found some material and a piece of curtain wire and we had a decorative covering for the window.

To celebrate we had orange squash and biscuits at our new table. Then we put out the beach deck chairs and lay back satisfied with our achievement. It had been so much fun putting our shed together. Now it was finished we were stumped as to what to do next.

'It's quite dark in here,' Liane said.

'We could paint it,' I suggested.

The following weekend we pooled our pocket money and met in Ryde. We went to Wood and Wilkins the local large hardware store. This shop sold everything for builders and decorators. They had a selection of wood and nails which were bought by weight. They also had a large paint department. We found our way to the bargain box where there was a small selection of paints. These were the unpopular paints that no-one would buy. We could afford yellow paint for the walls and gloss paint in turquoise blue for the wooden cross members. We hadn't enough money for the brushes and turpentine but we were sure that Daddy had all that.

Painting the shed took us a couple of weekends and when finished again we sat back to enjoy our work. It was still a bit dark so I went indoors and found some candles. We placed these around the shed and lit them. One of them was on top of the cabinet.

We sat back to admire our work.

'There's a strong smell of burning,' I said to Liane as we relaxed in our deck chairs.

'I wonder where it is coming from,' she replied.

We sat unperturbed and deliberated a bit longer when suddenly Liane jumped up out of her seat and blew out the candle that was sitting on the small seed cupboard. Above the candle was a small patch of black on the roof which was very hot and about to catch fire.

'Oh dear,' I said, 'I never thought of that.'

'Neither did I,' she replied.

We checked where we had put all the other candles and moved them well away from the walls.

'I don't think we will tell anyone about this,' I said and she agreed.

The following week it was pouring with rain we went to the shed. With the newly felted roof we were sure we would be dry there. I opened the door and discovered water on the floor just inside. Being at the bottom of the slope water had poured down into the dip and into our shed.

'The rain has to go somewhere,' I said, 'I'll dig a hole just in front of the door for the water.' I borrowed a spade from the garage and dug through the clay making a small hole about 12 inches deep. From the front porch I took the metal grating, deciding that no-one ever scraped their shoes on it any more as the road and paths were mud free. I laid this over the hole.

This worked well for a time, but the rain still kept falling. The sump that had now filled with the water was not draining away. It was overflowing and again seeping into our shed.

I understood the principles of an overflow system from my games at the sink in the kitchen. Among the rubbish from the shed I found a piece of lead piping. I set to work digging a small trench which sloped downwards towards the hedge away from the shed. I laid the pipe, which was luckily long enough, from the sump along the trench and through the boundary. I made sure that the water could flow freely from the sump and out through the hedge to the pathway on the other side. I then covered in the pipe with the earth and waited. It worked well. We used our shed a lot as we repainted it the following year. This time we had pink walls, and red woodwork.

Liane and I remained friends and our games matured with us. We played tennis in the garden and went for cycle rides.

We spent a lot of time together throughout our school days. We eventually split up when we went into separate careers. Liane went into Childcare and I went into an office, but we have remained pals up to this day.

On the last day at school when we no longer had to wear our school uniform dress, blazer, regulation shoes and silly Juliette panama hats I went to Liane's flat for a celebratory shout, scream and refreshment. We threw our hats around the room and I jumped up and down on mine. I stayed for a while and then picked up my hat gave it a shake. There was no damage to it so I plonked it back on my head and wore it home.

8 OUR PETS AND OTHER ANIMALS

'Come here! Look at this!' said Daddy one day. 'Look at that silly dog. He is chasing the cat around the rose bed in the middle of the garden.'

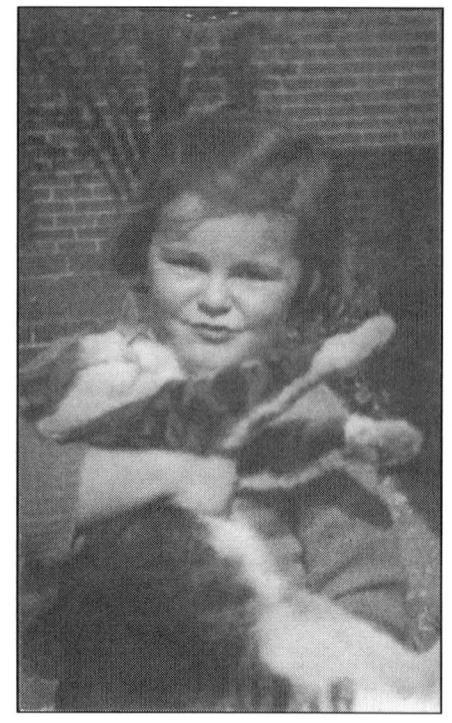

Willie Pickle our dachshund was scampering after Tigger our tabby cat who was running around and around the middle rose bed. The dog got no closer to the cat as they continued to run.

Just then the cat who had obviously had enough of this game scampered off and up the almond tree. It took the dog four more circuits to realise the cat was gone. Willie stopped looked left and right and then continued down the garden to sniff out who had been on his patch since he had last been there.

'Tigger is definitely the brighter of the two animals,' said Mummy.

Carolyn was given a kitten not long after I was born. He was named Tigger after the character A.A Milne created in the Winnie the Pooh books. He was a canny cat, unlike his scatty namesake who got into many difficulties with Winnie the Pooh. We had an enormous garden and fields surrounding the house in which he roamed. When Willie Pickle arrived he treated him with disdain. Mum said, 'Look, it's like he is turning up his nose at the dog.'

Carolyn with Tigger, her tabby cat.

Tigger hissed at him and then as the back door was open he went into the garden up a tree and away from this "silly little puppy".

Willie could not get out of the garden, so it was easy for Tigger to get away from him.

Willie Pickle belonged to all of us and fortunately our cat and dog became friends. They lay together happily in front of the sitting room fire. Tigger often held Willie Pickle down so that he could lick him clean.

After one of Tigger's sorties he came back with a swollen face. 'I think he has been hit by a car,' said Mum, 'but he has managed to get home. I'll take him to the vet tomorrow to get him checked over.'

Tigger unfortunately did not want to be taken to the vet. Subterfuge was employed. Willie, who was guilty of devouring any food put in a bowl on the floor, was shut in another room as a meal of Tigger's favourite "Kit e Kat" was left in his bowl. Tigger found his bowl, looked left and right before he ate happily.

'Willie is in the other room Tigger you don't have to worry,' Mum assured the cat.' As the bowl was nearly empty Mum took a large towel and wrapped up the struggling cat and put him in the cat basket.

Covered in scratches Mum was sneezing. 'I am a little allergic to cats,' she said.

Carrying the cat basket and sneezing periodically, Mum took Tigger on the bus into Ryde and to the vet.

'He's alright,' Mum said on her return. 'There are no broken bones and he appears to be O.K.' We were relieved and took the basket with Tigger inside into the garden and opened the wire door which held him inside. He shot out of the basket and up the nearest tree.

Michael and Rosemary Tenant lived in the bungalow which used to be my Great Auntie Maud's home. I knew the garden well as I played there before she died. Rosemary bred guinea pigs in the shed which she sold. I was once put in charge of looking after these when the family went away. I also had to feed the chickens. Where there had been a lawn was now a chicken coop. In return for my work I could have as many eggs as I liked. There weren't many and one was bad. I took my job seriously. I measured accurately the amount of food and water needed. It was noticed that I took this work very earnestly and reliably.

'I'm very proud of you, Jo,' said Mum when I had finished my week of caring for the animals. 'You have carried out your job very conscientiously.'

I liked that.

A few weeks later five guinea pigs were born. 'Mummy, can I have a guinea pig to look after?' I asked.

'Well you did look after the animals responsibly for them,' she replied. 'You must promise to look after it yourself, feed it and clean out its cage regularly.'

'Oh I will I will!' I shouted.

Carolyn heard this and came running into the kitchen. 'That's not fair, I want one too,' she wined.

'Of course Carolyn you can have a pet too. Do you want a guinea pig?'

She thought for a while and said, 'No. Can I have a tortoise instead?'

Daddy set to work to build a hutch for the guinea pig. He added a removable tray to help with cleaning out the cage. It had its own stand to bring the hutch up to my height and was placed outside the kitchen window.

'You just pull out the tray with the dirt on it,' he explained. 'Throw that away on the compost heap, wash it out, put it back with more straw and the job is done.'

A little hut with a fenced-in run was made for Carolyn's tortoise.

'Look, Carolyn I have found some spare chicken wire for the run,' said Daddy.

Once the hutch and the tortoise run were finished I called round to Rosemary's and chose a guinea pig. A trip was arranged to go into Ryde and buy a tortoise. Tucked away in a side street there was a pet shop. We walked up to the shop and noticed there were some kittens in the window.

'Aww,' Carolyn said, 'aren't they sweet.'

'No Carolyn you are not having a kitten. We have Tigger already and he will be hurt if we bring another cat into the house.'

'I'm glad the kittens have lots of water there,' Mum said. 'They must be hot in the window.'

The shopkeeper, Mr. Lovelace, came into the tiny shop from the back. As he walked in he was putting on his brown linen overall. 'Sorry madam,' he said, 'I hope I have not kept you waiting. I was having a cup of tea. Are you interested in buying a kitten?'

'Oh, no, we would like a tortoise and I was told you have just had some delivered,' Mum said.

'Yes Madam, if you would like to step this way they are at the back of the shop.'

We followed Mr. Lovelace to where there was a large flat tray with wire netting covering it. 'That's to stop that little one trying to climb out!'

'I thought tortoises were slow moving and docile!' Mum said.

'No, not that one!' he replied.

There were three tortoises in the box. 'Come on Carolyn, you chose one,' Mum said.

Carolyn looked in. 'The big one is doing nothing and he is ugly!'

'I didn't think tortoises could be ugly,' Mum muttered as she exchanged a smile with Mr. Loveless.

'Now,' Carolyn sighed, 'it's between the middle sized one and the small one.' The small tortoise continued to scuttle around the box and as the wire lid was removed he put his claw on the wall. 'Look he is trying to escape!' said Mr. Lovelace.

'He certainly has a bit of character,' said Mum.

'That's the one I want.' Carolyn pointed to the small one.

'Right,' said Mr. Lovelace, 'I'll get a box so you can take him home.'

Carolyn carried the box carefully as we made our way to the bus stop. 'We must think of some names for them mustn't we?' Mum suggested.

The bus was crowded and we all three sat in one double seat. 'Stop squashing me. Mind my tortoise!' Carolyn said.

'What have you got in your box?' the bus conductor asked as he collected our fare.

'It's a tortoise,' I said realising that Carolyn was getting all the attention.

'A tortoise eh? That's nice,' said the bus conductor. 'What is his name?'

'I don't know, we haven't named him yet,' Carolyn continued. 'What can I call him Mummy?'

'Anything you like. I am not sure what a tortoise should be called! I have never met a tortoise with a name before.'

The unnamed tortoise was introduced to his new home. Once in the run, he continued to crawl all over the area at great speed.

'My goodness he is a speedy tortoise,' said Mum, 'running around his cage like that. Anyone would think he is trying to do the four minute mile.'

'A mile in four minutes!' Carolyn said, 'who did that?'

'Roger Bannister. He is a student at Oxford where he ran a mile in under four minutes. He is the first man in the world to do so.'

'Well, that's what we will call him,' announced Carolyn. 'Roger Bannister.'

My guinea pig was white and had pink eyes. There was nothing about him that would connect him with anyone famous. We sat and looked him. He squeaked as I stroked him.

Mother pondered. 'The correct name for a guinea pig is a Cavy,' she explained, 'and to keep cavy is to be secretive. If we joined up the two words together he could be called "Keepey Cavy"'.

Keepey Cavy was put in his cage, fed and left to settle in.

Unfortunately I took looking after Rosemary's animals far more seriously than I did for my own guinea pig. Mummy did most of the feeding and clearing out.

'Jo!' shouted Mummy one Saturday morning. 'Come and clean out Keepey Cavy's hutch. Now!'

The hutch was placed in the front garden on the concrete drive way. I was handed a large bucket of soapy water, a scrubbing brush, rubber gloves and some bleach.

'Now get on with it!' Mum was very angry. 'He is your pet!'

I scrubbed out the cage and then put in the bleach. It made me retch and I was nearly sick.

'Carolyn doesn't have all this trouble.' I thought, 'Tortoises make a lot less mess.'

The first pet tragedy to occur was when the run that Daddy had so carefully made warped and lifted from the grass. Roger Bannister escaped underneath.

'Roger Bannister has got out!' shouted Carolyn one day.

We searched the garden, under the raspberry and black current bushes, in the hedge and rubbish heap waiting to be burnt. Roger Bannister was too fast for us. He was gone.

'Where do you think he is?' Carolyn asked.

'Darling I'm afraid that he has probably died owing to the very cold weather we have just had.'

Keepey Cavy also only lasted a short time. One day after school when I went to the hutch I found him, unconscious. I pushed him, but he didn't move. 'Carolyn!!!' I screamed. 'I can't make Keepey stand up.'

Mummy was at work and Dad was away. Carolyn took charge and brought him into the kitchen. She went to the sideboard and found a bottle of brandy.

'I've seen brandy being given to very ill people. It may work on Keepey Cavey,' she assured me. She put a trickle of brandy on a spoon and tried to put it into Keepey's mouth. The guinea pig lay lifeless. There was no response at all. Keepey Cavey was dead!

This was totally due to lack of my attention. I was filled with guilt. I sobbed and sobbed. Carolyn covered him with a tea towel and left him on the kitchen table until Mummy came home. She appeared sympathetic but was practical.

'It's all my fault,' I cried. 'I didn't love him enough. It's all my fault.'

Mother sighed but didn't comment. 'We must bury him. I've found a suitable coffin, a shoe box.'

Mum and I chose a space for the grave in the shady garden under the prunus tree. Mother got a large spade and dug a deep hole.

'There you are, Keepey Cavy you can rest here,' she said as she dug. 'You have been a lovely pet and friend of Jo's.'

I held on to the box sobbing. 'I didn't look after him properly did I?' I said.

'No darling you didn't but it is all over now,' Mum said firmly.

'I would be better next time, I promise.'

'No I don't think we will have another pet. Pass me the box please.' Mum said and she placed the coffin in the hole. 'We have Willie Pickle and Tigger the cat. They are our pets. We don't need any more.'

Willie Pickle, our dachshund.

Mum did not change her mind. We were not allowed to have any more pets. We asked but the answer was clearly, 'No, certainly not. You did not take enough interest in their welfare. Now that's an end to it.'

Willie Pickle had been a member of our family since I was five. I was 13 year old when Mother woke me up as normal and told me that Willie Pickle was not well. Carolyn and I got up quickly and went to the kitchen. He was in his box, there was blood on his blankets and he was very still.

Carolyn went over to his box. Willie lifted his head to greet her. 'What's wrong with him?' she asked as she stroked his soft head.

'I don't know,' Mum said quietly, 'I just don't know, I'll call the vet as soon as you have gone to school. Now eat your breakfast.'

We ate quietly, Mum made our packed lunches as we were both at St. Therese Presentation Convent School in Ryde. Willie lay silently in his box. 'He is too silent,' I said.

'Yes he is, isn't he,' Mum replied. 'He is very ill.'

I got home first from school and found Mum in the kitchen. She should have been at work. Willie Pickle's box was gone and the kitchen had been swept clean and the sideboard tidied.

'Willie's not coming home then?' I asked.

'No darling, his kidneys had failed. That was the cause of the blood we saw. The vet had to put him to sleep.'

I burst into tears. 'Oh Mum I'm never going to be happy again!'

'Yes you will, of course you will. I stayed with Willie while the vet injected him with a large dose of medicine to put him to sleep. I held on to him and stroked his head and he looked at me knowing that I loved him right to the end of his life.'

Mum went to the airing cupboard in the corner of the room and found a handkerchief.

'Now dry your tears and I'll make you a cup of tea.'

There were more tears when Carolyn got home.

'Shall we have another dog?' Carolyn asked.

'No not at the moment, I'm working full time. It wouldn't be fair on a new puppy and we can't afford one at the moment. With two sets of school fees to pay for there is nothing left out of my pay packet from Packs to buy a new one.'

Mother missed having a dog and a year later a new puppy arrived which Mother named Timmy. I suspect that her friend Ruth had bought it for her.

Tigger put up with the new puppy, but he was not as agile as he used to be, so the two pets seemed to ignore each other. Tigger was also put to sleep after he had another head injury and then a stroke. Mother, sneezing all the time, held her pet while the vet injected him.

'It was important not to desert my pets at that moment.'

Timmy was a great companion to us as we got older and our lives got busier. He was especially important to Mum when she was left a widow after Daddy died in 1967.

He was 14 years old when he became very ill. Carolyn was on the Island with her husband, David and daughter Clare when it was decided to take him to the vet.

'I suspect that he will have to be put to sleep.' Mum said quietly to Carolyn. Clare sat in Granny's chair stroking this much loved but very old pet. 'Will Timmy know me when I get to heaven?' three year old Clare asked.

'Of course he will,' said her Granny. 'I'm sure of it.'

9 ACCIDENTS AND INJURIES

We had been waiting all day. Clare was coming to stay. Clare Woodward was Mummy's first cousin and had been her best friend since they were young. Clare was five years younger than Mummy. Carolyn and I adored her as she loved us and was always interested in what we did.

Mummy had got Clare's room ready. It was swept and the furniture was dusted. The mat had been hung on the line and had been given an extra bash with the carpet cleaning beaters. Carolyn and I loved doing this. We took it in turns to take the paddle made of plated bamboo and to hit the mat as hard as we could. It would swing on the line as we hit it hard and dust would fly off everywhere.

Carolyn picked some flowers to put into her room. She put them in a turquoise blue vase.

Two year old Carolyn with Clare Woodward, mother's cousin.

'I wanted to do that,' I said.

'Go and pick some more. I'm sure Clare will like two vases of flowers,' Mum reassured me.

I went to the garden and picked a large bunch of bright yellow dandelions. I arranged them in an empty jam jar and placed them in her bedroom.

'She is on the three o'clock boat so she won't be here for a couple of hours yet,' Mummy said as we finished our lunch.

'That's ages!' I moaned.

'No its not it's just two hours,' said Carolyn.

Mummy sighed. 'Go and find something to do. She'll be here before you know it.'

I went to the garden and found my skipping rope. I decided to practise in the front garden on the concrete leading to the garage so I would be the first to see Clare arrive.

I was finally getting a rhythm with my skipping. I was up to 18 skips when I heard Carolyn shout. 'Clare's here! She's coming down the road.' Carolyn was watching from Mummy's bedroom window upstairs and spotted her Ford Popular car around the bend in the road.

Mum, Carolyn and Willie Pickle our dachshund rushed out from the house to welcome her.

Still carrying my skipping rope I was there first.

'Mind the dog,' shouted Mummy as Willie was about to slip through an open gate. Carolyn tried to pick him up but he struggled and wiggled.

'Put him down in the garden and I'll shut the gate,' Mummy said.

She held the car door as Clare climbed out holding tight to her miniature dachshund, Texi's lead. He was already barking and was desperate to get into the garden where Willie was.

'Shall I get your suitcase?' Carolyn offered.

'Clare!' I called out.

'Oh Betty it is so lovely to see you,' Clare said. Mummy gave Clare a big hug.

'Clare!' I called out again.

'Are your bags in the boot?' Carolyn called out.

'You look so well Betty. How do you manage to look so good all the time?'

'Clare look I can skip now,' I tried again.

'Let's take the dogs to the back garden,' Mum said. 'It's best they get to know each other again in a large open space.'

'I could take your bags for you?' Carolyn said.

Mummy looked at Carolyn who was about to open the boot. 'Let Clare get her breath Carolyn. We will unpack the car later.'

'Come on Texi, come on Willie this way,' shouted Mum. The dogs were barking as they rushed past Mum into the back garden. 'You've certainly brought the good weather with you Clare. Did you have a good journey?'

'Clare,' I entreated, 'can I show you? I can skip now!' I picked up my skipping rope ready to demonstrate.

Clare turned around and looked at me. 'Darling Jo I would love to see you skip but I have only just arrived. Show me later Darling. Texi! Texi! Come here you naughty dog!' Texi dashed around the garden. Willie followed at a slower pace.

Mummy, Clare and Carolyn followed the dogs into the back garden. Holding my skipping rope I started to follow but fell. My feet were tangled up in the rope and I tripped over on to the grass.

'Ow!' I screeched and then began to cry. Mum came back to me and helped me to my feet leaving Clare and Carolyn to sort out the dogs.

She picked me up and untangled my feet from the rope. Together we walked to the kitchen.

She lifted me to sit on the table. My crying was reduced now to a snivel. 'It's alright Darling,' Mum said, 'I'll put some nice soothing cream on it in a minute and it will stop hurting.'

Mum took a bowl which she half filled with warm water and added a capful of Dettol disinfectant. She pulled a small wad of soft cotton wool dipped it in the water and washed my knee. The used cotton wool ball was put aside. She pulled a fresh piece from the roll and repeated the process cleaning my knee.

'I thought you fell on the grass. What on earth made this cut? Perhaps there was a sharp stone,' she said quietly as she bathed my knee.

The dogs were still running around the garden but the barking had ceased. Clare joined us in the kitchen.

Mother stopped bathing my knee. 'Oh dear,' she said, 'I think this is going to need a stitch or two.' Clare and Mummy took a closer look.

'Yes I agree,' said Clare. 'It's a good thing I arrived when I did, I can stay here with Carolyn while you take Jo.'

'I'll take her to Casualty at Ryde Hospital. Being Sunday it shouldn't be too busy,' Mum said.

'Casualty! Hospital!' I thought. I felt really important. My knee didn't hurt that badly! Everyone was concerned about me! I liked that feeling.

She covered up my knee with a soft bandage. 'Now do you want to go to the toilet before we go?'

I was lifted down from the table and helped to the toilet.

'You'll be fine,' Clare said. I did not reply as I didn't know what to say. I knew that I would be fine and I was not afraid of going to hospital at all.

I sat in the back of the car with my injured leg stretched out on the back seat. 'Alright now? Try and keep your leg straight will you?' Mum was making such a fuss of me and I loved it.

We arrived at the hospital and were quickly seen. A nurse gently took off the bandage and examined my knee carefully. 'This will need a stitch,' she said to Mummy.

'That's what I thought!' Mummy replied.

'Unfortunately the doctor has to come in especially as he is off duty. I'll call him straight away.'

Mummy was ushered into the waiting room and I was laid out on a bed and there I waited. I was now in the hands of the hospital. Nurses dressed in blue striped uniforms, starched white aprons and white caps came in and out of the room all attentive of me. I felt so special.

The doctor arrived he walked into the room putting on his white coat. He was very tall and had red hair.

'Now what have we here?' he said to me. I said nothing.

'I think this will need a couple of stitches,' he went on. I still lay there without saying a word.

'You're a very good girl,' he said as he put on his white mask. 'This shouldn't hurt much at all,' he assured me.

I continued to be silent. He held a curvy needle with an instrument that looked like a pair of scissors. He then took some thread which he carefully pushed through the eye of the needle. 'I'm just going to prick your knee.' I stayed quiet. Lying flat on the bed I couldn't see what he was doing. 'And again,' he continued 'You are a very brave girl, aren't you?'

There was a nurse with him who also had a mask over her mouth and nose. Her job was to pass him scissors to cut the yarn once he had done the stitch. He repeated the action three more times, saying the same, 'I'm just going to prick your knee' each time and finishing with 'You are a very brave girl, aren't you?

I couldn't understand how lying still was being brave. Bravery was to me rescuing people in danger. I lay there silent.

The doctor covered the wound and the nurse put on a very long bandage which covered the knee, above and below it.

'She will need a tetanus injection,' the doctor said to the nurse.

Injection! I hadn't thought of that. What was an injection! Was that going to hurt?

The nurse returned with a tray. On it was this glass tube with a very long needle sticking out of the end. This was a syringe. There was also a small glass bottle of clear liquid. She checked the label on the bottle with the doctor and I was rolled over on my tummy, my knickers pulled down and I felt a sharp jab. 'Ow!' I screeched. That pain did not fit into my image of a hospital.

'There you are. All done,' said the nurse in a sing song sort of way. 'We will take you back to your mummy now.' The nurse lifted me from the bed and I walked with her back to Mummy. It was difficult to walk normally as my knee wouldn't bend at all as there was too much bandage.

'Mrs. Drawbridge,' the nurse said, 'the doctor has put in four stitches. Keep the wound dry and covered for a week and come back and see us a week tomorrow on Monday. Just come to casualty again and they will take the stitches out. If there are any complications please do come back and see us.'

On the way home in the car Mummy said again and again. 'You were such a brave girl. Does it hurt at all?'

'No not really.' I replied.

'I wonder what Clare and Carolyn have been doing all afternoon?'

I was helped out of the car and I hobbled into the house. We surprised Carolyn and Clare who were in the kitchen cooking.

'We are making scones,' Carolyn shouted excitedly, 'but they are not like the ones you make.'

'We thought it a good idea to make some scones for you as a surprise. I found the place in the recipe book. Look it's marked by a piece of card,' Clare explained, 'and we are following it exactly.'

'But they are not like the ones Mummy makes,' Carolyn insisted.

'Carolyn, you keep saying that all the time. I can't understand why not as I am following the recipe. Look!' Clare pointed to the open book.

The Good Housekeeping Cookery Compendium lay open on the table. There was the recipe for scones that Mummy always used on page 120. On the opposite page there was a recipe for Girdle Scones which Mummy had never made. Clare was making these!

Mummy put her hand over her mouth covering her smile, 'Clare,' she said 'Carolyn is right. These are the ones I always make, not those.' She pointed to page 120. But I am sure these will be just as nice.'

'Oh I'm so sorry Betty. So sorry Carolyn! You were right,' Clare said, 'I was looking at the wrong page.'

'Never mind, I'm sure they will be lovely,' Mum repeated. The attention had disappeared from me now and was placed on the wrong scones! I was disappointed as I liked Mummy's scones. Mum finished the cooking while Clare and Carolyn laid out the table for tea. I sat in Mummy's special chair with my leg propped up on a stool.

'Thank you Jo for the lovely flowers you gave me for my bedroom. I do find Dandelions have such a vivid yellow colour. I wonder what had cut your knee so badly.'

'It must have been something very sharp,' Mum said.

'Could it have been a piece of glass?' Carolyn suggested.

We ate the griddle scones with butter and jam. I did miss Mummy's scones but thought it polite not to say anything.

After tea we went out to the spot where I fell. Mummy and Carolyn knelt down and searched the grass for anything that might have caused the damage. They ran their hands over the earth. They pulled up some of the grass to see properly but they found nothing.

'There is definitely nothing here that could have caused that cut. There is only lawn,' Mummy announced. 'It will have to remain a mystery.'

Later that evening Mummy came to tuck me in at bedtime and she reminded me how good and brave I had been in the hospital. 'You were so well behaved and you were on your own.'

'Why didn't they let you sit with me when they were sewing up my knee?' I asked.

'Because it is felt that it is too upsetting for you. You have been in hospital before when you were a baby and I couldn't stay with you then, either,' Mum replied.

'Yes I know I was in Great Ormond Street Hospital,' I said confidently. I had always known that. 'Why was I there?'

Mummy sat on the bed and said, 'When you were born I collapsed and the midwife had to deliver you with forceps. Forceps are an especially shaped piece of equipment that fits around a baby's head. You were, unfortunately, left with a bruise on your face. This then turned into lump and an open wound that would not go away. I used to dress this with a powder, but the lump stayed. So they decided that you were to go into Ryde Hospital.

'It was awful. I left you there screaming. I was not even allowed to come and see you at visiting time, so Mrs. Dyer, our cleaner, used to go and visit. All you would say was "Where's my Mummy? I want my Mummy." It was a dreadful time. The wound did not heal. It just got worse so I went to Ryde hospital and insisted on a second opinion. They agreed and referred me to Great Ormond Street Hospital in London.

'Whilst you were in there I stayed with Clare's mother, Auntie Deedah, in Kingston south of London, but I was not allowed to stay with you.'

'Did I cry for you?' I asked.

'Yes, when I left, but they were such lovely nurses you soon stopped. They did a wonderful operation. Although the lump was on your cheek just below your left eye they managed to remove it and all you were left with was a scar at the side of your nose.

'The day you were due to come out I went to the ward to find you. You stood there in a short vest and nothing else. The nurse was trying to put your clothes on but you were more interested in the doll and doll's pram you were playing with. Your left eye and half your face was covered with a bandage. You turned around, saw me and said in a very nice voice, "Oh hello Mummy. Mummy this is nurse, nurse this is my Mummy." The introduction was perfectly and correctly done.'

Mummy laughed as she remembered. The nurse said, "Such excellent behaviour for one in such a short vest! How do you do Mummy?"

The author unable to sit owing to her injured leg after struggling into school for the photo

'Playing the game, I replied "How do you do nurse?" although I had met her before.'

'We had to traipse up and down to London to get this dressed over the next few months. The wound healed and you had no more trouble from it after that.'

I had forgotten about my injured knee and Mum smoothed the blankets, folded the sheet over the top of them and tucked them under the mattress so they wouldn't budge in the night. 'It's time you went to sleep now,' she said.

'Do I have to go to school tomorrow?' I asked.

'We'll see, we'll see,' Mum replied in a sing song voice. 'I want to spend some time with Clare now. Night night.' She kissed me, turned the light out and left the room.

I didn't go to school the next day. The bandages would not let me bend my leg. I said I was too unwell. However the following day there was to be a school photo and I struggled in for that.

10 BEACHES

A photograph of Binstead Beach taken by my father from the reed covered peninsula. We are standing in front of the tree we enjoyed climbing.

It was the sand in my shoes I mostly remember about visits to the beach during my childhood. My mother, father, my sister, Carolyn and I used to go to the beach often in the summer. When we had our car, this could be anywhere on the Isle of Wight. The beach offered us a fantastic playground, full of fun. We clambered over the rocks showing our nimbleness and balance. In the rock pools there were tiny shrimps and crabs to find which once they saw us would disappear. The crabs would bury themselves in the sand.

If I looked hard enough into these pools I could see imaginary tiny sea creatures who lived in caves near their own pool.

I had a collection of "Eye-Spy" small pocket books. These unglamorous books were printed on poor quality paper. They were illustrated but the colours were limited. They were designed to improve children's observation, enjoy discovery and were great fun to fill in. They were small enough to fit in a pocket.

My Eye-Spy the Seaside version was with me every time we went to the beach. I religiously marked off and dated things that I found. There was a picture of "the common Star Fish". I never found it and questioned how it could be common. I had looked for this star fish everywhere on every beach on the Island and never found one.

When the tide was out, there was a large amount of sand at Appley Beach. The beach was near enough to walk to when we travelled by bus and there was easy parking when we took the car. We created houses in the sand, and used stones and shells to decorate them. A castle with a moat around it had to have a flat stone to be the drawbridge. We tried to fill up the moat with sea water, but it would always drain away, before we managed to get back with the next bucket of water. Daddy taught us how to build a castle near the water edge.

'You are more likely to keep some water in the moat if you build it the nearer to the sea,' he explained. It worked for a while but then failed. The sea swamped the creation if the tide came further in and the water in the moat disappeared if the tide went further out.

We preferred it when the tide was in so that we could run up and down the beach and bathe in the sea.

'Don't forget your rubber rings,' Mummy said.

Carolyn picked up her blue one, I picked up my green one, and we blew them up. With her fingers holding the blow hole tight, Carolyn asked 'Can you help me first with the stopper please.' Mummy took the ring, gave it an extra puff, and then quickly pushed the stopper into the hole. Some air always escaped. Daddy had done mine. He seemed to have got more air in mine than Carolyn's.

Dressed in woolly swimming costumes, rubber hats on our heads, and rubber rings around us under our arms we were ready. We couldn't wait to get to the water's edge. There was always a line of shells or small stones that had to be walked over before we could fall into the water. Sometimes there was a line of seaweed, covered with small flies which rose up as we walked over it. No beach on the Island had pure soft sand right up to the edge. We were not allowed to complain about walking over the stones.

The Drawbridge Family in 1950 at Barton on Sea.

'The soles of your feet will toughen up,' Mother instructed us, 'You are Island girls.'

With bare feet we carefully walked over the obstacles and waded into the sea. We stayed in the water for ages. We swam on our front and backs; we danced and discovering the properties of buoyancy when we carried each other. Mother of course was on hand.

When she thought we had had enough, she called us in. 'You have been in the water long enough. Look, the skin on your fingers is now crinkly.' Mummy said as she handed us each a towel. 'Dry yourself off and we shall have our picnic.'

Picnics were well organised. We sat on the blue stripy rug; our food was put on plates, the sandwiches coming out of a tin sandwich box with a blue lid. The simple cheese sandwich was my favourite. Sometimes we would have leftover meat from the Sunday joint or boiled ham. They were neatly wrapped in greaseproof paper, or paper from the inside of a cornflake packet. Mother had often tucked in hard boiled eggs or whole tomatoes.

'Are you ready for a drink now?' asked Mum.

'Stop wriggling Jo, you are getting sand on my sandwich,' said Carolyn.

'I am not wriggling, I am perfectly still,' I retorted.

'Yes you are. Look Mummy she is doing it again.'

'It was only a little bit of sand Carolyn,' Mother calmly said, 'Try not to move Jo.' She poured orange squash from a glass bottle into our cups and then placed them in the "cup holder" she had created by pushing and twisting the bottom of the cup into the sand, so it would not fall over. Our cups were plastic and had a funny taste. With the salt air and the sea salt on our hands we were thirsty.

There was a flask of tea for Mum and Dad. Dad had a plastic cup and Mum had the lid of the Thermos Flask. The cork top of the flask had paper covering it.

'I can never quite trust that the flask won't leak,' Mum explained. However, she always made sure that the flask and the bottle were kept upright during the journey to the beach.

When it was time to go home mother packed up and helped us to dress. She held a large towel around me to ensure my privacy. I was terrified that I would show my body or my knickers to all those on the seashore. All packed up we walked up the beach in bare feet to the road. We did not put on our shoes until we got there.

Mother, the author, in a plastic bath hat, and sister, Carolyn lying in the shallow water at Appley Beach.

'The sand will dry your feet,' Mother reminded us.

A place to sit down was found and Mother brushed the excess of sand from my feet with her hand and put on my Startrite sandals. These shoes had a flower design cut into the leather on their tops. Shoes were not on ration but good shoes were expensive. These were always bought from Russell & Bromley's in Union Street, Ryde. Consequently buying shoes had to be planned and money put aside. As our feet grew mother checked every time where our toes were by pressing the top of the shoes. Once she discovered our toes were at the end Daddy cut a hole in the leather uppers of the shoes to relieve any pressure. Thus this extended the life of the shoes for that bit longer. To me this made them "peep toe" sandals, a fashion at the time. My mother had a pair of sandals which was designed to allow the big toes to show. Mine really didn't look anything like hers but they felt right.

With shoes tightly buckled up I could still feel a little left over grit between the soles of my feet and the sandals when I stood up.

We walked along the promenade from Appley to the Bus Stop near the pier.

'Now let me see,' said Daddy. 'It's ten past four I think the number 4 bus to East Cowes will be going first.'

With sandy legs and sunburnt body showing through our sun dresses we rode on the bus back to Binstead.

'Two and two halves to the top of Binstead Hill please,' said Daddy.

'Been to the beach have you?' said the bus conductor as he turned the handle on the ticket machine. 'It's been a lovely hot day. I bet you had a good time.'

Two very tired Drawbridge sisters stared back at him not saying a word.

My father who had not heard a word the bus conductor said looked at my mother who mouthed 'He asked if we had had a nice day.'

'Yes thank you, a lovely day,' Daddy said

'Yes thank you,' we chanted.

We staggered down the road and got to the house. Daddy opened the door.

'Take your shoes off in the porch,' said Mummy, 'and bang the shoes together to get rid of any leftover sand.'

The blue stripy beach rug was hung on the line outside, and was shaken vigorously and hit with the wicker carpet beater to remove the left over sand. It never did totally as the rug leaked sand constantly when it was brought back in doors.

We loved going to the seaside. Every summer we took picnics to various local beaches. Binstead beach was within walking distance, Appley beach was a bus ride away and Seaview which was Mummy's favourite was two buses away.

When Daddy bought the car the whole Island was opened up to us. We could go to lots of other beaches which had been inaccessible to us before.

'I can hear the Quarr Abbey bells clearly,' Mummy announced at breakfast. 'It's going to be a fine day.'

We listened and sure enough we heard the bells very clearly as if they were close by.

'How does that tell you that it is going to fine?' Carolyn asked.

'The sound travels on the wind and Quarr is in the west. If I can hear the bells clearly the wind is in the west and that usually means a fine day,' Mummy explained. 'If however I can hear the train going down the pier then the wind is coming from the east and there is a strong possibility it will rain.'

The choice of beach also depended on the temperature. We chose a sheltered beach on a cool day away from the wind. On a hot day we could go anywhere. An excessively hot day meant a trip to Freshwater was possible where the water was always icy cold.

It was important to me that the tide was in so I could go swimming. It didn't have to be a very hot day for us to go for a bathe.

Mum and the author standing in front of the remains of a demolished house at Seagrove Bay. This had fallen down owing to the clay and weak foundations (c 1956).

The state of the tide wasn't a problem at Seaview. After checking the weather Mother announced, 'Let's go to Seaview!'

Seaview is a select seaside town with many shops. We made our way towards Seagrove Bay which was the next bay along from the beach at the end of the shops. This beach had loads of rock pools and was covered in cobbles. 'It's too stoney for us to sit on,' mother said.

Daddy parked the car as near as we could in Pier Road and we walked carrying the picnic, the blue stripey rug and towels. We had our swimming costumes on under our clothes to save time. We passed the old suspension pier which was destroyed in the great storm in December 1951. The upright supports could still be seen but there was no walkway. We chose to walk along the road behind the houses and through the footpath by the toilets to get to the bay. We could have taken a shorter route along the beach, but decided the beach cobbles were too uncomfortable to negotiate.

We turned towards the sea and walked down the slipway past the small rowing boats; some had their oars in them, ready to go into the sea. Their occupants were probably in the café on the left. The café had an outside seating area. It sold ice creams and customers took beach trays out to where they were sitting. There was always sand on the floor. Customers didn't bother to put their shoes on or cover up beach wear in the shop.

Seagrove bay had a concrete wide walkway where the people who were mainly the locals sat.

'The tide's in,' said Carolyn slightly disappointed. There were big rocks which backed right up to the wall where we were going to sit. The waves were hitting the rocks and the water sprayed up, making our entry into the water difficult.

'We'll put our stuff down and then we will walk back to the slipway and bathe here.' Mother said, 'The sea is too rough for you to clamber over the boulders.'

We found a spot towards the end of the concrete in front of a demolished house which had a picket fence in front preventing people from entering. I wondered if this was due to the war and German bombing.

Dressed in our woolly costumes, rubber swim hats and our blue and green rubber rings, we walked back to the slipway and went for our bathe. Carolyn and I practised our swimming and floating while Daddy went for a long swim out in the bay. There was a diving board some way out to sea in front of the slip-way. Daddy climbed up and waited queuing on the ladder for his turn to dive in. He was a good swimmer and his dive was excellent.

'I wish he wouldn't go so far out,' Mummy said. 'But he is a strong swimmer, I suppose. He is far better than me.'

We could have stayed in for ages, but Mummy wanted to get back to the picnic.

'Darlings, I'm getting a little cold,' she said. 'You can get back in the water later after we have had our lunch. The tide will have started to go out by then and there will be some sand to play on.'

The rug had been put down on the hard concrete for us to sit on but there was no problem with sand. Mother had made a meat pasty for the picnic that day. We had had a steak and kidney stew the day before and she had minced up the leftover meat, added it to a pastry case and cooked it in the oven. This was a favourite whether we had it hot or cold. Today we had it cold with tomatoes.

I took a bite out of the tomato.

'Jo!' Carolyn shouted, 'You are dripping all the juice down your front!'

'Never mind,' I snapped back as I stuffed the very juicy tomatoes into my mouth. 'I can wash it off in the sea anyway.'

'You shouldn't talk with your mouth full either,' Carolyn retorted.

'Now, now girls,' Mother joined in, 'you shouldn't row on such a beautiful day like today.'

The cups for our orange squash sat safely on the ground, which we drank with a slice of homemade Victoria sponge cake.

We waited a while for our dinner to digest and for the tide to recede. I watched the rocks appear from being completely covered with water, then the cobbles showed, and finally some sand. The sandy area was now filling up with beach goers. There was a group of children building sandcastles, and a couple playing tennis. A game of "Rounders" was being organised for a group of adults and children. They used a cricket bat to hit the ball.

'Are you ready Dad?' shouted the bowler a young lad of about ten years old. There was grit and determination on "Dad's" face. He whacked the ball so hard it went into the sea and he started to run.

'Dad! You didn't have to hit it so hard!' scolded his son the bowler. The fielder nearest the shore ran into the sea, as "Dad" ran a rounder and then cheered.

'Can we get back in the water now please Mum?' I asked.

Mummy put our swimming hats on again, and we picked up our rings and climbed over the rocks in front of us which were now clearly visible.

As the tide receded the water was shallow and safe. Mummy watched from the wall as Daddy went to the café to get a pot of tea for two on a beach tray.

We played in the sea for ages as the tide went out further. Later on Mummy, unable to attract our attention, came down to the water's edge to call us in.

Walking up the beach together I looked at the remaining houses that opened on to the wall where we were sitting. All the houses were occupied with people obviously enjoying the seaside. There were oars leaning up against the wall, a boat upturned in front, children came in and out of the front doors. The windows were open. Each house seemed to have a party going on where everyone was having a good time.

I stared enviously, but then I noticed, 'Those houses are crooked!' I said. 'They are not straight.'

The houses were leaning to one side and triangular wedges had been put above the doors and window frames to fill in the gaps.

'That's because of the blue slipper clay,' Mummy informed us. 'They are all like that; they will have to be knocked down eventually. The house at the very end nearest the café is straight because the foundations go down further than the height of the house.'

It took a while for me to understand that. I had never seen a house being built, nor had I seen or heard of the word foundations.

'The people who owned those houses,' Mother said, pointing to the crooked ones, 'so I am told, tried to get money from the government for war damage. They stated that it was the vibration of the guns in Portsmouth that caused the buildings to be unstable.'

'Did they get any money?' Carolyn asked.

'No none at all. It was decided that the problem was caused by the instability of the foundations and the clay on which they are built.'

'I'd love a house this close to the sea!' I mused, envious of what I was viewing.

'Not one of those.' Carolyn said. 'They are likely to fall down.'

'No, not one of those,' I replied.

Mother brought me out of my daydream, 'Let's hurry up. If you are quick we'll stop and get an ice cream at the Boathouse opposite the old pier,' she announced.

We packed up quickly and with bare feet we walked along the beach on our way back to the car. We chose the short route as the tide had gone out enough to leave a sandy pathway between the cobbles and the water's edge. We walked and paddled along the beach, carrying our bags and our shoes which Mummy had joined together by doing up the buckles.

Carolyn, the author and Willie Pickle, our dachshund on a very hot day at Compton Chine. The cardigans, over our shoulders protect us from the searing heat. We are lying on the blue stripy rug.

'Don't go too deep girls,' shouted Mother, 'Hold the bag higher, Jo, the bottom of it is touching the water!'

Stopping at the wall in front of the pier, we put on our shoes. There was no sand to brush off. Daddy, Carolyn and I went to get the ice creams while Mummy waited with the bags. I chose a strawberry flavoured cornet, Carolyn preferred the vanilla, a chocolate one was chosen for Mummy. Daddy had a choc ice.

'Daddy,' said Carolyn touching his arm, 'You always have a choc ice.'

'I like a choc ice!' he retorted.

We ate our ices sitting on the wall. I noticed the large Pier Hotel which had a balcony at the front. Out of the windows were towels and costumes hung to dry. There was a woman, scantily dressed, her head out of the window shouting to a friend whose head was out of the next window. I thought the towels made it look untidy.

Daddy saw me looking at the hotel. 'I did a job in there once,' he told us, 'I helped replace the ballroom floor.'

'It's got a ballroom!' I said thinking that it was very grand. I pictured Cinderella in her beautiful dress in a ballroom. I couldn't quite put the holiday makers who shouted to each other, and who hung their towels and costumes out of the window, with the people in Cinderella type dresses.

Before I could ask, the ice creams were finished and we walked back to the car.

---oOo---

It was a stiflingly hot day. 'Let's go to Compton Chine today.' Daddy suggested.

'We'll have to take Willie. It will be too long to leave a dog all day.' Mum said. 'And we must take extra water for him to drink; it's going to be a very, very hot day.'

Extra drinks were packed, and a bowl was taken for Willie. Carolyn and I put on our new bathing costumes. Made of cotton, they were smocked with elastic behind to draw in the material and make them figure hugging. Mine was green and Carolyn's blue. Daddy loaded up the car. Mummy had put on her new sleeveless seersucker cotton sun dress over her costume too. She had sewn the dress herself. We loaded the car and started off on our journey to the other side of the Island. Carolyn sat behind Daddy, I was behind Mummy, and Willie was on the floor between her legs.

We had been on the road for about ten minutes, when Mummy announced, 'I've got that horrid feeling I have forgotten something. We have the picnic, lots of drinks, water and bowl for the dog and towels. Did anyone put in the beach rug?'

'Yes it's here,' Carolyn said, 'It's rolled up between us.'

'That's alright then,' she replied as she settled down for the journey. The windows were wide open, and a cool breeze flowed into the car.

To get to Compton Chine we needed to cross the Island. The chine is one of a series of bays situated on the Military Road, so called as it was constructed to link up fortifications during the 19th century. The French had threatened an invasion. The beach then, and is still today, without a café or holiday gift shops. There was, however, an area for parking cars in a field on the other side of the road to the bay. Daddy turned into the car park field.

'There are a lot of cars here today,' he remarked, 'Lots of people have the same idea as us.' He loaded us up with our bags and we crossed the road, climbed over the stile and walked on to the path to the beach across an open field. I looked around carefully for any cows that might also be nearby. Fortunately there were none. Carolyn and I ran on to get a look at the beach and the sea.

'We'll have a bathe first shall we?' Carolyn said.

'Can we bathe first Mummy?' I shouted.

'We'll see,' she replied.

We climbed down the rocky path and I jumped last step on to the beach. We waited for Mummy and Daddy to catch up with us.

'Which way?' I asked.

'Which way shall we go?' Carolyn corrected me.

Mummy looked around and we turned to the left. A place was found near the cliff.

'The tide is going out,' Mummy said. 'That'll give us lots of space to sit. We'll lay out the rug and get organised and then you two can go for a bathe.'

We quickly took off our dresses and ran down and into the sea. We walked into the surf up to our knees then we fell into the water and relished in the cool pleasure. The water was shallow and with our hands "walking" on the bottom we went back towards the shore.

Mum and Dad joined us. Daddy in his baggy bathing shorts strode in and swam out to sea. I caught sight of Mummy standing with Willie paddling at the water's edge in a new brightly coloured costume. It was covered with brilliant red flowers and was silky smooth.

'That looks like satin,' I said to Mum.

Carolyn and I were still lying on our tummies in the surf, when Willie swam out to us. It was lovely to hold a warm wriggling creature in the water.

Whilst we held Willie Mummy dipped under the water, swam a few strokes and cooled off.

'That's better now, I'll take Willie, get dried and get the picnic ready. You stay a bit longer. I do wish your father wouldn't swim so far out.'

'He's a good swimmer Mummy,' Carolyn reassured.

'I know,' she replied, 'Far better than me. Did I ever tell you I taught myself to swim?'

We were amazed. 'Really?' I said.

'Yes, there were no lessons for me as a child so when I was a lot older than you I taught myself.'

Mummy walked up the beach, put Willie's lead around her ankle ensuring he was in as much shade as she could and got the picnic ready.

She called us in. Daddy was back from swimming too far out.

'I wish you wouldn't swim so far out!' she scolded. 'It's so hot girls, put your cardigans over your shoulders. I don't want the strong sun to burn your backs.'

After we had finished our cheese sandwiches, Mummy picked up four bowls, 'I have some strawberries and cream for a pudding!'

She shared out the strawberries making sure she had been equally fair to all the bowls. She then picked up the cardboard carton of double cream. Getting the lid off was proving to be tricky. She pulled on the little tab to lift the round circle of cardboard from the top. Unfortunately her grip on the pot was too hard and as the lid came away she squeezed the pot and out poured some of the cream on to her leg.

'Oh dear, never mind, not too much spilt,' she said as she shared the rest out between us. Willie was quick to take advantage of the accident. He jumped up, came over and licked the cream from Mummy's leg.

'Thank you dear,' Daddy said to Mummy, 'That was a lovely feast.'

All of a sudden, Mummy stopped. She put down her bowl and picked up and searched in each bag separately and frantically.

'I know what I had forgotten,' she announced.

'What?' we asked.

'My knickers!' she replied.

Carolyn and I were horrified! To mention the word "knickers" on the beach with people around was not the way to behave. 'Shush Mummy!' said Carolyn, 'people will hear.'

Mummy mouthed the news to Daddy, they started to giggle and then they both laughed.

We returned to the sea for another bathe and then explored the rocks and pools that the receding tide had left visible. We negotiated the rocks, some of which were covered in slippery seaweed. It was easier to get over the rocks on all fours.

'Why are you walking like that?' Carolyn said. 'You look silly, you look like a dog.'

'I don't look like a dog,' I snapped back, 'and I don't want to fall over.'

We saw shrimps and crabs which always made us squeal.

'The crabs won't hurt you,' Mummy said. 'They are far too small and we won't get much of a meal from those tiny shrimps.'

I collected some shells and gave each one to Mummy, 'This is a pretty one,' I said as I handed my gift to her. 'Lovely, quite lovely,' she said.

Mother helped us change under the large yellow beach towel out of our wet costumes and into dry underwear under sun dresses. Her costume was also wet so Mother changed and put on her seersucker dress. We packed up the picnic and made our way up the path and back to the car. Mummy walked tall, confidently and completely without her knickers.

---oOo---

My love of the sea and swimming has extended throughout my life. When I was 12 years old I went swimming with my school friend Liane at Ryde. There were council run changing huts in an area along from the pier and a set of steps into the sea.

We paid our money for the hire of a hut, got changed, left our clothes in the basket provided with the man in charge and went down the steps and into the sea. The tide was in and there were lots of swimmers. A raft was moored in front of this area. The deck of it was high out of the water and there was a ladder for climbing on it. Around the side were looped ropes for people to hold on, similar to those found on the seats on the paddle steamers.

Mummy had explained that if the boat was to sink the seats would float and people could hold on and be rescued.

I was watching the boys dive from the raft. In they went head first, then up they came, climbed back up and dived again. Some climbed on without even using the ladder.

'I am 12 years old,' I thought. 'I should be old enough to be able to do that.'

I watched the boys diving off again and again, screeching confidently as they took off. It looked so easy. I scrutinised them as carefully as I could and then I plucked up enough courage to copy. I took off, flew through the air and landed on my chest, as flat as a pancake. It was the best belly flop of the day! My chest took the full force of the landing, and it hurt. I said nothing and pretended I was O.K. I was somewhat subdued for quite a while until the stinging feeling wore off. I then climbed back onto the raft and proceeded to screech as the boys did as I jumped in. 'Going feet first was much safer,' I decided, 'and certainly was without pain.'

I had no prior technical knowledge of what I was going to do whatsoever. Learning from my experience, I didn't try to dive again, until I was in my 30s, where I had a teacher to guide me in a safe swimming pool.

11 SHOPPING AND RATIONING

When the ration book was open on the kitchen table I guessed we were going shopping. All post war shopping trips were preceded by its appearance. Mother sat with the book, pencil in hand and an old envelope that had been carefully opened out fully. On this she wrote her list meticulously.

It was a dull day so we took a bus to the parish church in Ryde, and then walked up to the Health Food Store at the top of the town. This was our allocated grocery shop during rationing. As we entered the shop, the bell which was attached to a bent springy piece of metal at the top of the wooden door, jangled.

The shopkeeper greeted Mother.

'Good morning Mrs. Drawbridge,' he said. 'Won't keep you a minute.'

Seated on the chair in front of the counter was a large woman. Mother knew her. It was Mrs. Chandler-Smythe, an acquaintance of Mummy from the Mother's Union, a group connected to our Church.

'Good Morning Mrs. Chandler-Smythe,' said Mother.

'Good Morning Mrs. Drawbridge,' Mrs. Chandler-Smythe's voice was deep and booming, 'Hello girls.'

'Hello Mrs. Chandler-Smythe,' Carolyn chanted.

'Hello Mrs Smythe,' I said.

'Chandler-Smythe,' Mummy corrected me.

She was a big woman whose immense frame protruded so much over the sides of the chair that I wondered how the poor little chair could cope. Her large brown handbag was on her lap which she held with one hand together with the list. Her other hand was busy pointing to what she wanted and where she thought it was. She was dressed in a tightly fitting brown suit. Her skirt went just over her knees. She was wearing thick stockings and stout brown lace up shoes. She didn't have a waist as her huge shape went all the way from her shoulders to her bottom. A dead red fox was draped around her shoulders. The tiny head lay down over one side of her large chest and I could just see a paw appearing under the long tail on the other side. Her grey hair was neatly pinned into curls around her hat which was brown and made of felt. It had sculptured long swirls in it.

'How do they get those dips in her hat?' I asked Mummy.

'Shush my darling,' Mummy said. 'I'll explain later. You mustn't talk about people's clothes when they are here. It is rude.'

The grocer, Mr. Barton, was scurrying around the shop at her command.

Mrs. Chandler-Smythe referred to her list. 'I would like some cereal please. What have you got now?'

'We have Kellogg's Wheat Flakes, Weetabix, Shredded Wheat, Cornflakes and Quaker Puffed Wheat.'

'Well I don't want Shredded Wheat, that gets under my plate. I'll take some Cornflakes.'

'What plate?' I asked Mummy, thinking of our blue and white dinner plates we had at home.

I was shushed again.

Mr. Barton went over to the shelves on the far side of the shop, climbed up the ladder and picked up a packet and returned to the counter.

'I'd like some cocoa, the Bournville Cocoa I prefer. Have you got some?'

'Yes Madam,' said the grocer as he walked over to the same set of shelves climbed the same ladder again and picked up a packet.

'I'll take some Bird's Custard powder!' she called out, obviously aware of the repeated journey.

'Yes Madam, here it is. Is there anything else you need from this side of the shop?'

'Ah now let me think.'

Mr. Barton stood on the ladder and waited. Mrs. Chandler-Smythe scrutinised her list carefully.

'Do you need any coffee?' Mr. Barton tentatively suggested. 'You usually have a bottle of Camp Coffee.' There was a long pause. 'What about some cornflour? Coleman's mustard? Powdered Milk?'

'No but I'll have a jar of Marmite.' She turned to us. 'That's very good for you girls. Do you give the girls Marmite Mrs. Drawbridge?'

'Yes I do. It is very good for them,' Mum agreed.

Mr. Barton got down from the step ladder and returned with the items.

'Do you have a tin of Fray Bentos corned beef? And I'd like some Nestle's Condensed Milk.'

'That's my favourite,' I whispered to Mummy.

'But not very nice with corned beef,' she replied.

We giggled quietly at our silly joke.

Mr. Barton returned to the counter.

'Do you need any Oxydol washing powder?'

'No thank you I use a laundry but I will take some Lux flakes,' she replied. She looked at Mother and mouthed. 'For my smalls!'

'That'll be all! Thank you Grocer.' Mrs Chandler-Smythe boomed out.

'Do you want this delivered?'

'Of course, yes please, and make sure your delivery boy goes to the tradesman's entrance this time and not the front door.'

'Yes, definitely, I will tell him.'

Mr. Barton took the ration book and cut out some squares and then started to add up the cost of the purchases but before he had finished Mrs. Chandler-Smythe butted in.

'Put it on my account please. I shall be so glad when this rationing is completely finished.'

Mr. Barton reached under the counter and pulled out a large black book. He added up the purchases and turned to Mrs. Chandler-Smythe's page.

'Won't we all,' Mummy said, 'but it's not as bad as it has been. Things are improving.'

'Yes I suppose so. But it so tiresome, don't you agree?'

Mummy nodded her head.

'Excuse me Madam,' Mr. Barton interrupted, 'I will add this to your account, but I would be grateful if you could settle this as it is mounting up.'

Mrs. Chandler-Smythe coughed and cleared her throat very loudly. 'Yes certainly,' she stuttered as she cleared her throat again. 'Put the bill in with the delivery and I will settle up with a cheque when I next come in.'

Getting up from the chair Mrs. Chandler-Smythe quickly went to the door. Mr. Barton moved towards the door. 'Let me open the door for you.' But she was too quick. She pulled the door open, the bell rang loudly as she slipped through sideways and rushed off down the high street.

Mr. Barton returned to the counter.

'Mrs. Drawbridge it is so nice to see you. May I just put these groceries away in a box ready for delivery? I would hate to get Mrs. Chandler-Smithye's order wrong.'

'Of course, you carry on.'

Mother put her basket on the long counter. In front were large tins of biscuits. Carolyn and I peered in. 'Which are your favourites?' Carolyn asked me. I considered for a while looking through the glass tops.

'Those,' I said pointing to the Fig Rolls.

'I like the bourbon ones,' she said.

Mother ever conscious of the price, chose the Nice biscuits. 'I'll take half a pound of the Nice biscuits please.' Mr. Barton carefully ripped a brown paper bag from the collection on the wall, and holding them tight, placed them in the bottom of the paper bag and placed them in the bowl on the scales. He took an eight ounce weight and placed it on the flat side of the scales. He waited for the scales to stop rocking, and added one more biscuit. He waited again until there was no more movement and the scales balanced.

'That makes eight ounces exactly Madam,' he said. Then he took the top two corners of the bag and swung them over twice shutting and sealing it. He placed the bag carefully in Mother's basket.

I stood on the chair so I could watch him work. I could see better a little higher up.

'Jo! you shouldn't stand on Mr. Barton's chair. Get down!'

'That's alright let her stand there if she likes. I'm sure the chair will take her weight.'

Mother referred to her list.

The grocer broke the silence. 'Do you need any flour madam?'

'No thank you,' Mother replied, 'But I will take some tea - Typhoo if you have it. So glad it's off ration now.'

'Are you sure about the flour?'

'Yes I am quite sure, but while you are there I will take some Bird's Custard Powder,' Mother said.

He collected the packet of loose tea and custard powder.

'Have you got any canned pineapple?' she continued.

The grocer looked at the shelf containing the canned fruit. 'I don't think so, I'll check in the store room.' He scurried out of the shop.

'I am very sorry I'm afraid I don't. I do have pears, peaches and prunes.'

Mother turned to us and let us choose. It took a very little time for us to decide that prunes with their strong flavour, was not a favourite and we had a pear tree in the garden so we did not need them.

'Peaches, peaches!' we yelled.

Mother corrected us. 'Peaches, please.'

'So nice not to have rations on canned fruit now isn't it Mrs. Drawbridge?' the grocer said in passing.

The ration books lay on the counter, 'I'd like to take our ration of cheese please'. The large semi-circular chunk of cheese was placed on the white marble slab. There was a wire attached to a wooden handle at one end and the marble slab at the other.

'I'll take the full allowance, four ounces please,' Mother said

The grocer took the wire over the cheese and pulled it through, revealing a triangular slice. He picked it up and placed it onto the greaseproof paper on the flat scale.

The weight was just short of the four ounces so he added an extra piece. 'Is that alright with you?'

The scales were placed on the counter facing and in full view of the customer and the grocer. On this the weight was displayed in pounds and ounces. There was a bar attached at the bottom in the middle and moved sideways across the display of weights listed. Similar to the way a windscreen wiper moves.

'That'll be fine.'

The cheese was wrapped up tightly in greaseproof paper, efficiently and neatly, with sharp folds. Mother paused and checked her list.

'I think I might make some sweets for the girls. I would like two pounds of sugar please.'

'Sweets girls!' the shopkeeper smiled, 'What sweets do you make?

'My version of fudge,' Mother answered.

'You are lucky to have such a clever mother.'

I loved it when sugar was bought. This came in big containers hidden from my view behind the counter. The grocer took the large silver bowl from the scales in which he had weighed the biscuits and with a smaller scoop ladled the sugar into it. He placed it back on the scales.

'There you are, two pounds exactly,' he said. Then he took a piece of blue sugar paper and folded it so it made a bag into which he skilfully poured the sugar.

'I see you have some eggs. How fresh are they?' Mum asked.

'They are straight from the farm this morning Madam,' he replied.

They referred to the ration book.

'You can take your full allowance,' the grocer said.

'Then I'll take four eggs please and I'll also take some powdered egg for cooking.'

With care he took the eggs one by one from the tray and placed them in another paper bag and into Mother's basket.

Mr. Barton crossed the shop to collect the powdered egg from the shelves. There were lots of jars and tins on the shelves on the left. Carolyn and I looked and decided which were our favourites.

'I would like to have cornflakes and cocoa and condensed milk.' I said.

Carolyn agreed but added coffee for Daddy as he liked it. There were packets of flour, plain and self-raising. There were also sacks on the floor and an opened one revealed potatoes, grubby with earth.

'They came from the same farm this morning as the eggs. I don't usually sell them but the farmer insisted. Would you like some?'

Mummy inspected them, 'Yes I'll take a couple of pounds.' Mr. Barton measured them out and was about to put them straight into Mummy's basket, when they remembered the biscuits and eggs. Mummy took them out before he slid them into the bottom.

'I'll take a jar of marmalade please,' she said. The shop keeper bustled around from the counter to the other side of the shop again.

'And while you are there, two cans of Heinz baked beans,' Mother continued. She did not need any jam as she made her own from the strawberries in the garden, and the blackberries from the hedgerows.

Mother's basket was almost full. Carolyn and I waited, patiently, never asking for anything. Rationing forbade it. There was no point to any request.

Our patience was rewarded.

'Would you each like a Banana Bar?' asked mother

What a treat!

'Yes please,' we replied eagerly. These were added to the basket.

'These are not to be eaten now,' Mother reminded us, 'You may have them when we get home. One does not eat in the streets! It is just not done!'

Banana Bars have long since vanished. Sweets have now become more sophisticated. A Banana Bar was very humble. Made of mashed bananas with their natural sweetness, they were made into oblongs of brown sweet banana flavoured heaven. It had the texture of a soft undercooked biscuit, which had been taken out of the oven before it had time to crisp. Soft and yet solid, it was wrapped in cellophane. It was sweet and delicious, and I have not tasted anything similar since.

We had to wait longer for our treat as there were other groceries to buy. We went down the High Street past the Catholic Church and School and Hills the dress shop. A lovely smell greeted us as we went into the baker's shop next to Woolworths. Carolyn and I stared at the Danish pastries and the tray full of pink and white iced buns.

'A large loaf please,' Mummy said and left without going near the buns.

Further on down the hill we went into the butcher's.

'Morning, Mrs. Drawbridge, what can I get you today?' Again the ration book was produced.

'I'd like to take my ration in some stewing steak please. Have you any shin of beef?'

'Yes Madam, how much would you like?

She laid her ration book on the counter. 'I'll take all our rations in stewing steak.'

'Certainly, do you want me to cube it for you?'

'Would you please? Thank you. Can you weigh in two lambs' kidneys as well,' Mother continued.

Mother pulled out a string bag from her basket and the meat wrapped in paper was placed in it.

'Will that be all madam?'

'Yes thank you. Come on girls. Good morning.'

We walked back to the bus. Mother took great care of her basket and of the eggs which were placed on the top.

Once indoors, the shopping was put away and we were given our Banana Bars. We took them into the sitting room to enjoy. We nibbled at these so we could make them last longer. Carolyn and I would compare how much we had left. The winner was the one who could enjoy her banana bar the longest. I was impatient and therefore I never won.

Mother was clever with rationing. Her imaginative mind created lovely meals that filled us. We were never hungry and we always cleaned our plates. We were taught to mash potatoes into the remaining gravy, or to use a spoon to get the last drop of food from the plate. I scraped the plate with my spoon.

'Leave some of the pattern!' Daddy said.

We were allowed to pick up chop bones and gnaw at the remaining meat.

'You should never pick up the meat bone if you are out for dinner or eating in a restaurant,' she said. 'It is considered very rude. It is just not done.'

Nothing was wasted. We ate the skins of baked potatoes, but while they were in the oven, mother was cooking something else so as not to waste any power. She made stews out of shin of beef and lambs' kidneys. There wasn't an awful lot of meat because she would serve half of it at one meal and keep the rest to make a pie the next day. As she minced the beef for the pie she added a slice of bread.

'This cleans every last drop of meat and gravy from the mincer so nothing is wasted.' She told us as she mixed the bread into the beef.

There was always lots of gravy. She served the stew with dumplings, boiled potatoes, carrots and onions which were grown in the garden.

I used to eat my meals in order of preference. Firstly I would consume the onions and carrots, then the small amount of meat and finally the dumplings. Made of Atora Shredded Suet and self-raising flour, with the right amount of salt and water, these lovely light balls of suet pastry soaked in gravy were my favourites.

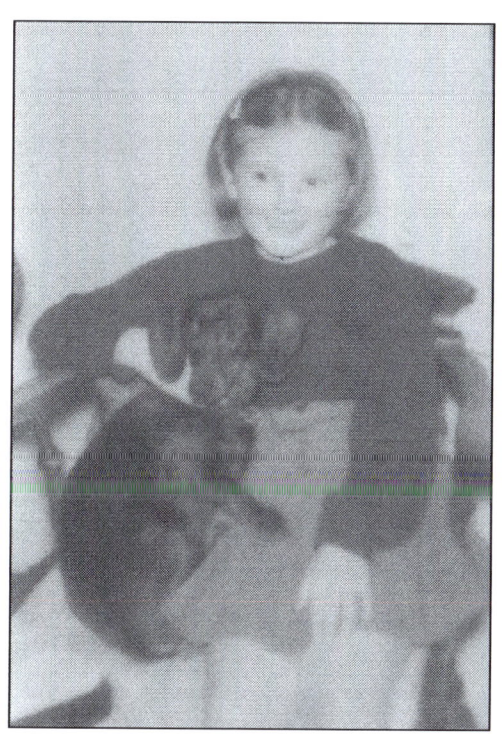

The author sharing the large carver chair in the kitchen with Willie Pickle

When we had a roast on Sunday, Mother served up enough meat to leave some for Monday to have cold with salad. On Tuesday what was left was minced to make into a

Shepherds' Pie. Baked beans were added to make the meat go further. I thought the baked beans were to add to the flavour which I loved.

One morning Daddy was at home, and we sat at breakfast. Mother gave me with my toast, a spoonful of marmalade, and a small oblong of butter which was my ration. I loved butter.

I placed the butter on the toast and then with my knife I cut out a piece of toast the same size as the oblong of butter. This I left on my plate with the butter on top. I then proceeded to cover the rest of the toast with marmalade and eat it, crusts and all. When I had finished I picked up the small oblong of toast and butter treat and ate that.

Daddy looked over his newspaper and said. 'Jo, what are you doing? Betty, she shouldn't do that. That is not the way she should eat her toast, butter and marmalade.'

Mummy looked crossly at Daddy and said firmly. 'It is her toast, her butter ration and she can eat it as she wishes.'

---oOo---

Willie Pickle our dachshund was loved and on the whole a very good dog. But he blotted his copy book one Sunday morning.

'To be fair it wasn't all Willie's fault.' Mummy said afterwards.

Daddy had come down early to get Mummy an early morning cup of tea in bed. He laid the tray, took the milk out of fridge and poured out two cups of tea. He put the milk back in the fridge and took the tray upstairs.

Unfortunately Daddy had not shut the fridge door properly. When it was pushed correctly it clicked as the lock took hold. Daddy could not hear the click. It was not shut properly. The fridge door was left ajar.

When Mummy got up and brought down the tray she noticed the fridge door open. The precious leg of lamb meant for lunch that day was missing. Mother went to the dog's basket and there at the side of a very miserable looking dog, was the joint. It was covered in fluff, biscuit crumbs and dog saliva.

'Oh Willie, you bad dog!' Mother shouted. Willie looked even more miserable. He had eaten a large chunk out of the raw meat and looked ill.

The family gathered in the kitchen. After we had all said, 'Willie you are a bad dog.' Daddy said 'It's Sunday! The shops are shut, what are we going to have for lunch?'

'I'll sort this out,' Mum said. She picked up the joint and went to the sink. The joint was submerged in the washing up bowl full of clean cold water. Here she cleaned it of the fluff and biscuit crumbs. She made sure there were no bits left on it. Out of the larder she got the vinegar and poured it into a bowl. The joint was submerged in the solution.

'That'll sterilise it,' she assured us. 'All will be well. Now run along and get ready its nearly time for church. Willie you are a bad dog!'

We all went to church leaving the joint soaking in the sterilising vinegar solution. Mother checked the fridge door was shut more than once.

Poor Willie was chastised every time we went into the kitchen before lunch. He was given nothing to eat all day as he was definitely bloated and feeling uncomfortable. He only left his basket when Mother ordered him into the garden.

Mother roasted the remains of the meat. 'It's in a very hot oven, that too will help to sterilise it,' she assured us.

The roast had a slight tang that day. 'That's the vinegar, it won't hurt you,' she said brusquely. 'Eat up! You'll be hungry later if you don't.' We were all very quiet as we ate our dinner that day.

Eating my meal in order of preference, I decided to eat the meat first to get it out of the way and finish with the vegetables. The crispy roast potatoes were last.

Mummy saved the day, she had made an apple crumble for pudding which was served with custard and it was delicious!

Willie recovered the following day as did our attitude towards him.

'You were such a naughty boy yesterday,' I cooed at him, kissing his soft smooth head. 'What a naughty boy.'

He gazed at me, I was sure he loved me as we sat sharing the large wooden carver chair in the kitchen.

'He is never going to live that down,' said Mum.

12 CELEBRATIONS

I was five and three quarters when I discovered that Mummy was Father Christmas. It was Boxing Day and all of us sat at the kitchen table having breakfast.

'Jo, you are old enough to write thank you letters,' Mother said. She sounded serious, 'You were given the presents now you must write and say thank you.'

I groaned as I hated writing. I had seen Carolyn's neat letters and I was sure mine were not going to be good as them.

'I'll help you. We'll do it together. They don't have to be long,' she suggested. After a pause she added, 'You were given writing paper and envelopes in your stocking from Father Christmas.'

I continued shovelling cornflakes into my mouth. 'I won't have to write to Father Christmas will I?' I asked, glad as that was one less I had to do.

Carolyn stopped eating. 'You don't think that Father Christmas can get around to all the houses all over the world do you?' she declared. 'It's Mummy that fills the stockings.'

I had nearly finished my cornflakes and got to the lovely sugary milky bit at the bottom of the bowl. I slurped it up.

'Why don't people tell me these things?' I said.

Despite rationing and the lack of goods in the shops Christmas was always a lovely day.

Mother put aside some of her rations, and money was saved so we could have a sumptuous meal. After the main course we had Christmas pudding and custard. This had been made well in advance. It was the first preparation for Christmas in our house.

On a cold November day the Good Housekeeping Cooking Compendium was open on the kitchen table. 'Would you like to help make the puddings?' Mother asked us. It was always fun to help with the cooking. We didn't need to be asked twice, there were often treats to sample and a bowl to clean out with spoons.

'Get the scales out Carolyn please. They are in the cupboard,' Mother instructed. 'Jo you can help me grease the bowls.'

With margarine on my fingers I rubbed the inside of the bowls and Carolyn measured out the fruit. Currents, raisins and sultanas were added to the scales in equal measure. Mother picked up a small pot of candied peel to add to the mixture.

'Oh look it is already chopped up. Last year I had to cut this myself,' she told us. 'I didn't have to cut up the suet as this is already prepared in a packet too.'

'Would you like to sample the glacé cherries?' Mum offered. 'One each! No more!'

My bowls were greased and Mummy told me to wash my hands. 'Now would you like to help me make the breadcrumbs?'

She had set aside some of yesterday's bread which was now hard and stale. A grating machine was attached to the table with a large clamp which was screwed on tightly. At the top of this was a square box which opened at the bottom on to the circular grater. The stale bread was added to the box and a square piece of wood with a round knob on the top exactly matching the box was placed on top.

'Press down gently onto the stopper and turn the handle clockwise,' she said.

I turned it the wrong way. 'Other way darling.' She said.

Out of the shoot at the front came the bread crumbs.

Orange and lemon peel had also to be grated. Mother had an upright grater for this.

'You just need the zest so stop when you get to the white bit,' she explained.

There was also nutmeg to grate. This had its own little container which doubled up as the grater. Holding the nut in one hand she grated it against the course side of the metal container. A powder came out of the bottom onto a saucer. 'There! That's enough,' she said. She put the nutmeg back in the container and shut the lid firmly. Carolyn and I smelt the nutmeg, mixed spice and cinnamon before Mum added them to the mixing bowl.

The large yellow china bowl was filling with all these lovely ingredients, but it was still all very dry. Mummy broke each egg separately into a cup before she put them into another small bowl and beat them with a fork.

'You must make sure none of the eggs have gone off before you add them to the precious mixture,' she instructed. To this she added half a glass of brandy.

She poured egg and brandy mixture to the bowl. The smell was gorgeous.

We made wishes as we stirred the lovely smelling gloopy mixture. Once in the bowls each one was steamed for four hours.

The build-up to the big day continued with a Nativity play performed at Binstead school.

When Carolyn was 11 and had moved to the Convent Senior School, I was nine years old and still at Binstead Junior School. The carol concerts for both schools were on the same day. Fortunately mine was in the afternoon finishing at three thirty and Carolyn's was in the evening starting at six o'clock.

'I can come to both,' said Mum. 'Jo, after yours has finished we will quickly go home and have a small tea and then we will have time to get to Carolyn's carol concert in Ryde.

In Binstead Church the school assembled to sing all the Christmas favourites. There were readings and songs all pronouncing the birth of Christ and how His birth brought peace and joy. After it was over, Mum and I raced up the road. Carolyn had already arrived home from school and had let herself in via the back door. Mum had put the key was under the mat on the shelf in the porch. She gave us a sandwich and a cup of tea. 'You have both had school dinners so a sandwich will be enough for now.'

We were still in our school uniforms but Carolyn was given a clean shirt. 'You must look your best,' Mum said.

We took the bus to Ryde and walked to the top of the town to the Ryde Youth Centre. The hall was packed with Convent School girls, their parents, siblings and friends. We heard the same readings and sang most of the carols that Binstead School had sung earlier in the afternoon.

Mother swapped the usual pleasantries with other parents and the nuns before we disappeared into the night. It was a crisp cold night. There were stars shining brightly as we talked about the star that had been shining at Jesus's birth on the way home. Mum gave us a supper of a glass of warm milk and a marmalade sandwich.

'What a lovely day I have had,' Mum said, 'I love to hear the carols and listen to the readings.'

'Didn't you mind that you heard most of them twice?' Carolyn said.

'No, no, of course not,' Mum said, 'Today has been the start of Christmas.'

I don't know what caused the row, but Carolyn and I went into a real fury of shouting, screaming and banging doors. We took our grievances to Mother who was resting in her chair in the sitting room. She was laughing!

'Why are you laughing?' we both said.

'It's not funny!' I snarled.

'No it's not fair!' Carolyn said.

Mother looked at us both and sang 'And praises sing to God the King, and peace to men on earth.' And then she laughed again.

We decorated the house with holly and ivy that we had gathered from the woods around us. Mother bought a tree which was planted and placed in the sitting room. We decorated this with silver balls and tinsel. The Christmas fairy for the tree was woken up, taken out of her box and tied on tightly to the top branch. She was a small doll with stiff legs and moveable arms and dressed by Mummy. Her outfit was white with a tinsel belt and headdress.

In the school assembly we sang carols which were repeated in the service of Nine Lessons and Carols at Holy Cross Church. I loved this because the church was decorated and there was a big Christmas tree at the back. There was a large model of a stable set in the corner of the North Aisle. There was fresh straw for the models of Mary, Joseph, Baby Jesus, shepherds, a donkey and a cow to settle in. It always looked so cosy I thought. The Three Kings arrived after Christmas at Epiphany. The three pillars on the north side at Holy Cross Church had ivy wound around them. Every window had greenery in it and a log in which there were two red candles. These remained lit even when the lights were put out for the sermon. The whole church was full of a magical atmosphere of Christmas.

We always sat in a pew on the south side of the church half way down. Carolyn sat at the end and I was next Mummy. This was near a large painting of the Virgin Mary and baby Jesus, which I thought was lovely. Daddy was still on the mainland at work.

However long the sermon was, it was always too long for me. Suddenly I turned towards Mummy to see her standing on the pew in her yellow coat. She made no noise, as she got up from her seat, and climbed on to the seat. She reached up into the window display where the greenery had caught light and there was a small fire. Mother blew out the candles, spat on her fingers and patted the evergreen until it was put out. There was a certain behaviour we were expected to show in Church. We had to be quiet, still and respectful of others. We were certainly not allowed to stand up on a pew in the sermon and put out a fire. Carolyn and I sat mortified that Mummy was standing on a pew, in full view of the whole congregation in her yellow coat.

Carolyn and the author in Daddy's bed on Christmas morning 1955

'Everyone could see her,' I thought. 'What would they think?'

The small fire was extinguished, and with every ounce of her deportment Mother stepped down from the pew, arranged her coat, sat down and turned her head to the pulpit to listen again.

At the end of the service there was a quiet buzz of people wishing each other a Happy Christmas as they left the church. No-one mentioned the fire; I did not hear a word about it. It was as if it had never happened.

'I saw the candle burn down and watched it catch a little bit of holly which would have been enough to set the whole display alight.' Mummy told us on the way home.

'I suppose so,' said Carolyn still slightly embarrassed by the incident.

The slightly burnt display remained the same throughout the celebrations that year.

On Christmas Eve we left one of Daddy's socks at the foot our beds for Father Christmas to fill. We woke up early on Christmas day to discover a lumpy package on the quilt over our feet. There began the usual conversation.

Carolyn and I stood at the foot of the stairs, 'Can we open our stockings now Mum?' each of us asked in turn. 'No, not yet, it is far too early,' Mummy replied. 'Go back to bed and wait awhile.' Mother was able to drag this out until seven o'clock and we started to take out the presents from the socks.

'OK, put your dressing gowns on to keep warm,' called Mum. 'You can get up now but please be quiet.'

'Thanks Mum,' said Carolyn.

'We will be quiet,' I shouted.

'Shush, be quiet Mum said,' Carolyn instructed. As quietly as we could we tiptoed back to our bedroom.

Father Christmas always gave us sensible presents. There was Basildon Bond writing paper and envelopes, a new flannel, some pretty smelling soap, coloured pencils, nuts and a mandarin orange in the toe. This year he had given us two large books which could not be stuffed into the socks.

'Let's go upstairs to show Mummy and Daddy,' Carolyn suggested.

'Right!' I said gathering up my presents and clutching them in my arms.

Bryan's great grand-daughter and Carolyn's grand-daughter, Charlotte, plays with the green wooden engine made by Bryan in 1948 for the author and carried home from Birmingham on public transport.

We tiptoed upstairs and peeped around the corner. Mum and Dad were both asleep. Carolyn put her finger to her mouth.

'Shush, they are both asleep.' We crept further into the room.

In a loud whisper I said, 'Mum can we show our presents?'.

Mummy stirred and lifted her head.

'Look Father Christmas has left us books which were too big for Daddy's sock!' I said. 'Can I show you the lovely pictures?'

'All right you two, I give in. Show me what you have got,' Mummy said as she sat up in bed.

Daddy lay blissfully asleep unaware of the activity happening around him, until Carolyn jumped on his bed. 'Look Daddy! Look at my presents!'

He yawned. 'Right you are! I think it is time I went downstairs and got us a cup of tea.'

'Get into Daddy's bed, it'll be warmer in there,' Mum said. I was unaware of how cold I was until I got into his warm bed.

Daddy returned with a tray of tea and his camera. 'Stay still you two,' he said, 'I want to take a picture.'

We had breakfast and after that was cleared away and mother was ready, we all went to the sitting room for the main presents. We gave our gifts to each other. Carolyn and I had bought small items for Mummy and Daddy from the school or church bazaar and had wrapped them up. I loved this time as Mother was always so very pleased.

'Oh thank you darling, that's what I really wanted,' she said. 'How clever you are to find this.'

We were then given main presents which were always equal. In 1948 my father carried home from Birmingham where he was working, two homemade wooden toys for his daughters. Toys were scarce, so he made a wooden wheelbarrow for Carolyn and a steam engine for me. Carolyn's wheelbarrow was painted blue and my train was green. The boiler of the engine was a National Dried Milk can. He put the train into the wheelbarrow and fixed them together with belts and string. He then fashioned a large loop out of webbing which he fixed to the package, and carried it over his shoulder. This generated a lot of conversation on the trains, the paddle steamer and the bus as he carried his precious gifts carefully home.

One year we both received a gold cross and chain. I loved this and thought it very grown up.

Another important present was from Mother's cousin, Clare Woodward. She came to stay often with us but rarely at Christmas. As she was unmarried and without other children of her own she took a great deal of trouble buying presents for us. They were always exciting. One year she gave me a glove puppet. I soon got the hang of how to make it come alive. 'You are so clever,' Mum said. 'It's very easy. You just put your fingers in the head and arms and make it work.' I explained.

When I was eight years old, I was given a recorder and a book on how to play it. Mother helped me with the first few notes, and then I picked this up quite easily. Very early on Boxing Day I went up to Mummy and Daddy's bedroom.

'Can I play you a tune Mummy?' I whispered because they were asleep.

Mum opened her eyes and very encouragingly said, 'Oh yes how lovely of course I would love to hear you.' I jumped into her bed; my feet were cold so I put them against Mummy's warm legs.

The Author with her new puppet given to her by Clare Woodward on Christmas Day circa 1954

I had learnt seven notes and was able to play a tune.

'You are such a clever girl,' Mummy praised. I didn't think I was clever at all, it wasn't difficult.

The Christmas pudding made in November had to be steamed for a further four hours on Christmas day. The house was filled with mist in the morning; condensation ran down the walls and windows. Mother boiled up four sixpenny pieces to sterilise them and then when she had turned the pudding out on to a dish she placed each coin evenly into the pudding, where she could find them when she served it. It was important that we all got one.

To accompany the pudding we had Christmas Custard. This special sauce was made with evaporated milk and tasted very superior to ordinary custard.

We always had a capon for Christmas which had to be bought from Barnets in the Ryde High Street. Mother didn't like turkey. 'The meat is too strong,' she said. She prepared the bird by covering it with streaky bacon.

'That is to prevent it burning on the top,' she told us as we helped carefully lay individual rashers on the breast of the bird. A small amount of stuffing was put into the bird and the rest made into stuffing balls. This was accompanied by slices of hot gammon (cooked the day before and reheated with scalding hot water), chipolata sausages, roast potatoes, sprouts, bread sauce and gravy made from the giblets.

The making of bread sauce was a particular treat. The delicious mixture of white breadcrumbs, milk, an onion studded with cloves, and a large knob of butter was a favourite. Mother put the ingredients, without the butter, into a bowl over boiling water in a saucepan.

'I'm not putting in the butter until we are about to serve it up. There would be none left as we shall go on pinching a taste all morning,' Mother instructed. 'Now run along and play, I'm very busy.'

We disappeared into the sitting room where Mother had lit the fire. We laid out our presents. Carolyn was keeping an eye on the cooking in the kitchen. She suddenly returned and said in a loud whisper, 'Quickly Mummy is putting the butter into the bread sauce!'

I jumped up and together nonchalantly we strolled into the kitchen. 'Can we help you take anything into the sitting room?' Carolyn said

'Yes please, could you lay the table?' Mummy answered.

We picked up the cutlery, table mats and glasses. The plates were being warmed under the grill. We laid the table and returned to the kitchen to catch Mummy tasting the bread sauce.

'Oh,' she said, casually, 'Would you like to taste it too? I think it needs a little more salt. What do you think?'

We lined up with dessert spoons to taste and give our opinion. We each took a large spoonful.

'Delicious,' I said.

'Delicious,' Carolyn repeated as we were about to take a second tasting.

'Now, now don't be greedy. Leave some for lunch.'

The whole family sat down around the round table for Christmas Lunch in the sitting room.

Mother had carved the meat in the kitchen. 'I want to make sure there is enough for two more days.'

1st Binstead Brownie Pack. Carolyn is standing just behind Brown Owl fourth from the right. The author, in the same row next to the girl kneeling, is not yet in uniform.

We were wearing our Sunday best clothes, mother was in her special twin set, and wore tiny earrings and pearls but she left on her apron.

I didn't like sprouts!

'But they are good for you,' my pious sister said.

That made no difference to me, I still didn't like sprouts. Mother never made us eat anything we didn't like.

'I had enough of that as a child,' she confided to me one day.

Mother was however very clever.

'Carolyn would you like some of the delicious juices from the capon over your sprouts? I kept it especially for that,' she said.

I realised I was missing out on the delicious meat juices. 'Can I have some sprouts and meat juices too, please?'

'Of course, I thought you didn't like sprouts.'

'Oh yes I do,' I argued.

I had been conned. The meat juices made the sprouts just bearable. I ate them first to get them out of the way.

Just before serving the Christmas Pudding, castor sugar and brandy was poured over the pudding and it was set on fire. Mother always looked very serious performing this operation and we were told to keep away.

Christmas Day afternoon was quiet. We played board games and then we had a very light tea of cheese and biscuits with a Christmas cake. We lit sparklers from the fire and made patterns in the air in the sitting room.

Lastly we collected all our new possessions and carried them to our bedroom. It was only a small pile.

---oOo---

Carolyn and I were Brownie Guides and we met at the Drill Hall in Binstead every Tuesday. There was a Christmas party to which the mothers donated the sandwiches and cakes. Mother made two chocolate flavoured Victoria Sponge cakes, but it had chocolate flavoured butter icing in the middle and on the top a further thick spreading of chocolate icing. Carolyn and I loved this.

'Now girls,' Mother said before we left for the hall, 'you must eat the cake that is in front of you. You must not ask for my chocolate cake.'

'No we won't,' we promised.

We played games, a version of Hunt the Thimble, where we had to find Brown Owl's hat. We played team games where we had to pass a balloon over one head and under the legs of the girls behind, the girl at the end had to run back to the front of the line and the whole routine had to be repeated until all the girls had done it. The winner was the team who could do it faster and sit down on the floor. To calm us down, we played "Chinese Whispers". The message whispered to each girl around the large circle was totally different from the message on the card.

We were all told to go and wash our hands in time for tea. Carolyn and I ran as fast as we could and washed our hands quickly. We returned to the hall where the food was laid out. One of Mummy's chocolate cakes was at one end of the table and the other cake was in the middle. I chose my seat in the middle in front of one, and Carolyn sat at the end by the other cake. There were cakes all the way up the long table, but none of them compared with Mummy's cake. All the other cakes were decorated, one had sweets on it. Unfortunately the dye in the sweets had run into the white icing. There were lots decorated with silver balls. My mummy's cakes were the best by far.

When we had eaten our fill of sandwiches, the cakes were cut and I was offered a slice.

'Yes please.' I said, taking a slice of the cake in front of me. It was my Mummy's chocolate cake. I looked to the end of the table and Carolyn's plate also had a slice.

One school Christmas Party ended in tears. I was five years old. We had a nice tea of sandwiches which were made by the parents. There were cheese ones, some egg but mostly they were spread with Shippam's fish and meat pastes. Afterwards we had jelly and blancmange. The teachers at Binstead School thought it a good idea as entertainment for us was to watch black and white silent movies.

After tea the children were restless. The tables were put away and the children ran about, shouting at the tops of their voices. Benches were put out in lines and a big white screen was put on the raised stage. A large projector was brought in and placed at the back of the room. Mr. Pack busied himself with a large flat circular box. He opened out two arms on the projector and he put on an empty wheel on one and out of the box a full wheel on the other.

'The film is about to start. Sit down and be quiet please,' said Miss Brant the headmistress.

Mr. Pack didn't have the experience of being a projectionist and it took a long time to get started.

'I've got to thread the film through this sprocket here and then through here,' said an exasperated Mr. Pack. 'Children I am being as quick as I can.'

The children were brought to order again and the lights were put out.

'Turn on the light again please,' said Mr. Pack, 'I can't find the switch to start the film.'

The film was finally going. The sound of the projector was whirring and to start with the children sat quietly. There was laughter as the seven men with odd faces one with a squinty eye were running around the country side. I couldn't understand what was funny. There were words put on the screen between the scenes. I couldn't read that fast and didn't understand what was going on. For some reason they all lost their clothes and had to make holes in an advertising hoarding and put their faces through the holes and run along the road. The picture on the advertisement board was of seven men dressed in clean clothes.

This was too much for me and I burst into tears.

'They have lost their clothes,' I wailed. 'That is horrid. That's not funny! I want my Mummy!'

Mother was in the kitchen clearing up with the other parents and I was delivered to the kitchen door. Mummy smiled at me and as the reason for my leaving the film was explained she giggled.

'It is not funny they have lost their clothes!' I said.

I sat in the kitchen and watched as the mothers did the washing up.

'The film was broken too, you couldn't hear what they were saying.' I said.

'It is meant to be like that,' said one of the other mothers 'it is a silent movie.'

I sat quietly until the film was ended whereupon the room erupted with noisy children running around the hall. Mummy collected my coat, found Carolyn and we walked home quietly.

'What did you think of the film Carolyn? Did you enjoy it?' Mummy said

'It was rather boring I thought and very old fashioned. Couldn't they get a film with people talking in it?' Carolyn replied.

'It was silly and horrid,' I sniffed.

'Silly, boring and horrid,' Mummy agreed.

---oOo---

We followed the Church year and joined in with celebrations and events. We gave up things for Lent, usually chocolate. This wasn't difficult as we didn't have much money to buy it.

I gave Mummy flowers on Mothering Sunday. I picked these in the woods and hid them in various places throughout the years. The best place I thought was between my piano and the wall near the window. At bedtime Mummy came in and pulled the curtains carefully not looking at or seeing the hidden jam jar of flowers. The next morning I would give her my flowers and she was astonished! 'Oh how lovely, what a surprise. You picked them in the woods, I do love wild flowers.'

The church was decorated for Easter with a garden arranged on top of a large board laid on the pews at the east end of the North Aisle. A tomb was made of stones to represent where Jesus was laid. There was a light cunningly placed inside and a round stone in front of the cave. This covered the entrance until Easter Day. The whole garden was covered with moss. We gathered primroses from the woods in Quarr Road. Carolyn and I knew all the best spots. There were never enough and we picked extra from the grounds of the Keys, the large house behind the church. Carolyn and I walked the length of the drive to the front door and knocked.

'Please may we pick primroses for the Easter Garden?' Carolyn asked.

The answer was always positive but we had to ask. There were lots of plants there.

We took these back to the Holy Cross Church and took our baskets full of primroses to where the Easter garden was being made. There were empty Shippam's paste pots set in the garden. We filled these with water and stuffed them with the primroses.

On Easter day I gave Mummy another bunch of picked woodland flowers hidden overnight between the piano and the outside wall. Mother put food dye in the water for our boiled eggs which turned them pink. We were given a card and a small gift. One year she was able to give us each a paper maché Easter egg, inside which was a pretty embroidered handkerchief.

The church was decorated for Harvest Festival in the Autumn. Food was donated to the church to be handed to the needy. Mummy always gave a homemade sponge cake. This was displayed every time on a shelf just inside the door.

One year we had a harvest supper organised by the Church. The Methodist hall in Chapel Road was hired and we ate a Bread and Cheese supper followed by apple pie and cream. All the women in the church made the pies. The apples came from various trees in people's gardens. Unfortunately unlike the Brownie party and Mummy's chocolate cakes we were unable to get a piece of Mummy's pie and had to put up with what we were handed, a plate with a piece of pie and cream already on it.

I was 14 years old when we went to my cousin Elizabeth's wedding. Owing to Elizabeth's father, Uncle Percy, having to go away to his job in the Merchant Navy they had got married in a registry office in London the week before. The ceremony we attended was just a blessing of their marriage. Uncle Percy had left during the week between the wedding and the blessing.

I didn't have a choice as to what I was to wear. Mother had made me a dress. The material was of dark olive green wool. It had a boat neck with a roll collar which was broken by a small bow just below my left shoulder. It had a drop waist and was long enough to cover my knees.

My hair was brushed and Mother had found a matching large hair ribbon to tie part of my hair back. The ribbon lay the full length of the rest of my hair which was well brushed and flowed down my back.

'Your hair is a lovely blonde colour and this shade of green really sets it off,' said Mummy.

'Yes,' I replied, 'thank you.'

I was a modern teenager and it was 1961. I hated all of it. The colour and the style of the dress and my hair tied back like a small child. Didn't she understand I was 14 years old and far more sophisticated? I didn't argue.

As a member of the choir at Holy Cross I had sung at lots of weddings but I had never been to one for a member of our family. We went by bus to Seaview and walked up to the church. We took our seat but didn't have to wait long before Elizabeth arrived and strode in with her husband, William Cottrell. She wore a green shot silk dress with a hat. 'Why isn't she wearing white?' I whispered to Mummy.

'Because she is already married and this is just a blessing.'

When the ceremony finished we walked the few yards to Auntie Betty's flat which was near the beach. We politely waited a few minutes before going in. There was a receiving line. I didn't know anything about this.

'What's this for?' I asked Mummy.

'Shush,' Mummy replied, 'just follow me.'

Mother gushed her greetings to various people she knew.

'Lovely to see you my dear. I trust you are keeping well? Yes she does look absolutely lovely.'

We were one away in line to be introduced to William the bridegroom when she turned to me and in a strong rather aggressive but whispered voice said. 'Kiss the bride!'

'What?' I said.

'Follow me!' she instructed.

I watched Mummy as she gushed her congratulations to William and kissed the bride.

In my dreadful green dress, my long flowing hair and old fashioned green ribbon I shook hands with William and kissed Elizabeth.

The food was nice and Uncle Tat, my father's brother, played the piano. Mummy didn't like him very much and was a little rude about his playing. At the end William and Elizabeth left for their honeymoon in a lovely car. Mummy, Daddy, Carolyn and I went home on the bus.

13 PNEU AND BINSTEAD JUNIOR SCHOOL

I looked at myself in the large mirror proudly. I was dressed in school uniform, the same outfit as Carolyn's. I was about to experience my first day of school. We had to go by bus from Binstead as it was in Partlands Avenue, Ryde. It was a private school for five to eight year old children and was based on the educational principles of Charlotte Mason who created the Parents' National Educational Union. In this PNEU school, I learnt my alphabet from a poster which I considered as correct. It was a fee paying school which I attended for only a year. I did not understand at the time that it was because Daddy was ill and not working, that there was not enough money to pay the fees. Mother's richer friends offered to cover the costs for a while but she was too proud and declined the offer.

At PNEU there were two teachers whose names were Miss Queen and Miss Ella. As they were sisters with the same surname the younger of the two used her Christian name as a surname.

There was a mixed curriculum. We repeated the alphabet regularly and learnt our times table by reciting them. There was a lot of learning by rote. In the corner of the large main room there was a piano and a large box of percussion instruments. There were triangles, bells on sticks, tambourines and drums. I wanted a drum.

'Can I have a drum please, Miss Ella?' I asked

'No dear there aren't enough,' she said quietly. 'Have this large shiny cymbal instead.'

Miss Ella showed me how to hold it and I couldn't wait to practise. I clanged these two large metal cymbals together and I liked the sound.

'Jocelyn! Can you please just wait until all the class is ready?' Upset at being told to stop playing I did not hear her telling me when I was to clang my cymbals. I was too busy looking at these shiny round plates, as I realised I could see my face in them.

Miss Ella took her place at the piano and started

PNEU school photo. The author is kneeling in the second row seventh from the left, her sister Carolyn is standing one row behind fourth from the left.

to play. The drums drummed; the bells shook vigorously; the tambourine players bashed their instruments and the triangle players knocked the metal at the bottom to make a chinking sound. With full enthusiasm for my part in the band I clashed these two shiny round plates together as soon as Miss Ella started to play.

She lifted her hands from the piano keys and waited for silence. 'Enough! Enough every one! Quiet please! Stop playing your instruments!' She waited until there was complete stillness.

'As I told you before I started to play the piano, Jocelyn, we only need one cymbal sound at the end of the music please,' she said.

I felt cheated. I was only allowed to play my instrument just the once when everyone else was playing their instruments all the time. 'Why can't I play my cymbals all the way through the music?' I asked.

'Because that's what the music tells us to do,' explained Miss Ella.

I sulked. I did clash my cymbals just the once at the end of the music, but it was without any gusto or enthusiasm at all.

When the lesson finished it was Milk Time. We collected our milk in cups and sat down to drink it.

---oOo---

'You are going to a new school today,' said Mummy. 'It's just down the road; a very short walk. And you have got a new school uniform.'

Mummy dressed me in a new white blouse and on top she slipped a tunic over my head. She did the buttons up on the shoulder. This navy blue dress had three box pleats at the front and back. 'Oh, I nearly forgot the tie,' Mummy said.

She put this under my collar, tied the knot and pulled it gently up under my chin. 'There you are, precious. Don't you look smart?' She kissed my forehead.

'Why can't we go to the other school?' my sister asked. I didn't listen to the answer; I was too excited to get to the new school. Mummy, Carolyn and I walked down Arnold Road from our house at number nine to Binstead Church of England Junior School My new uniform tickled my legs.

Binstead school photo. The author is seated with a book, ironic as she couldn't read at this stage.

We walked through the small gate opposite the main door and along the concrete path. It was the 3rd of September, 1952, I was five years old. Other new children milling around me were chattering. There was a large playground on a slope marked out with white lines, and a smaller one on the other side of the path at the top. Children were playing in the smaller playground, throwing balls at the wall and catching them. There were no windows on this wall. I wanted to join them; but they were older than me and I didn't know them.

We went up three steps and through the front door and walked along the corridor. It was dark but I could see there were pegs for children's coats on both walls. The corridor had a sharp turn to the right. It was brighter here and I saw more coat pegs. This corridor was under cover but open at the side to reveal a small courtyard and a bank of wooden doors.

In the classroom at the end, Mother met the teacher and after a lot of conversation between Mummy, the teacher and me, I was left. I didn't mind, it was all too exciting. I was used to school. There were tables in rows with activities on them. The day was busy and full of new experiences. We recited together the alphabet with the aid of the poster on the wall. I was cross that this was not like the one at my previous school. That poster had "F", "L", "R" and "W" finishing each line, and the XYZ was in the middle at the bottom. This was different. Didn't they know it was wrong?

It was comforting to know that there was a milk time at Binstead School as well. At this new school we were given milk in small bottles which we drank with a straw. One after another the children went to the teacher, Mrs. Gibbons, and asked, 'May I be excused please?' I decided I would join them and asked the same question. I queued up outside the bank of wooden doors. When it was my turn I was surprised to discover what was behind the mysterious doors. These toilets were like nothing I had ever seen in my short life.

Inside each little cubicle there was a plank with a hole in it. It wasn't difficult to work out how I was to use it. When I'd finished I stood up and I turned around to look for the chain to pull. There were two hooks and a piece of string which supported the toilet paper hanging on the wall but there wasn't a chain. Just then I heard a swishing sound coming from the hole. Water was rushing past it. I peered down into the dark abyss and watched the water flow by. Every so often this process occurred which left clean water beneath.

In our house, we had upstairs a bathroom, with a basin, bath and a toilet with a chain to pull. These toilets at Binstead School were not pleasant but I soon got used to them as the need to visit to the toilet periodically throughout a school day was greater than my qualms about using it.

There were many houses in the 1950s without inside toilets. Often outside toilets were attached to the house and had a cistern above and a chain to pull. However, there were a few which were more primitive. These were to be found in little huts at the bottoms of the gardens. They were often referred to as the "privy". Inside the hut was a box with a hole in the top, and underneath was a pit. Most of the effluent drained away into the soil and a small amount of earth was added to keep any smells down. If this filled up a new hole was dug, and the little hut was moved to a new spot. I asked a friend who had this system what was it like.

'It's O.K. really. You got used to it. As it was in our orchard we did have very good apples.'

After a busy day there was a crush of children all leading to the door. Coats were taken from the hooks and arms thrust into sleeves. Some didn't bother to put on their coats and draped them over their shoulders. Some just carried them and dragged them on the floor. This crush was greatest as I got to the front door where the other class had joined the throng.

'Excuse me please!' I said as a boy stood in front of me. He turned and looked at me and pulled a face.

'Ooo hark at yooouu, 'scuoose me please,' he said imitating my rather refined voice and then pushed me down the steps. I picked myself up. I was very cross but I saw Mummy and ran to meet her.

I related all the experiences of the day to my Mum but did not mention the fall down the steps. She had already seen it.

The next day at school I listened to the way they spoke, and without thinking I spoke using the same accent. I made friends quickly.

At the end of each school day I would shout out 'Bye! See ya t'morra.' to my new friends in the way they spoke, and then say 'Mam!' as I met her. Then I remembered who I was with and changed it to "Hello Mummy", and told her about the day's activities in the way she spoke.

---oOo---

After the war service men returned to their wives and with the prospect of long term peace there was a baby boom. As a result schools like Binstead School filled up. The Methodist hall opposite was requisitioned. I was now in the class 3 that used this temporary arrangement. There were benches stacked up at the back of the hall on which our coats were thrown. At the front was a raised stage the full width of the hall. I thought this was very exciting. Perhaps we might do some acting.

There were two toilets outside placed back to back. The men's was first used by the boys and then the women's used by the girls. They were identical. Near the door of the women's toilet was a window to the hall. This had a bolt in the middle which allowed the window to swing open. The girls were queuing up to go to the toilet and a group of boys were crowded around the other side of the window, giggling and jeering. David swung the window open. I was indignant at their lack of respect for us as we wanted our privacy. So I shut the window.

Another boy, Malcolm, opened it and I shut it again. This continued until I shut it so firmly that it broke.

There was no honour in the class that day and the boys named me for breaking the window. I tried to argue my case with Mr. Pack.

'The boys were swinging the window too,' I said stating my evidence.

Mr. Pack did not listen.

'Jocelyn be quiet and sit down,' he said firmly

I sulked. I sat at the desk at the back of the classroom, folded my arms, and did nothing.

'Stop sulking! Pick up your book and pay attention,' said Mr. Pack. I tried again to argue my point and again I was told to be quiet.

'Well!' he continued, 'if you are not going to join in the lesson, you may as well go home.'

I sat for a moment and thought Mummy would listen to me. So I stood up went to the back of the hall, picked up my coat, put it on and walked out of the door. I was half way along Chapel Road when Mr. Pack came running after me.

'Where do you think you are going?' he shouted.

'You told me to go home! So I'm going to find my Mummy!' I replied. As I had stopped walking I tried again to plead my case. 'It was not my fault the boys were playing with the window too.'

This made no difference and I was marched back along the road into the back gate of the school up the long playground and into the class room where Miss Brant the headmistress was teaching.

I stood humbly in front of the top class whilst my wicked deed was related by Mr. Pack.

'She has broken a window in the hall.' He left out the fact that the boys were playing with the window too. Although I was angry I stood with my head bowed and did not restate my case. She was the head mistress after all.

I don't think Miss Brant could be bothered with this much as I received a short lecture about being good and told to get on with my work. We walked back to the classroom and nothing more was said that day. The window remained broken for the whole time I was in that class. The matter was never mentioned again.

As a Church of England School we had regular visits from the Rector. All four classes were crammed into the largest classroom which was for the top form. As we entered, the Reverend Gum was standing at the front, holding a medicine bottle full to the brim with a pink liquid. This was put down on the table at the side of him.

After we had sung a hymn we had a prayer. Then the Rector gave us a lecture on the evil of swearing.

'Saying offensive words is not the way to behave,' he preached. 'It upsets every good person who hears them. God does not like these words.' There wasn't a sound in the room every child terrified that they were in trouble for saying "swear words". I was not sure what a "swear word" was.

The Headmistress, Miss Brant, then called out officiously.

'Terry White! Come and stand by me at the front facing the school.'

A terrified Terry stood up silently. He slithered between the boys and reached the front of the room between Miss Brant and the Rector. Terry's shirt was half hanging out of his short trousers. He had outgrown his sleeveless woollen top which had holes in it. His socks were down around his ankles and his shoes were scuffed. His face was red and his ginger hair seemed to stand on end. His head was bowed and the Rector pointed at him and shouted, 'This wicked boy has sworn and said swear words in Miss Brant's hearing.'

He picked up the bottle and turned to Terry and continued.

'This is not the way you should behave especially in front of your excellent and hardworking teacher, Miss Brant.'

Terry shivered, terrified of what was to happen next. The Rector unscrewed the top of the bottle. A gasp went around the room. The open bottle was thrust under Terry's nose. His face contorted and he turned his head away. 'This special liquid is to wash out all swear words from your foul mouth.'

I stood terrified that maybe had I said one of these words. Was I going to be next?

The Rector continued, 'Terry what should you say to Miss Brant?'

Cowering, Terry still looking at the open bottle, said in a terrified whisper, 'I'm sorry.'

'What did you say?' shouted the vicar. 'I did not hear that!'

Terry now near to tears said in a louder voice 'I'm sorry.'

'I can't hear you!' yelled the Rector.

Between sobs he garbled, 'I'm sorry, I'm sorry.'

'I'm sorry who?' said the Rector.

'I'm sorry, Miss Brant.'

The Rector wanted more and prompted him to say, 'And I won't do it again.'

'I'm sorry,' said the now sobbing Terry through his crying, 'and I won't do it again.'

He could hardly speak as he gasped for air in between bouts of sobs.

'Say it again!' The Rector's face was close to the small boy's face, he was now roaring.

'I'm sorry,' Terry gasped, 'I won't do it again.'

The children all heaved a sigh of relief when the lid was returned to the bottle and put on the shelf behind Miss Brant's desk.

'The bottle will remain there to remind you not to say rude words or swear,' announced the Rector. His voice was officious but still loud. Miss Brant agreed, nodding her head dutifully.

We then had a closing prayer which began with the words "The love of God ….."

Prompted by Miss Brant, in unison we thanked the Rector for coming. The pupils filed out to their classrooms.

---oOo---

When I was eight, I went with the school to Lakeside Pool in Wootton Bridge for school swimming lessons. We travelled by foot from the school, along Chapel Road to get to the Southern Vectis bus stop at the bottom of Binstead Hill. We waited only a short while before the bus arrived. We filed on and sat downstairs while Mr. Pack bought the tickets.

'One whole and 14 halves to Wootton Bridge please.' It was a trophy to get the long strip of tickets. He gave these ticket strips to a different child each week.

After a short journey, we got off the bus at the bridge and walked the last few hundred yards to the pool which was clearly visible from the road, my excitement was building.

The pool was situated on the far side of the Mill Pond. We marched in a crocodile up some low wide steps past the café and dance hall and across an open space to the entrance of the pool.

Lakeside Swimming Pool in Wootton Bridge, where the author was taught to swim.

The Mill Pond was full as the sluice gates were closed. There were dinghies, canoes and punts moored up at the jetty bobbing gently. I wondered what a trip in a boat would be like, if we went up the creek I could discover what was there. That thought left me as we approached the swimming pool. My excitement grew as I could see the pool and the diving boards. We walked up the slope to the entrance. Mr. Pack spoke to the man behind the counter and we were handed a wire basket for our clothes. It was about two feet tall and at the bottom was a small space for shoes. The top was shaped like a coat hanger.

We walked further in and saw there was a semi-circular terrace which looked down on the pool. There was a fountain, which was not on when we were there. To the left of the pool there were long, wide steps designed for seating. On the other side of the poolside there was an area for deck chairs. The changing cubicles were on the terrace. The girls went to the right, the boys to the left.

'Get changed quickly,' said Mr. Pack.

The class disappeared into the cubicles and I quickly took off my clothes and pulled on my costume. Initially I found basket fiddly and irritating, as I was anxious to get into that water.

We came out of the changing cubicles and gave our baskets in to be hung up. I had a plain woollen navy blue swimming costume, and on my head a white rubber swimming hat with an adjustable strap that went under my chin. These hats came in different sizes and were designed to keep the water out. It never did. Whilst we were getting changed, Mr. Pack had arranged benches, set out in neat rows, upon which we lay and were taught the breaststroke leg action. I did not concentrate at all as I could see the water and I just wanted to get in. We were used to swimming and playing in the sea. To get to the water at our local beach in Binstead I had to negotiate spiky shells and stones. When I reached the water I lost my feet in blue slipper clay which squelched up between my toes.

Lakeside pool was all concrete! The difference between the two situations was like silk is to sackcloth.

When we finally got into the pool, without my rubber ring I had been wearing for the past few summers, I felt almost naked. We went through various exercises; we held the bar and practised our breaststroke leg action.

'Turn your feet out like a frog as you kick hard back,' encouraged Mr. Pack.

It took little time for me to learn to swim, I was used to sea water in my face but this was pool water, and so much nicer. I got to the stage where I was able to "swim" using the correct leg and arm action, but I did not move. I struggled and counted the number of strokes I could do before I put my feet down on the floor of the pool.

At the end of the lessons, we collected our baskets and dressed. If we got ready quickly we were able to go into the dance hall that was on our route back to the bus. The juke box played all the current hits as the staff did the cleaning. "Rock around the Clock" by Bill Haley was the favourite.

We crossed the road and waited in line for the bus to take us back to school. It was obvious where we had been as most of us had wet hair, our clothes were twisted and some cardigans were buttoned incorrectly, but all of us carried our costumes neatly rolled up with our towels under our arms. Mr. Pack had taught us how to do this. Mr. Pack had been in the army.

Behind us was the Watermill. Mr. Pack explained how the water from the mill pond with the tides powered the millstones which ground the grain which made flour for our bread, pastry and cakes. The building itself was unremarkable. It was three storeys high and quite ugly I thought, unlike the 'Sloop', the pub next door; which looked more inviting. It backed on to the creek the other side, where goods were shipped in and flour was taken out by boats.

Mr. Pack continued, 'The millstones are turned by the tide. This water power using a system of pulleys, levers and trap doors hauls the sacks of grain up to the top of the building. Here they are poured through the chutes down to the millstones for grinding.'

These were not visible to us. I wondered whether the miller, having to work with the tides which I knew changed every day, would have to grind flour in the middle of the night when I would be in bed.

'The mill is not now in use,' said Mr. Pack. 'It stopped milling flour a long time ago.'

The bus came and we all got on. Again we fought for the long ticket. We were quieter going back to school.

There were two moments that summer of 1955 in my learning to swim experience that I clearly remember. My mother taught me to float at Seaview. I lay back on the water, on her arms. I was flat with my ears in and head looking up. It was sunny so I shut my eyes. She then gently let one hand go and then the other and I was floating. I could feel the gentle rise and fall of the sea. It was very comforting. She lifted her hands above her head.

'Jo you are floating!' Mum called out to me. 'Look, my arms are above my head.' I did not believe her until my sister told me.

'It's true, you are floating.'

I was still struggling counting the number of strokes I was doing. Each time I would tell Mum.

'I've done eight strokes Mum.'

'Well done,' she said. She had said this consistently every time I told her.

At the weekend, Daddy was home and on a very hot day we went to Freshwater a beautiful bay, with water so clear that I could see the stones under my feet. There was little sand. The sea water was always very cold, whatever the weather. It was not a beach to go to if the day was cool.

I couldn't wait to get into the sea and start practising my swimming. I was ready, I had put my costume on under my clothes. I stripped off and waded in and started counting my strokes again.

'I've done nine now Mum,' I shouted.

'Well done!' she said.

I stopped calling out the number of strokes when I realised that I was traveling towards the cliffs while Mum and the beach was travelling the other way. I was moving. I was swimming. I could do it!

Binstead School was part of a community and one of the teachers, a Mr. Marler who had never taught me, met Mother at a social event.

'How old is Jocelyn now?' Mr. Marler asked Mummy quietly, when she was on her own.

'She's eight. Why?'

'I think you ought to know', he said almost whispering, 'that Jocelyn is behind in her reading.'

Classes were full, teachers were busy and for reading lessons, we were set in groups of six to read in turn to the group. We sat facing each other on the desk lids with our feet on the flip seats below. I was with a group of jeering boys which I hated so I didn't bother to join in.

Mother's shock was obvious but Mr. Marler was ready. He lent mother a reading book and during the summer holidays very patiently she taught me to read.

-------oOo-------

The National Health Service began 1948 and there was a surge in looking after the health of the children. The school nurse made regular visits to the school, which were often to check for nits in the children's hair. All nurses throughout the UK were nicknamed "Nitty Nora". We lined up and stood in front of her and she used her fingers to part our hair looking for these blood sucking insects.

At the age of seven we went through an eye test. We were gathered into another classroom where on the wall was pinned a chart with letters on it graded from very large to very tiny. We lined up and in front of me was Jackie who was a very pretty girl with long blond hair right down her back. Jackie had a slight fault in one of her eyes and this was noted down. It came to my turn. I knew I could not see properly out of one eye. That is how I could tell left from right. If I winked with my left eye I could see clearly out of my right eye. If I shut my right eye I saw a blurry picture so I already knew the eye I was trying to see out of was my left.

A ruler was held over my left eye and that was fine and I read to the bottom of the sheet. She then she covered my right eye and I could not see any of the letters clearly at all. I told her.

'Stop lying,' she snapped.

'I'm not,' I protested.

She took my hand turned it over and hit my knuckles with the ruler.

'Don't you dare lie to me! Get out of my sight!'

I said nothing to Mum. I had been told off at school and that was bad. It wasn't until I was explaining how easy it was to tell the difference between left and right that my mother found out.

I had had an operation when I was 18 months to remove a cancerous lump from my face. My eye was covered for some considerable time. Up to the age of two the eyes are developing and my left eye did not develop correctly because it was covered. I was sent to an optician at the age of eight but he could do nothing. However, I was given a pair of round pink wired framed National Health glasses. I continually forgot to wear them as they did not improve anything.

The school dentist called regularly. He set up his surgery in the kitchen of the Methodist Church hall. We went in individually and our teeth were inspected. Those who did have problems were called back on another day for treatment that was carried out in the same room.

Mummy was there when it was my turn. I had a bad tooth which needed filling. I was called from the classroom and went into the kitchen. There was no injection and the bad tooth was drilled and filled. The drill was on an articulated arm and on each section were pulleys. This was operated by a foot pedal. I did not cry. My Mummy was there and I was safe. I did not experience any pain.

-----oOo-----

I left Binstead School when I was ten years old. My sister had passed her 11 plus exam, but as there were only places offered for one girl and two boys from Binstead School to go to a grammar school my sister missed out. Her score for the exam was high but not as high as another girl. Mum decided to get a job so she could send Carolyn to St Therese Presentation Convent in Ryde. I joined her a year later when I was ten years old.

'I've got a job at Pack and Culliford, the dress shop at the top of Union Street,' Mum told us. 'You are old enough to look after yourselves when you get home from school. I'll be home by six o'clock.'

I enjoyed being at Binstead School although I had so much enjoyment that my learning suffered.

'Your school work interfered with your having fun,' Mother said.

My proudest achievements at Binstead School were learning how to swim, being voted in as second therefore being an attendant at the May Day celebration, and winning the Rector's prize for "Religious Knowledge". This was a book which had been chosen by Mummy and was about making things out of paper. I never used it practically but proudly kept the prize.

14 MAY DAYS, CARNIVALS AND DRESSING UP

The bottom drawer of my chest of drawers was for "Dress Ups". This was tightly packed with all sorts of stuff. There were old velvet curtains that became robes for kings and queens. There were net curtains that became veils for brides and highly fashionable ladies. There were a couple of Mummy's old dresses and a skirt for someone with a very tiny waist.

'You can have that for your dress ups,' Mum said. 'I don't think that will ever fit me again. I was very slim when I met your father.'

There was my old kilt that I wore when I was mistaken for a boy and Daddy had difficulty doing it up when it fell off at the bus stop. As I grew taller and bigger it still went around my waist and became an ice skating or dancing skirt. There were two old fashioned hats, a large one with a wide brim and a small one made of blue felt.

We made up stories of being kings and queens where we would be crowned, dressed in Mum's old dresses and wearing robes. We knew all about that from Queen Elizabeth's Coronation Day in 1953.

'Mum,' I asked one day, 'we need a crown for our game. How can we make a crown?'

Mum thought for a minute, disappeared upstairs and into the loft. She returned with some tinsel from the Christmas decoration box.

'Right let me have that old blue felt hat.' She picked up her sewing box and threaded some blue cotton into a needle, made a knot at the end of it. She picked up the hat and held it up.

'Now! This is going to be a very regal and unique crown.'

I watched fascinated as she attached the tinsel around the brim and across the top. In a very short time she turned the old hat into a crown.

'Now crowns have to be displayed and handled carefully,' Mum said joining in with the game. 'There is a red velvet cushion in the sitting room on my chair.' Carolyn ran and collected the cushion. Mum shook it and plumped it up into shape and then regally placed the crown on it in the middle. I followed Carolyn who was carrying the crown into the sitting room. We walked ceremoniously. We decorated a chair with velvet curtains and found some left over tinsel to put on the back.

'I crown you Princess Jocelyn,' Carolyn said as she put the crown on my head. 'Your majesty!' she added bowing and walking backwards.

I waved regally and then got up with my train flowing behind, walked to the sitting room door and disappearing outside to take off my regal clothes and come in as the courtier who was to crown Queen Carolyn.

Carolyn had by now put on her regal train and was seated on the throne waiting to be crowned by me. I walked in slowly and put the crown back on its cushion. Once I had put it there I bowed and then I picked it up.

'Your majesty, I crown you Queen Carolyn,' I repeated as I plonked the crown on her head. We then took on other characters.

'Let's have some dancers to dance in front of the queen,' I suggested.

We pushed back the chairs and laid the crown on the throne and got dressed to be the dancers.

We made up our own routines and sang the music as we cavorted around the room at the same time. We were shop girls, ice skating champions, dancers in top theatre shows or Hollywood stars in a musical in which we sang made up songs. How famous we were in our imagination. Dressing up and performing was a favourite game.

One day we collected all the shoes in the house and arranged the sitting room as a shoe shop. We were making a film which was also to be a musical. With the aid of the hat previously used as a crown, we created the difficult customer, Mrs. Plumb-Ponsenby, who could not make up her mind as to which shoes to buy. All was well in the end and we finished the movie with a rousing chorus of a song whose main line was "We say goodbye to the shoe shoe shop!"

---oOo---

The author wearing her Daffodil hat and green dress is sulking because she wanted to have the pansy hat belonging to the girl next to her. David in his cockle shell is between the silver bell and the girl with the pansy hat.

At school we happily joined all events that involved dressing up. Binstead School were very successful in the Ryde Carnival. Mummy was clever with her sewing machine and the Parent Teachers Association at the school took advantage of this. I hadn't appreciated all the work that Mother had done. She had made a lot of the costumes and had designed the display. It was her idea. My sister dressed in a red homemade tutu was part of the display of an artist and his paints. A boy dressed in a paint splattered smock with a moustache drawn on his face and a brush in his hand faced an easel. Around him clustered a group of girls in colourful tutus who were the paints on the palette.

The first year I was involved the school entered as "Mary Mary Quite Contrary How Does Your Garden Grow". Around the edge of the flat bed lorry there was a canvas painted as a wall. Above that there was a small picket fence behind which sat girls dressed in green dresses each with a hat shaped like a flower. I was a daffodil and the girl next to me was a pink and purple pansy. I loved her hat as the colours were more interesting than mine. Her mother had embroidered details of the flower on each of the petals. Boys sat in the beautifully created cockle shells and two girls sat in two cones, their heads peering out over the top denoting the silver bells in the nursery rhyme. David was a cockle shell and sat behind me.

'It's a hot day David,' said his Mum. 'You don't need your shirt on. You'll be more comfortable like that.' David said nothing.

We arrived at the school just after lunch on the first Thursday in September 1955 and were put on the back of the flat bed lorry. On this we went to Ryde. Mummy and some adults on the lorry were with us but no-one was tied on. We were told to sit near the middle. We had just passed the bridge at Binstead when the back wheels bounced into a dip. This dip filled with water when there was heavy rain.

Dressed as a fire fairy, the author is leaning over to make sure she was seen in the photo, Carolyn her sister is standing at the back on the right hand side of the fire place.

It startled me. 'Mum I'm going to fall off,' I said.

'Hold tight,' she said. 'I've got you.' She pulled me further back towards the middle of the lorry.

Lorries from all over the area with their contents of bright costumes, scenery and excited children arrived at the top of Ryde in Adelaide Place. Our lorry was ushered into its allocated parking space.

'Children get into your places, we are about to be judged,' said Miss Brant the head mistress. We shuffled around until we found where we should sit or kneel. 'Molly stand up nice and tall! There's a good girl.' Molly, who was "Mary Mary" in the rhyme, stood in the doorway of the cottage front with leaded windows.

'And smile everyone,' she shouted.

The three judges walked up and then back again. Their heads were together as they were in deep discussion. There was no ceremony to announce the winner. We were just handed the cup. Then the photographer came and we shuffled into places and smiled.

The lorry paraded around Ryde ending up at the Simeon Street Recreation Ground where we were met by our parents. David's Mum was there. 'Do you want to go around the fair David?'

'Yes please Mum!' David loved fairs. 'Where's me clothes? I've only got my pants on under this.'

'Oh dear I forgot them!' she replied. 'Never mind it's such a hot day you can go around in your pants.' David paused and thought. 'I don't want to. People will laugh.'

'No they won't!' His Mum tried to reassure him but she soon realised that was not possible so she suggested, 'You could wear your costume then.'

'Mum!' David wailed, 'I will look stupid! People will laugh!'

'Do you want to go around the fair?'

'Yes I do!' said David.

'Then it's your pants or the shell. You decide!'

David chose the shell. A wire frame had been made and covered with paper Maché and painted to look like a cockle shell. It was heavy and was held up by two straps over David's shoulders. It reached down to his knees so his modesty was preserved, as his pants could not be seen.

As we walked around the fair I caught glimpses of a walking cockle shell with an unhappy David peering out of the top.

After the parade I never saw the shell again, but my green dress ended up in the Dress Up Drawer.

Mother was also behind the idea for the next carnival entry: "The Fire Fairies". All the children were dressed in flame coloured costumes with net over the outfits in the shape of orange, yellow and red "flames". There were extra flames sewn on them around the necks. The girls had Alice bands with "flames" fixed on made of the same net. These flames were wired to make them stand up. The boys' flames were hats made of sugar paper. These too were cut with spikes. One girl, Valerie, was dressed in her pyjamas and holding a book as if she was going to bed.

Carolyn and the author hold down their net collars for this special picture.

It was the same routine. We travelled into Ryde on the back of the lorry and parked at Adelaide Place and we won the cup again.

The last carnival I was involved with was not Mother's idea, but she settled down to make my costume from a roll of pink stretchy fabric.

'Where did you get this stuff?' I asked picking up the pink stretchy material that looked like a dishcloth.

'From a butcher's,' she replied. 'It covers the meat to keep it clean.'

'A butcher's!' I cried. 'What are you making with it?'

'It's a top for you to wear in the carnival. It's the nearest material we could find that would look like skin. You are going to be a mermaid!'

I was upset when told where this material was from. I remembered seeing it around large carcasses last time we went to Dewhurst in the High Street. 'Ugh!' I said.

Mother laughed and assured me again and again that it was unused and washed.

My legs were to be entombed in a fishtail, my feet in the two fins at the bottom. I did not like this costume at all.

'Push your feet down into the tail,' said Sarah's Mummy who had made all of them. I did as I was told.

'Mum! My feet don't stick out like the tail of a fish,' I argued.

'Yes you are right! Don't worry it won't matter. Let me put on your crown.' This was very heavy. Daddy had made the crown shape out of garden wire and Mum had decorated it with large ormer shells which she had collected from our holiday on Alderney in the Channel Islands many years previously. The fish from these shells helped keep islanders alive during the German Occupation in World War II.

The author as King Neptune's queen seated on her tea chest throne, covered in sea shells from the beach.

I was the wife of the Neptune the Roman God of the sea and I was to be seated on a rock made from a tea chest on which some diligent parent had stuck individual sea shells collected by the children on visits to the beach. It looked nothing like a rock at all.

'It looks like a Tea chest covered with shells Mum,' I moaned. 'And I can't move in this fish tail. It's uncomfortable and hot.'

'Shush!' she said, 'someone will hear you. You mustn't be rude.'

We went to Ryde on the back of the lorry up to Adelaide Place, parked and were judged. We didn't win. The cup went to Gatten and Lake County School whose float 'Automation' was decorated with space men and a science fiction space craft.

After the parade the lorry arrived at the Simeon Street Recreation ground, but Mummy was late. All the other mothers were there but mine wasn't. I cried. I was stuck in this uncomfortable fish tail, dressed in a material that should be around a carcass of meat, supporting a very heavy crown on my head, seated on an uncomfortable Tea Chest and I couldn't move.

'I want my Mummy,' I wailed.

It was not long before she turned up.

'What are you making that noise for?' Mother spoke firmly. She helped me take off my fishtail and I put on my skirt. Then she removed the heavy crown which was fixed firmly to my head.

'Ow! You are pulling my hair!' I started to cry again.

'Sorry, sorry,' said Mum. 'And you can stop that noise! There's no need. No need at all!'

Now I was free to wander around the fair. There were lots of stalls to entice us to part with our money. Games that required different skills, balls were thrown or rolled down a slope to a target. There were hoops that when thrown had to land so that the whole of the hoop went right over the prize otherwise you didn't get it. I had a go at the game with a fishing rod. Everyone hooked a duck, but the duck had a number underneath which had to match the number on one of the prizes. I didn't win. Mother was very selective as to which game I was allowed to play.

Carolyn was crowned May Queen in 1955, the author is standing, third girl from the left, and wearing the green dress seen previously on the Mary, Mary Carnival float.

We went to the centre of the field, where an area was marked off with rope. There we stood still and watched a display of a band playing as they walked up and down.

I was standing very still when suddenly I felt this thorn go into my wrist. 'Ow!' I screeched and began wailing. Crying was easy that day.

'Ah poor dear,' said the lady next to me. 'She has been stung by a wasp.' She quickly brushed off the insect.

'She'll need some vinegar,' said another lady trying to be helpful.

'No best thing is ice to stop it hurting,' said the first.

'There, there don't cry,' said a third lady as all three peered over my arm.

Mother came to my rescue. 'Here,' she said. 'It's all right. I've got some special cream. This is magic and it will take the pain away quickly.' She gently rubbed the Sting Relief cream into my wrist and the pain disappeared.

---oOo---

Every year the school put on a celebration of May Day. This had little to do with the Pagan festival of Beltane which was marked on the 1st of May. The school chose the nearest convenient Wednesday at the beginning of the month.

The position of May Queen was voted for by the top two classes of the school. Leading up to the voting day, Mary Ann had been bragging that she was going to be the 1955 May queen. She told everyone that her mother had made her dress. The class was a bit fed up with this and voted for my sister Carolyn by a large margin.

It was the job of the May Queen's Mum to dress the queen and make her a crown decorated with a flower of her choice. There were a lot of primroses at the time so Carolyn became Queen of the Primroses.

Carolyn receives a gift as May Queen from the Rector's wife.

Mummy made a dress of white lining, with a yellow netting top skirt. She had a long yellow train. Daddy made the wire frame for the crown. On the day before May Day we scoured the woods and picked every primrose we could find. This was not enough so we stripped the garden and those of our neighbours of polyanthus as well to fill out the crown. The regal party also carried posies of primroses.

The afternoon began with a procession around the village. We went out of the school, along Chapel Road and up Binstead Hill. We turned left at the top and continued along Newnham Road, down Kings Road, along Sand Path and back into the school playground for the crowning ceremony and celebrations.

The author as an attendant to Jackie Bailey who was queen of the lilac.

My role in this event was to be an attendant. I had to carry a bamboo pole which had ribbons attached to the top connected to a further pole held by another girl. On these adjoining ribbons were flowers sparsely placed. There were six attendants. The green dress that had been worn for the Mary Mary carnival float was taken from the Dress Up Drawer. It was washed, ironed and worn for this important part I took. I had a headdress of flowers.

The May Queen was crowned by Molly Barton who had held the position the previous year. Carolyn was presented with a silver locket by the Rector's wife. There were celebratory country dances in the playground and around the May Pole. This was firmly held by the Rector. It had ropes attached to the top. There were two attachments: the top one moved around as the children danced. The other one was fixed and during the dance we plaited a pattern. I thought the rope ruined the effect.

'Why don't they have ribbons like the pictures?' I asked Mum. 'And why does the Rector have to hold on to the pole in the middle? He looks stupid.' The Reverend Gum did look silly as he stood and clutched the white pole tightly as the girls danced around it.

'Because that is how they made it,' was the only answer Mum gave.

I was not to be a May queen. When it came to my year for the celebrations, I was to be an attendant. Carolyn's dress was recycled. Mummy took off the yellow over skirt and replaced it with a white one. My hair was put up in a bun on the top of my head and flowers were put around the bun.

There was the usual country dancing around Maypole in which I did not take part as I was in the regal party. I just watched. After the festivities there were stalls of white elephant bits and pieces to buy, games to risk your money playing and teas and cakes.

A lot of effort was put into creating this day. The mothers busied themselves making dresses and outfits. All the children were in fancy dress. People were adept at sewing, having just emerged from rationing, during which clothes were altered to fit rather than using precious ration points to buy new. Clothes were expensive; making an item of clothing was a lot cheaper. Mothers were expected to stay at home.

This was the last May Day I attended, I left the school that summer and went to the Convent.

The green dress made a further appearance in the play about a duchess and a lost cat that Mr. Pack had written for our class. The green dress was taken again from the Dress Up Drawer, washed and ironed and I wore it as Lady Sarah. It was a very simple story, the main parts were a duchess, a maid, a cat and a sofa. I played the Duchess, Lady Sarah and my friend Timothy played the cat. The rest of the class had various small and non-speaking parts. The sofa was three chairs put together with a rug covering it.

In Scene 1 the Duchess entered and went to centre stage, her head in her hands, 'I have lost my cat,' I wailed, as Lady Sarah to the maid who comforted her. At this point I acted as accurately as I could "real" tears. 'Oh where is my pussy cat?' I searched around the stage. 'Oh Tibbles where are you?'

Other members of the cast also searched throughout the play, each time coming back on stage to tell me where they had searched and that they too could not find the cat.

I sat down on the sofa crying profusely.

'I am so sad will I ever see my Tibbles again? I am tired now I am going to lie down and have a rest on the sofa.'

In character as a duchess I yawned.

'Cor that was a good yawn,' said Peter.

'Yeah where did you learn to do that?' Roger joined in.

'I only yawned!' I said.

'Yes it was a very good "yawn" Jocelyn. Now be quiet everyone and get on with rehearsing. It's your line Mary, the maid says 'I'll get a rug for you.' said Mr. Pack

'I didn't know I was good at acting "a yawn",' I thought

I as the Lady Sarah fell asleep on the sofa only to be awakened by my cat appearing from behind the sofa and the play ended happily. The cast came to the front of the stage and bowed. The audience applauded enthusiastically. I liked that.

The play was performed on the stage in the Methodist Hall to the school and parents, after which the green dress went back into the Dress Up Drawer. However my career as an actress did not take off.

15 GOD AND THE CONVENT SCHOOL

God played an important part in my childhood. As a convent girl He was this unseen being that had a notebook in which He recorded all my misdemeanours that I committed, "mea culpa, mea culpa, mea maxima culpa." said the prayer. I was convinced that the longer the list, the longer I would stay in Purgatory when I died. God at that time to me was not a God of Love. Being a naturally lazy pupil, I was sure that my poor performance in school, my talking in class and my being in an out of bounds area was all adding to this list.

As a pupil at the convent and a member of Holy Cross Church, I spent a lot of time on my knees as a girl. I was a member of the girls' choir at church, singing every Sunday at Sung Eucharist at 9.30 am and at Evensong at 6.30 pm. I was Church of England! The Convent was Catholic. I learnt about the Pope in Rome, the head of the Catholic Church whose decisions were infallible. It took me a while to understand the meaning of the word "infallible".

Praying was also an important part of the Convent School life. We prayed every day at assembly, before every lesson which was run by a nun or a Catholic teacher; we also attended Mass on Wednesdays and Benediction on Fridays. If we had a nun teaching us at noon we had to stop what we were doing and say the Angelus.

On the 10th of September 1957, I was 10 years old when I entered the Convent in Junior Four, the last class before going to senior school. The class teacher was Sister Ursula. She was small in stature and most of the class were taller than her. But she had a commanding presence and a shrill voice. The first lesson on that September day was Religious Education and Sister Ursula preached for the first 15 minutes that God was everywhere.

'God is in flowers, the trees, the hills and vales. Everywhere.' Her sharp piercing voice was evident even when teaching.

I accepted that quite easily.

'He is especially in the Sacrament,' she went on.

'What's that?' I thought

'The bread and wine at the Mass,' she informed the class

'Ah, they have bread and wine like us.'

Then she added, 'God is not in the Non Catholic Church. And,' she paused, 'not in any Non Catholic Sacrament.'

I was bemused. She continued with this statement for the remaining 15 minutes of the lesson.

'How could He not be everywhere? Of course God was in my Holy Cross Church.' I thought. 'She can't know what she is talking about. How could He be everywhere but pick out small patches on the earth and chose not to be there.'

My immediate reaction was that she didn't know what she was talking about. It was ludicrous for me to think that God wasn't in my Church. There were lots of Non-Catholic buildings everywhere. I decided that she was daft.

She was very strict, and screeched repeatedly at anyone who disobeyed her stern rules. 'You are a very bold girl!' Her voice was like a witch in a pantomime.

Binstead School was no preparation for the Convent and Sister Ursula! I found the work hard. I was the last to finish. I couldn't add up, take away, multiply or divide at the same speed as everyone else. I felt useless and so I gave up trying. I sat still, my elbow on the desk supporting my chin.

I turned to Mary who was sitting next to me. 'Tell me what the answer is please,' I pleaded. 'I just don't get it.'

'Jocelyn Drawbridge!' she shouted. I was spotted! 'Stop talking! You have not listened to what I am saying, you are always dreaming! You will never learn if you don't pay attention! Get outside!'

I wanted to say, 'I don't understand.' But I didn't dare. I humbly stood up and walked to the door. I knew asking for help from her was a waste of time.

Except in summer, standing outside was cold as well as embarrassing. The classroom was in the basement, with frosted glass doors leading directly to the outside. We were not allowed to get our coats for this punishment nor to put on a jumper. This was meant to be humiliating and uncomfortable.

I turned to collect my jumper which was hanging over the back of the chair.

'You can leave that!' Sister Ursula yelled. 'Hurry up, Hurry up, get outside.' There was a pause. 'Now!'

Once as I stood outside for this reprimand, I was caught by Reverend Mother. I looked away ready to hang my head in shame if a further telling off was going to come from her as well. She just smiled and whispered without stopping, 'Oh dear.' Nothing more was said and she walked quickly away. 'She is too busy to stop,' I thought. There was always a pupil outside Junior 4's classroom. It happened a lot.

My standard of listening did not improve as a result of this chastisement. I was just more aware of the ways I could avoid getting caught, incurring Sister Ursula's wrath and being told to 'Get outside'.

There were a lot of sums done at speed, mostly dictated, as Sister Ursula was preparing the pupils to take their 11 plus exam. It was all very new to me and I couldn't keep up. I was expecting sums to be written on the blackboard. This was nothing like Binstead School; I was far more comfortable there.

One day after another chastisement for not getting enough sums right, she simply asked me if I wanted to take the 11 plus exam. Without any thought, I simply said.

'No.'

I didn't tell my mother until a few weeks later when it was too late to apply. She was not consulted by the school over this decision which was made solely by her 10 year old daughter.

Sister Ursula ran the tuck shop in her cupboard at the side of her old Dickensian style desk. This was popular; the girls queued up between the desks. Order was kept by her harsh voice which was heard over everything else. There was always a crush so I got my sweets before school from a local newspaper shop.

Humiliation was at the top of the list in my education at the Convent. Any feedback we were given was very negative. I was never praised in class for anything. I continually got a five or six out of ten and a roasting for bad work. Very rarely did I get a better mark.

The worst humiliation occurred at the end of term. There were the exams and then the scores for all the exams were added up by us in class. These were dictated to us without the name of the pupils who had got the marks. With the list of numbers in front of me, I tried to add them up. I would be half way through when some horrid girl would shout out the answer. This took up a whole lesson, and all I learnt was the feeling of stupidity. I never thought any other girl might feel the same.

Then there was "Mark Reading". The whole school was assembled in the hall and we sat in our classes on low benches. One class stood up at a time. The name of the girl who came top of the class was read out first. Her marks were the envy of most girls, especially me. There was no applause; she sat down. Then the list went on, until those that came lower down the list were still standing feeling very exposed. The humiliation was complete.

Not only were we chastised for not doing well by the Reverend Mother, we had to experience all the other girls in the school seeing that shame. I survived Sister Ursula's class and was glad to leave it. My school reports were never good, but Mummy was ever faithful and loving when these were read.

I started off each new term with a determination to do better, but any new resolve was soon destroyed by the negativity. I was constantly told how stupid I was. I was never praised. This continued throughout my time there. Later on when I was in Senior Form 2, I had patiently traced a map of Norway and Sweden and then transferred this to my book. It took me ages as there were many inlets in the coastline. When my book was returned I found I was given 8 out of 10. I was amazed I looked up at the teacher, Sister Regis, but she had moved on and said nothing. This high mark did not motivate me further. I never felt that this result was worth working hard to try and aspire to again.

When any work was returned to me my efforts were rewarded with, 'You will never succeed if you don't work harder.' The pages of my books were covered with red ink.

---oOo---

I moved up to the senior school which was in the main building. There were many stairs to climb up and down. For the next two years my class was on the top floor.

In Senior Form 3 we moved down a flight of stairs to a large classroom with big windows overlooking the back playground, the nun's garden. There were broken paving stones, a few bushes and a large walnut tree. Any exposed soil had been stamped down by endless convent girls' regulation shoes.

I walked into the Senior Form 3 classroom on the first day of the autumn term, to discover my class mates leaning out of the window. I joined them to be greeted by the view of a building site in the playground. There was dust and bricks lying around. The classroom to the left of the building was being demolished. The noise was deafening as a large ball on the end of a chain swung and hit the building. We had a grandstand view. The swinging action of the ball and chain was made by a large crane and this powered into the building smashing the brickwork and on the second hit pushing the bricks through.

The classroom had been for the "Infants" and Junior 1. The walls inside were now clearly visible by the hole the ball had just made. The decoration was pale yellow and brown and there were a few pictures that had been done by the children the previous term remaining on the wall.

'They could have taken them down,' I remarked.

The walnut tree had been cut down and the old science block which stood further down was no more.

However, most excitingly for us at 14 years old there were builders, and better still, it was hot and they were all stripped to the waist. The good looking ones were young, bronzed and had visible muscles.

'I didn't know they were going to knock down the classroom,' someone remarked

'I wonder what they are building in its place?'

'The science classroom has gone! Does that mean we won't have science this term?'

'Oh good, I didn't like it anyway.'

There was a lot of gossip, gasps, sighs and giggles; we were making a great deal of noise. Suddenly we heard the thump, thump, thump of shoes coming along the corridor. Together with the rattle of large rosary beads, it was easily identified as a Nun, and the rhythm of her feet told us it was Reverend Mother.

She stood at the door:

'Young ladies,' she bellowed, 'come away from the windows!'

We all slid away back to the desks and sat down. She then gave us a short lecture about our behaviour and left the room. We returned to the windows. We were a great deal quieter this time.

For the whole of that term, the building and our viewing went on. Occasionally we heard the thump, thump of Reverend Mother's shoes and the rattle of her rosary beads, and we all hurried back to our desks quietly. She didn't have to say anything, she just rattled her beads and we knew.

One day I was given a letter by Reverend Mother. My name was on the front. It had been opened and obviously read. I took it and realised it was from one of the builders, a good looking young man called Freddie. He had sharp blue eyes, deep auburn hair and his back was bronzed. I was flattered that he had written to me. I took the letter home, but said nothing to Mother. I was sure she would not have approved, especially as he had written that he thought me a "mice gril".

I was desperate to hide this from Mum, so I met him in the daytime. He took me to the pictures at the Commodore to see "West Side Story", the award winning film about two lovers from different gangs in New York. The cinema was empty except for the two of us in the back seat. I was meeting him clandestinely; it was a little like the film, two lovers having to meet in secret. One Sunday I walked with my sister to church. She went in and I went on to Ladies Walk where I could meet my boyfriend.

My sister did not approve and she told Mother. She was cross but understood.

'If you have to meet him in secret and you are too ashamed to bring him to meet me,' she gently said, 'then he is not right for you. And you know it.'

We were obviously not suited and it fizzled out quite quickly.

---oOo---

St. Therese Presentation Convent School, situated in Ryde High Street next to the Catholic Church, had only a tennis court sized playground. On this the games mistress, Mrs Major, organised netball and rounders. I was not popular with Mrs Major as I was no athlete. I was not a good runner but I was excellent at hitting the ball, so I was always picked early for teams.

'What about Jo?' said the selected captain of the team, Margaret, to Kathleen, her best friend, who had already been chosen, 'She can smash the ball an awful long way.'

'Yes good idea,' said Kathleen.

'We pick Jo!' they both said.

It was my turn to bat. 'OK everyone,' said Susan the captain of the opposing team. 'It's Jo's turn! Spread out, she hits it hard and the ball can go for miles!'

Saying that I was "to bat" is incorrect as there was no bat. We made a fist and hit the ball with our lower palms and clenched fingers.

I was good at this. I could hit the ball either to the left around the school building and into the Nuns' Garden or to the right through the gate and into the road.

At that moment I chose to hit the ball to the right as there were a lot of fielders on the other side and two in the Nuns' garden. I hit the ball accurately as it went over the wall and down the road.

'She has hit it into the road!' the captain shouted. 'Get it Nicola! You're nearest! Run! Run!'

Nicola, the fastest sprinter in the class, ran out of the school gate. I had managed to get the ball into Warwick Street. I easily ran my rounder.

'Mrs Major can I go again?' I asked. 'She is taking ages to come back.'

Eventually Nicola returned, puffing, she threw the ball to the bowler. 'The ball,' she said as she puffed, 'had rolled down the hill. I was nearly at the bottom before I could get it!'

The phrase 'Health and Safety' was not in use in the early 1960s. Fortunately there were few cars. The playground was covered by large square sections of concrete which were uneven, making a game of tennis more interesting as the ball could bounce anywhere. These large square slabs had lifted over time and there were numerous places where we could trip. We also played netball on this pitch as the playground was marked for netball and tennis. Neither the teachers nor the pupils thought about any possibility of stumbling.

To accommodate all the girls when teaching tennis, which I loved, we walked down to the Mead Tennis courts. This was a short walk from school located in Church Lane at the back of shops in Union Street. Although I was not very good, I enjoyed these lessons.

Our safety was not considered at all when it came to hockey. I hated Thursday afternoons in winter as we had to make our way up to the playing fields in Playstreet Lane. We walked there in small groups unaccompanied. It was a lengthy hike which took at least 20 minutes or longer if we dawdled. We came out of the school walked up the High Street into Swanmore Road past Ryde Hospital, over the road and right into Radcliffe Avenue, left into Pellhurst Road and right again into Playstreet Lane. Not only did we carry our hockey sticks we also took our games kit and our school bags as, at the end of the lesson, we went straight home. My hockey boots with the laces tied together hung over my school satchel.

We changed in the large wooden hut on the playing fields. There were no showers so if it was muddy we had to go home covered in dirt. More importantly for me there were no toilets!

'Just go around the back of the hut,' Mrs Major said in an embarrassed whisper.

I did not like hockey. The pitch was too big, the ground too messy and I hated the hockey boots. These boots made out of black canvas covered our ankles and had two rubber round pieces designed for protection. Dressed in a gold Airtex shirt, a pair of culottes and long socks under these boots I joined the class on the field. I looked awful!

'It's cold today,' I said to Mrs Major. 'Please may I put on my jumper?'

'No you can't!' said this gym mistress dressed in a short gym skirt showing off her red tinged weather worn bare legs, and a large long sleeved top over a shirt. Her ensemble was complete with a long scarf. 'You will warm up when you get going.'

She blew her whistle, called the class together and after the teams were picked we were placed in our positions.

I never understood the game except that it was the job of the team to get the hard ball through the two white wooden posts at each end by means of hitting it with the wooden sticks.

Aware of my ankles I kept out of the way, but I knew I had to look as though I was joining in. Stephanie, who was very good at this game, hit the ball really hard and it went way down the pitch towards the goal. I ran after it with a keen look on my face. By the time I got there Margaret had hit it back hard and it ended up near the other goal. Again I ran after it looking equally keen. Fortunately someone got to the ball before me. I was nowhere near the ball throughout the game as I kept to the side lines moving out of the way if the ball came anywhere near me.

The pitch was muddy with puddles which despite my keeping out of the way covered my legs in a thin coat of sludge. Every time a group got closer the other girls' boots hit the puddles and covered me in muck.

I spent the 40 minutes cold and miserable running short distances up and down the pitch. I was so glad when the game finished and we did the obligatory three cheers.

The captain of the winning team muttered, 'Hip Hip.'

'Ray,' we shouted back without any passion. This was repeated three times.

The losing team unenthusiastically repeated the process.

These three cheers were said and at the same speed at which we rattled off the "Hail Marys" at school. We raced to the unheated hut and wallowed in the shelter of being out of the cold.

The calls of 'I'm freezing!' echoed around the room.

'Me too!' I shouted. 'Why couldn't we wear our jumpers? Old Meanie!'

The room went silent suddenly as Mrs Major had just walked in. With my head down trying to look inconspicuous I put on my gym slip, my school jumper and then my gabardine coat. For more warmth I left my culottes on. I screwed up my school shirt and stuffed it into my games drawstring bag with my school tie. Finally I took off my hockey boots, tied them together and slung them over my satchel. I pushed my feet into my regulation shoes, wiggled them to the ends without undoing the laces until the backs were free for me to pull up with my finger.

'Jocelyn Drawbridge!' Mrs Major called out.

I shuddered as I thought she had heard me call her a "meanie".

'Yes Mrs Major,' I said innocently.

'Where is your school hat?'

I looked around and then spotted it. I picked it up from the floor, gave it a shake and plonked it on my head.

My inability to play hockey and tennis well was recorded on my reports and added to my feeling of being 'a stupid and lazy girl' with which I had been labelled.

There was just one teacher at the Convent who was encouraging. Mrs. Olive Palmer Felgate taught us French. Despite my finding French a little difficult, she was always inspiring. I tried hard for her. I didn't get many high marks for my work, but she was kind and helpful.

The school decided that I take only five GCE 'O' Levels, English Language and Literature, Domestic Science, Art and French. This would free up some time during school hours in which I could study and do my homework. This suited me as I could enjoy peaceful evenings at home daydreaming and watching the TV.

I didn't think I worked hard, but I began to find learning easier on my own without the continuous chastisement.

Convent school photo. The author is standing in the second row, second from the left. This original photo is signed by all the girls on the reverse.

One day I was sitting at a table in the library, my books were open in front of me and I stopped work as I listened to two other girls talking.

'Have you heard, Mary,' Bernadette said, 'Rodney is going out with Ann?'

'Is she?' Mary squealed. 'He may go to the grammar but he is not that good looking.'

'He is growing his hair to look like a Beatle but it's all greasy.'

'And he has loads of spots,' Mary continued as she put her finger under her nose. 'And he smells!'

I knew Rodney so I turned towards the girls to join in the conversation.

'Mind you Ann is not that pretty.'

Suddenly I heard a voice, 'You are here on trust to get on with your work.'

I looked up and saw Sister Regis' face looking through the window opposite me from the room next door. 'And I find you playing around and wasting valuable time.' She was taking an elocution lesson and was standing on a chair looking through the high window. 'You, Jocelyn Drawbridge, will never succeed! You are talking and not studying. I shall report this to Reverend Mother and she will hear how disloyal you have been.'

Later that day Reverend Mother stopped me in the corridor and told me that following the incident I was not to go to the library again and was to stay in the classroom to study. I felt at the time that I was being punished, but in retrospect I think it was the right course of action. Mary and Bernadette were very disruptive and I was easily distracted.

In the quiet of the classrooms, undisturbed and in the right learning environment, I got my work done. I only did what they told me. I did nothing more, except in English Literature. The education system was such that we were never taught to think for ourselves. We had to consume all the knowledge they gave us and spew it out in the exam.

I was given a reel to reel tape recorder for Christmas 1963. I wanted it to record all my favourite songs from Top of the Pops to the Brian Matthews programme on Saturday mornings called Saturday Club. The reels were expensive but I managed to buy some with my pocket money.

'"Twelfth Night" is the play on the Radio tonight,' Mum said. 'It certainly is an opportunity to hear it performed properly by good actors.'

What an opportunity to hear the whole of the Shakespearean play we were studying in class on the radio. I could listen to the play instead of reading it. What a good idea. 'If I recorded it on my reel to reel I could listen to it again!' I thought.

I told Carolyn and Mummy to be quiet as I had to hold the microphone to the radio. I missed a bit as I had to turn the tape over but that didn't matter.

I had listened to the play when it was broadcast on the radio. I then told the teacher what I had done and she asked me to bring it into school. I lugged my heavy tape recorder on the bus and the class listened to it. The lesson was not long enough to hear the whole play so I had to do the trip twice. Each time I followed the words in my textbook and suddenly the whole play came to life. Gone was the stilted reading by the girls in the classroom and out came the humour and the colour of Shakespeare's play.

I listened to it again at home as part of revision. The result of this was that I gained a 'C' grade for English Literature, my best mark. I could quote from it and knew the play very well. That part of the exam was easy. I had not studied "Northanger Abbey" by Jane Austin in such depth. I didn't know any of Tennyson's poems.

A week before the exams were to start, I was sitting at my desk in the classroom and was listening to a conversation the other girls were having. Reverend Mother had one final attack.

'Jocelyn Drawbridge! When will you ever learn that you will not succeed if your head is not in a book? You should be studying. Get on with your work,' she snapped.

I ended up with four 'O' levels. However this result was better than most of the girls who had sat down earlier than me at the dreaded "Mark Reading".

---oOo---

Music, which is still a love in my life, was developed at the Convent. I had piano lessons from Mrs. Clarke. She too was a stern lady and arrived for my lessons at 4.00 on Monday and Thursdays smelling strongly of tea. The school finished at 3.50; she only had a short time to grab her drink before my lesson.

Convinced I was never any good at anything I never really worked at it. I was lazy about practising, leaving it to the very last minute. However, I managed to get to Grade III in both practical and theory.

Through the school I was asked to be an usher at a classical concert at Ryde Town Hall. I went along in school uniform and loved what I heard. The beautiful sounds washed over me and I was hooked. I didn't let the other girls in my class know; they were into pop music and classical music was not 'hip' or 'with it'.

I asked Mum for a classical record for my birthday and received 'Swan Lake' which I played and played on my Dansette record player.

There was a popular pianist at the time called Russ Conway and his record "Side Saddle" was in the charts. He had made a classical LP called "My Concerto for You." This cost 35 shillings, £1.75 in today's money. I dutifully saved my five shilling – 25p - pocket money for six weeks. I had only one week to go and one more pocket money to add to my savings.

'You have done so well,' Mum said, 'I'll give you the last five shillings.'

After school I ran down to Teague's Music Shop at the bottom of Union Street in Ryde with my savings safely in my purse. The shop had a selection of musical instruments; there were two grand pianos in the windows. Towards the back was the record section with cubicles in which the customer could listen to the record to make sure they wanted to buy it.

I was glad that the shop was empty of anyone who might pass on the information to my school friends that I had bought a classical record. 'Please may I have a copy of "My Concerto for You" by Russ Conway,' I proudly asked the shop assistant. He went to the back of the shop and spoke to the manager.

'I'm sorry we don't have that in stock,' he said, 'but we can order it for you.'

My disappointment was difficult to hide but I did.

'It will take a week,' he continued. 'Come back next Friday.'

I had waited six weeks for this record and now I had wait a further seven days. The music from that record was all the more sweet having had to wait.

Mrs. Clarke also took us for singing lessons but she was second rate compared with Miss Black. This large woman was well known on the Island. She had been the music teacher at the other private girls' school in Ryde which closed so she came to us. She always wore plain blouses and grey cardigans, grey straight skirts and sensible lace up shoes. She had been teaching the piano and singing for many years, she had pupils who became teachers and their pupils were called "Miss Blacks Musical Grandchildren".

When she came to the Convent there was a major difference. She knew her subject so well and was passionate about it. I loved her lessons. She broke down the songs we were to sing, getting each musical phrase correctly performed. She taught us how to pronounce words properly when singing. She showed us how to position our heads when singing top notes and how to sing quietly with a lung full of air allowing the breath to be used for a crescendo at the end.

Every year in October Miss Black hired out Ryde Town Hall for her annual concert. In the programme there were piano recitals and some children sang solos. The musicians were her pupils and some were her "Musical Grandchildren". The choirs taught by Miss Black also sang a couple of songs and the whole event was finished with the hymn "Jerusalem".

It was tradition that the head girl should conduct this as Miss Black played the organ for this one song. The head girl in 1963 was Elizabeth Snellgrove. She stepped forward and Miss Black ceremoniously handed her the baton. As Miss Black walked to the organ which was already open, Elizabeth slowly processed forward to the front of the stage. Miss Black slithered along the bench at the organ; her face appeared in the mirror above the keyboard. She placed her hands on the keys, her arms and legs were wide to reach the notes and pedals.

The St. Therese Presentation Convent Choir stood silently, seriously and patiently waiting for the new conductor to be in her place and to raise her baton. Elizabeth taking her duty as head girl seriously stretched up until she was fully to attention. She proudly turned to face us and then screwed up her nose, twisted her mouth to the side and stuck her tongue out. We stifled a snigger. We were used to her pulling funny faces but did not expect her to pull one at this serious moment. She lifted her two arms, waved the baton to tell Miss Black to start playing. Miss Black played the introduction and at the right moment Elizabeth waved her baton-less hand to tell us to start singing.

As Miss Black swayed with the music which magnificently filled the whole hall, Elizabeth kept a regular four beat movement with the baton as her other arm remained up at shoulder height. The acoustics in Ryde Town Hall were magnificent and thrilled me as I sang the hymn.

This was October 1963 and I was to leave in the summer after my 'O' Levels.

'This is the last time I shall sing with the school,' I remarked to my friend, Liane after we had sung "Jerusalem". I shall remember this for ever.'

The Convent education was authoritarian but thinking back it was the right school for me. I was not an academic and I didn't work hard at all. I could have achieved more. Was that my fault or the school's? I was bullied by the teachers and I only learnt the basics. I didn't put any effort into studying. If I had gone to the local Secondary Modern I imagine there would be no-one to push me and there were far too many distractions. It was also co-educational and I was interested in boys!

However I did win a school prize which I felt I didn't quite deserve. When I was in the third year aged 14, I used to ring the lesson change bell. This was an irritating job but it did mean that I could leave any boring lesson early to go to stand by the clock and ring the bell on time.

My other responsibility was to set up the microphone which relayed the morning assembly up to the classroom on the top floor. Not realising that it took time to warm up I turned it on as Reverend Mother arrived. I don't think the pupils upstairs minded but they only got half of the assembly notices. To counteract this I turned it on very early. I didn't tell anyone that I had done this, but they soon worked it out as I did not return to the microphone when Reverend Mother came in.

Before she arrived the fun began. There were renditions of the latest pop songs, sung as they were performed on the television; impersonations of the teaching staff which included one "important message stating that everyone in Senior Form II had a detention that day unless they wrote a six page essay; there were news reports which included who was going out with who and, of course a few weak jokes. Surprisingly enough, the nuns and teachers did not stop this. Maybe they didn't know or maybe they saw this as harmless fun. I could have turned the volume down until Reverend Mother arrived and then turned it up again, but it was good entertainment at that time in the morning.

I also worked out if my friend and I did jobs for the school we could stay in the warm instead of going out for cold fresh air in the playground. There were always books in need of repair. I offered to do this thus forgoing my midday break. We used to sit with a pile of books, sticky tape and scissors. There we would chat and mend books in the warmth of the classroom. For this and my other responsibilities I received the prize for 'Services to the School'.

16 HOLY CROSS CHURCH

In 1969 a fire caused massive damage to my church, Holy Cross Church, Binstead. On Saturday 7th of June in the evening, a neighbour discovered the fire and called the fire brigade.

'I saw smoke coming out of the roof by the bell tower,' said the neighbour. 'By the time I got back from ringing the fire brigade there were flames spreading over the whole roof.'

The fire brigade arrived and got to work immediately as large flames shot out of the 50 foot pine roof. Ladders were mounted up against the building and hoses were aimed at the source.

People gathered to watch the drama unfolding. 'I was surprised just how quickly the fire took hold of the whole roof.' said the neighbour. 'It is such a shame: the roof was repaired extensively a few years ago.'

This photo of Binstead Church was taken in the morning after the fire which destroyed the roof in June 1969.

The little lane leading up to the church was blocked with fire engines and a large extendable ladder. Working tirelessly, the firemen were able to stop the fire at the end of the nave and prevented it from spreading to the chancel roof.

Once the building was relatively safe members of the Parochial Church Council and parishioners helped firemen rescue books, music, vestments and furnishings which they took home by car to dry out and repair.

'It looks like the organ is totally destroyed,' said one bystander.

'That must have been the area where the fire started,' someone replied authoritatively

'An electrical fault in the new organ,' another person suggested. 'It was new, wasn't it?'

'No,' said the man who spoke with most authority. 'Hardly new! It was 10 years old at least!'

'Could have been the sun through the window catching on to a piece of paper,' another spectator suggested. 'There is always a lot of sheet music in the gallery.'

'Could be, could be,' they all murmured.

'Arson!' someone suggested. 'I reckon it was started deliberately! Arson that's what it was.'

'I hope not!' the small group agreed.

'Who would want to burn the church?' a parishioner said, holding back her tears.

'I'm sure it was insured!' said Mr. Authority. He put his arm around her shoulder. 'They'll repair it, don't worry.'

The local paper, 'The County Press', reported

"The fire was extinguished before it reached the sanctuary, chancel and vestry, the oldest parts of the church, thought to have been built more than 800 years ago, and the north aisle roof.

Firemen remained on the scene for five hours. They returned on Sunday morning to probe through the debris in the hope of finding the cause. So far it remains a mystery"

'It was dreadful, the damage was extensive and the church was certainly not able to be used. We were offered space to hold our services in the Methodist Church in Binstead and at the Abbey in Quarr,' said Hillary Spurgeon who at the time was a member of the church choir. 'We were very grateful.'

'Within a few weeks the north aisle was blocked off from the damaged section and able to be used for services. Late comers were always a little embarrassed as entry to the area was made by the vestry at the east end thus facing the congregation as they went to find a pew.'

A further report in the County Press in December of that year reported that a meeting was held at Binstead CE Primary School regarding the plans for the re-building of Holy Cross Church.

It took 14 months to complete the repairs and the church was rededicated on Saturday, 20th February 1971.

Mr. & Mrs. Drawbridge stand at the door of Holy Cross Binstead on the 19th June, 1943. At the time of writing the rose over the door is still thriving.

'The rededication service was wonderful,' Hillary told me. 'The choir was resplendent in their new robes. The Assistant to the Bishop of Portsmouth, the Right Reverend Laurence Woolner, took the service. There wasn't a seat free, the church was packed. I remember the large mixed choir sang Psalm 122 in procession! As well as the building everything was rededicated, the font, the extension, the improvements and the organ. There were four hymns. The last one "The Church's one foundation" was sung so loudly that it nearly raised the newly repaired roof. It was truly a wonderful day.'

'The builders and craftsmen did a good job with the repair,' I commented. 'I love the wooden structures in the roof.'

'The wood when it was just completed was much lighter and looked vulgar, like a bordello.'

I didn't question her as to how she knew what type of decoration was in a bordello.

When the fire occurred I had long since left the Island and was living in London but too sad to visit and see the damaged church which had held so many happy memories. It was a place of stability; it was there all the time during my childhood and I didn't want to see its ruined state.

I did not get married there. Mother didn't want it as the last time we were all in Holy Cross was for Daddy's funeral. There were too many memories for her. I respected her wishes and Robert and I were married in the Norman church of St. Edmund's, Wootton. This was Mum's new parish church.

Holy Cross had been Mum's church since she came to the Island in 1927. It was the obvious choice for Mum and Dad's wedding in 1943. They were regular members and they took Carolyn and then me for our christening there.

Both of us wore a long Victorian christening gown made in Manilla in the 1880s. This precious dress had been handed down to Mum for us to wear. Its long skirt was made of handmade lace. It had two short butterfly sleeves. The little bonnet had a frill at the back which was the fashion in hot countries to protect the back of the neck from the sun. The

Carolyn Mary is held by Auntie Vonnie at 2 Church Road, after her christening at Holy Cross Church June, 1945.

silk lining had worn badly and Mum replaced it for my son Philip's christening in 1971. It was also worn by my daughter and Carolyn's two daughters for their christenings. It has now also been used by the next generation, my daughter's children. The last to wear it was Carolyn's granddaughter Charlotte Carolyn in September 2015.

The church was constantly a part of our lives. Mother used to clean the brass regularly. There were two crosses, one that stood on the altar and the other at the top of the processional pole. There were also eight candlesticks. One day in the school holidays we went with her. Willie Pickle our six month old dachshund puppy had just come to live with us.

'We'll have to take Willie with us,' Mum said. 'It'll be alright in church. With the door shut he won't be able to get out.'

Carolyn and I had great respect for the church. However we were allowed to wander around inside, leaving Mummy to get on with the cleaning in the vestry.

'I won't be long and then we can go into Ryde and get the shopping,' she said.

'Can we go and play outside?' Carolyn asked.

'Of course, but make sure you don't let the dog out as you open the church door,' Mummy warned.

'We won't,' replied Carolyn as she lifted up the latch to the heavy door. We went through and she made very sure it was firmly shut behind her.

The churchyard was packed with many tombstones. I did not consider that each stone represented a body buried there. We looked at the "Smuggler's Grave" erected by grateful parishioners as he was "cruelly shot on board his sloop by the Customs Officers of Portsmouth on the 15th of June 1785." We marvelled at the dates of some of the others. They were just memorials, we didn't think of the human body beneath.

We went around to the back of the church, and there were some large flat gravestones on which we could climb. The respect we had for the church, God's house was not extended to His yard.

'These graves were for the richer people.' Carolyn informed me.

'Oh really,' I said as I jumped off one and clambered on to another.

Bored with the game we returned inside.

'I'm just finishing off now, darlings,' she called out hearing the door open.

Carolyn again firmly shut the door behind her.

Mummy finished the work, shut the vestry door, and picked up her bags ready to walk into Ryde.

'Where's Willie Pickle?' she asked us.

We called and called him as we raced around trying to find him. 'He can't have gone outside,' said Carolyn. 'I was very careful, Mummy.'

We checked under every pew and in and under the pulpit. Mummy was becoming a little worried. 'He can't have gone far,' she said. 'He has to be in here somewhere.'

Mummy had already shut the iron gates to the chancel.

'We have checked everywhere. I'll just check here.'

She opened the gates and walked through. The chancel was where the choir sat during services. It had a gate so it was forbidden for Carolyn and me to go through. She looked behind the tall boys' choir stalls, then she went into the sanctuary and looked under the altar.

'It's all right!' she called, 'He's here, under the altar.' There was Willie Pickle curled up and fast asleep.

I looked at Carolyn and she looked back at me.

'Willie was under the altar!' We were horrified, 'Mummy, Willie shouldn't have been under the altar!'

'Oh I'm sure God won't mind, girls,' Mummy said reassuringly, 'He is one of God's creatures after all.'

Holy Cross played a great part in my childhood. I attended Sunday school for a while. My class was at the back in the north aisle. My teacher was Mrs. Sibbell, an elderly widow whose husband had died during the First World War. Every year she commemorated her wedding anniversary by having a special meal.

I was part of a group of five for the very young. We sat in one pew. Mrs. Sibbell stood in front of us and told us stories. The school started at two o'clock on a Sunday afternoon. The session began and ended with a hymn.

It was the Sunday before Easter and Mrs. Sibbell had told us about Jesus' crucifixion. At the end we sang the well-known hymn, "There is a green hill far away". Mrs. Sibbell stood at the side of us, and I turned and looked at her, just as she sang the last verse. 'Oh dearly, dearly has He loved, and as she sang, her top lip stuck out like a beak on the word 'dearly'. I stared at her and decided, 'I shall remember this for the rest of my life.'

Holy Cross Girls Choir c 1955 before I joined. Carolyn is seated in the front row at the end on the right. Four girls had borrowed the boys' cassocks as there was only money for seven blue ones.

She was a loyal member of Holy Cross, a tradition that remains today with a continuing congregation of willing volunteers.

When I was old enough I left the Sunday School and joined the choir. Binstead Church was progressive and one of the first on the Island to have a girls' choir. One family left All Saints Church in Ryde because they would not admit girls into their choir. The Holy Cross organist and choir leader was a Mrs. Pudan. She was very strict. The organ was placed against the west wall so Mrs. Pudan had her back to the choir. There were 12 girls in the choir. At choir practice we faced the organ and perched on the balcony's balustrade below which was a fall of about ten feet. No-one thought that we might topple over the top.

If she heard chatting, she turned around and hit the offending girl with a hymnbook. I have no recollection of this happening to me. Perhaps I was a good girl. I was a Convent girl and I was a little scared of God and I was in His house.

At Sung Eucharist service every Sunday, after the Agnus Dei, those in the choir who had been confirmed clattered down the stairs to take communion. This left just three of us waiting upstairs.

I decided to be confirmed and took classes. On the day of our confirmation, all the girls were to be dressed in white. I didn't want to have a white dress, and Mother agreed thinking it impractical.

'I cannot think of a time when you will need to wear a white dress again. They have got some concertina pleated white skirts in Pack's, would you like one of those?'

'Yes please,' I said.

'Call into the shop after school tomorrow and I'll get someone to help you.'

I wore this with a white blouse on the day. We went to the Old Parsonage in Church Road to put on starched white veils. These were triangular and had a cross embroidered on them in white. This cross had to be dead centre just above our foreheads. They were held on by tying two white strings at the nape of the neck. We walked round to the church and at the appropriate point in the service we processed up in twos and knelt before the bishop who was seated just inside the chancel. He put his hands on my head and I was confirmed. I could now go down with the choir after the Agnus Dei and take communion like the rest of them.

"Songs of Praise" was coming to All Saints Parish Church in Ryde and we were invited to take part. It was filmed in November for broadcast in January 1964. It was strange to sing the hymns which celebrated Epiphany when we had not had Christmas.

We practised for two evenings at the All Saints Parish Church. The recording took place on the following day. The choirs arrived first at 6.00 pm; the congregation arrived shortly after. The car park was full of large grey lorries with BBC printed on the side. I felt quite important. Mummy made me a new dress. It was turquoise blue as we had been advised to wear pastel shades as this would make a clearer picture when it was broadcast in black and white. Only the All Saints choir wore their robes.

Mummy sat at the back but we were with the other choirs occupying the reserved front seats. There was a rather large soprano who had come to sing two solos. She had a wobbly voice which I didn't like.

We sang the hymns in the order printed and we sat to listen to the soloist. We were half way through the next hymn when we heard a loud bang and the sound of falling glass and a few screams and shouts. The church suddenly became dark as we were left with just the Church's lights. Then there were gasps, shuffling of feet and we stopped singing. We all turned around to try and see the cause of the loud bang and the lighting failure.

'Ladies and Gentlemen if you would like to sit down I will let you know what is happening as soon as know, and we hope to resume recording as soon as possible.'

Some men from the BBC were near some pews at the back of the church and were moving people away from the area. One said, 'If you would like to come this way, thank you, keep moving please.'

'What was the bang?' I said.

'It sounded like an explosion to me,' said Angela, my friend from number seven Church Road.

'What on earth has exploded?' I continued.

Turning around, we knelt up on our seats to try and see. There were a few empty pews. People were standing by the door. Two men from the BBC stood on the empty pews looking up at the extinguished lights.

'Oh,' said Angela. 'A bulb has popped.'

'Popped! I think it was more than a pop!' I said.

'They just have to find another bulb,' Angela went on assuredly. 'Ours pop at lot at home, Dad just replaces them with new ones!'

We continued to wait patiently and then were told that the recording could not continue that evening as new lights had to be found and installed.

'Then it was more than a popped bulb,' I said to Angela

'We shall resume tomorrow evening at the same time.' There was a pause as another man from the BBC whispered to him. The two men stood head to head in deep discussion. The more important of the two then announced, 'Ladies and Gentlemen would you remain seated as our guest soprano cannot return tomorrow and we have found enough light to record her piece.

'Oh, how lovely,' I groaned sarcastically.

'What a shame there was enough light,' Angela agreed

We all sat dutifully and listened to the wobbly soloist with her wobbly voice.

The local press got hold of the story and made it a little bigger than it was with a report stating that the congregation was showered with glass.

The next night we returned. Some of the girls wore different dresses in the hope that they would appear on the television in two different shots wearing two different outfits. It didn't occur to Carolyn and me to be naughty.

We watched the broadcast on Sunday 12th of January. There were a few long distance shots of me but there was no hint of the drama of exploding lights.

---oOo---

I was nine when I joined the choir. The men, boys' and girls' choirs got together to produce a show. It was to be mixture of songs and dances. The whole choir sang "Petro the Fisherman", but Carolyn, Angela and I were put down to sing the Gilbert and Sullivan song from the Mikado, "Three little maids from school". Mother was particularly proud of this decision, as her Aunt Louie Rene sang with the Doyly Carte Opera Company, and knew Gilbert and Sullivan personally. Aunt Louie's pet name was Oolou.

'Your great Aunt Oolou would be very proud,' she told us. 'She was their principal contralto and sang as Katisha in The Mikado.'

'Was she famous?' asked Carolyn.

'Oh yes, very famous. She sang with the company for 10 years, and had lots of major parts.'

Angela already had a kimono. Mother took a long look at this and copied it. She bought the material from Fowler's in Union Street Ryde. She chose a cotton material printed with bright flowers which she felt conveyed the look of Japan. Carolyn's was predominantly blue and mine was green. Mother bound the edges with wide bands of blue and green lining material. She copied the long oblong pocket at the end of each arm.

'What are these for?' I asked Mummy.

'I haven't the remotest idea darling, but you all need to look the same. Maybe it is to carry a very small dog.' I liked that idea.

We practised very hard and we got it right. On the night Mother made up our faces with stage make up and put black lines from the outside corner of our eyes pointing up.

'This is to give the effect of being Japanese,' she said with authority.

Dressed in our kimonos we went on stage at the Drill Hall in Binstead. We sang the song "Three Little Maids from School" perfectly and performed the little dance we had practised again and again in the middle.

The applause was tremendous! We had performed without a fault and the audience loved it. They shouted for more.

Mother prevented us from coming off stage. 'Well done you three! Go and do it again,' Mummy said.

'Why?' I replied, 'Didn't we get it right the first time?'

'Yes you did! But darling they liked it so much they want to hear it again. So we did an encore. I loved the experience and refused to take off my make-up that night. Mummy let me go to bed and sleep in it.

It was during the build-up to this concert that the village suffered a terrible shock. The rector's wife committed suicide. When Mummy heard she disappeared around to the rectory but there was nothing anyone could do to help.

Mummy carefully explained what had happened. 'Mrs. Gum was very unhappy and thought she didn't want to live any more. So she turned on the gas tap in her bedroom and went to sleep. Gas is a poison and kills if left without a flame. She had a change of heart and was trying to turn the gas off but it was too late and she died.'

After that Mother had all gas removed from our house. All our power was from electricity. She replaced the old gas cooker with a new electric Belling cooker. This was plugged into a large socket on the wall which Mummy made a point of turning off when she had finished cooking. The Belling Cooker too had its dangers.

'The hot plates stay hot for a long time after they have been turned off,' Mummy explained, 'so you must never touch them.'

Carolyn was not touching the stove but she moved closer to see if it there was a light under the saucepan. She knew she shouldn't touch it so she held her arms behind her as put her face nearer and nearer the stove.

'Carolyn! You are too close!' Mummy shouted.

It was too late the frill which went over the shoulder on her dress caught alight. She screamed. 'I'm on fire, I'm on fire!'

Mummy patted out the fire with her hands. 'Stand still! Don't move!' Mummy shouted.

I stood still too. Because Mummy was so quick putting the fire out it had just burnt the frill and nothing else. Carolyn was unhurt.

'There, there, it's all right now, no harm done.' Mummy breathed sigh of relief, she paused and then laughed. 'Well, only to the frill on your dress.'

17 TEENAGE YEARS

It was Flint McCullough of "Wagon Train" that told me that I was growing up and changing. One day I was day dreaming about being on a Wagon Train in the Mid West of America in the mid 1800s. I dreamed I was bumping along in an uncomfortable covered wagon, eating my meal from a tin plate at the back of the wagon and sitting on a log next to Flint McCullough at the side of a camp fire with a rug around my shoulders. The Indians would attack but although I was hit in my shoulder by an arrow I survived to be swept up by Flint McCullough on to his horse.

Almost the next day I couldn't understand why I was more interested in the actor Robert Horton than the part he played. I would now imagine myself with him in his Hollywood house with a swimming pool and every luxury imaginable.

Liane Brown was my close friend in my teenage years. A holiday was arranged for Liane and me to go and stay with friends of her mother's. I was 14 years old and Liane was 13. This was the first holiday I had taken without Mum and she carefully packed for me. The plan was to fly from Bournemouth Airport and a coach was arranged from Portsmouth Harbour to drive us directly there.

Clare Woodward was staying with us for a holiday. 'Betty dear, why don't I,' said Clare, 'drive you to the airport with the suitcases? We can see the girls off on their journey.'

'That's a good idea it you don't mind Clare,' said Mum, 'The girls won't have to carry their heavy bags.'

'After a car ferry crossing from Fishbourne we arrived at the Portsmouth Ferry Terminal. We then took the short journey in the car to Portsmouth Harbour where Liane and I got on the coach.

'We'll see you at the airport,' said Mum as she waved to us.

'Enjoy the journey,' said Clare.

Our journey was long as the traffic was bad. The coach crawled along and then came to a stop. 'Look at the time,' Liane said looking at her watch. 'I hope we don't miss our flight.'

'Yes,' I replied. 'The plane takes off in half an hour and I haven't seen a sign for the airport.'

The journey dragged on. The coach's journey was so slow with so many stops that we soon realised that we were going to miss our plane to Alderney.

'There'll be other planes, girls,' said the man in front of us. 'Don't worry you'll get there in the end.'

'Yes, that's right,' said Liane who was a seasoned traveller. She had flown to Alderney before.

We agreed that it was good that Mum was going to be at the airport, as we would not be alone to sort out a plane to get to Alderney.

Clare and Mum however had had a good journey, arrived at the airport and were waiting for us.

Instead of greeting Mum with a "hello", all Liane and I could say was 'We've missed our plane! What are we going to do?'

'I know, I know,' said Mum. 'It's all been sorted out.'

'We went to the check in desk,' Clare explained, 'and booked you on a plane to Jersey which will stop there and you will get off and go into the air terminal. You will then get on another plane which will take you to Guernsey, where it will drop off some passengers and finally it will take you to Alderney.'

'Do we get off at Guernsey?' Liane asked.

'No you stay on the plane,' Clare assured her.

'You will be able to say you have been to all the Channel Islands!' Mum said with a cheery smile.

'Your luggage will be looked after throughout the journey,' said Clare, who had taken many flights to all parts of the Continent.

'I am going to go to all the Channel Islands!' I announced.

'Yes Jo,' said Clare, 'but you will not see much of any of the other islands, only their airports.'

Mrs. & Mrs. Minton who shared the ownership of an old German Bunker with Phyllis and Jack White with whom Liane and I stayed in 1961.

We booked in our cases, and said our 'Goodbyes' to Mum and Clare and proudly walked to the departure lounge.

Liane and I sat together on the large plane to Jersey. It was quite luxurious. I felt really grown up and mature. We were travelling alone and without our parents.

We sat back to enjoy the journey. 'Are you two little girls travelling on to Alderney?' said a rather glamorous air hostess.

'Little girls!' I thought. 'How dare she!'

'Yes we are,' said Liane.

'Well there is no need to worry, I'll make sure everything goes well and direct you to the right plane when we get to Jersey.'

'I wasn't worried before she spoke,' I thought. 'I look mature and not like a little girl!'

We got off at Jersey and the air hostess directed us to the departure lounge for the plane to Guernsey and Alderney. I looked out of the window at the airport hoping to see some of Jersey. I didn't, I just saw aeroplanes.

The plane which took us on the final part of our journey was very small. Squashed up we landed in Guernsey and waited whilst other passengers got off and more got on.

Owing to the delay in our arrival in Alderney there was no-one to meet us at the airport.

'We could ring Uncle Jack and get him to come up and fetch us,' said Liane, 'but that will cost us money. Or we could walk. It's not far.'

'Let's walk!' I said ever conscious of our precious holiday spending money.

We picked up our suitcases that we had not touched since we left the Island and lugged them down the hill to the Alderney Cottage. The "Cottage" was two dwellings with one connecting door on the ground floor and two sets of stairs. Our bedroom was on one side and Auntie Phyllis and Uncle Jack slept in the other.

It was a lovely two weeks. Every beach around Alderney is perfect. Being such a small island we were able to walk to different beaches every day.

Mum had given me a weighted beach ball which refused to be thrown straight. I took this on our first day to Braye Beach. We made friends with another holiday maker, Lorraine, on the beach and was playing with the ball when I decided to show her how well I could swim. I deliberately threw the ball into the sea. Lorraine sensibly said, 'I can't get it.'

'Don't worry,' I said confidently, 'I'll get it.'

'Don't be silly,' said Liane, 'it's gone too far.'

I waded into the sea not listening to others imploring me not to go. I swam towards the ball, but the current was pulling the ball just out of my reach. Liane and Lorraine's shouting attracted others on the beach. I spotted them waving and looking out to sea when I turned around.

The author with her friend Liane at Telegraph Bay in the Channel Island of Alderney.

A crowd had gathered and everyone was beckoning me to come back. With misplaced self-assurance I swam a little further out. My pride wanted me to get the ball, but it continued to go further away. I turned again. 'I am rather a long way out,' I thought as sense suddenly prevailed and I decided to swim back. The ball was eventually picked up by a boat but we never saw it again.

On Sunday we went with a couple called the Mintons who took us to their bunker at

Saye Bay. These were built during the German occupation between 1940 and 1945. The locals had taken these over and had tidied them up to make a place to store beach chairs, cooking stoves and everything needed for a day on the beach. It was fascinating to think they these were built by prisoners for German soldiers. The Mintons had cleaned and painted it white in an attempt to hide their real purpose. It had a large window which looked out on the bay. 'That is a lovely spot to relax in when the weather is cold,' said Mrs. Minton. 'It's beautiful today so we'll sit outside.'

We had a lovely day, swimming and exploring the beach.

We had our household duties to do during our stay. We had to keep our bedroom tidy! She never inspected our room: if she had she may have found most of our dirty clothes under the chest of drawers and bed. We also had to wash up after every meal. There was no hot water tap in the kitchen. The used cutlery was put to soak in a saucepan or bowl. The plates were scraped of food and stacked up. Once the kettle had boiled and poured into a bowl in the sink we set to washing and drying up. We only ever used one kettle full of boiling water for each meal.

There was one beach to which we were not allowed to go alone, so Uncle Jack took us to Telegraph Bay. Access to this bay was via roughly hewn steps down the cliff. Once there we swam, enjoyed the sunshine and ate our picnic.

'Right you two, sit on the rock over there and I will take your picture,' said Uncle Jack.

Liane and I got to the rock and sat down. Our feet were stuck out in front and our hands were behind us as we slouched.

'Come on you two, sit up straight,' he said. Instantly we sat up and instantly he took the picture. This snap still is one of my favourites of the trip.

The journey home to the Isle of Wight was uneventful. Uncle Jack took us to the airport and we boarded the right plane which took us directly back to Bournemouth. From there we got on a coach to Portsmouth and a boat to Ryde and a tram down the pier. Liane walked home up St. Thomas's Street and I took the bus.

---oOo---

Having been educated at an all girls' Convent School I was not at ease with boys. I did not see them as my equal. Women had not yet been 'liberated'. It was the male of the species that had to make the first move. There was no sex education in school. The nuns were certainly not going to enlighten us. I picked up the basics from a girl who was younger than me in the junior cloakroom at school when I was ten. I returned home and told Mummy as she was getting tea.

'That part of a man,' she said as she cut a slice from the large white loaf, 'Goes into that part of a woman.' Obviously uncomfortable to discuss further, she continued to cut individual slices from the loaf which she had already buttered. I was relieved that she had confirmed that this strange procedure was true!

'Now I'm really tired,' she said clearly hoping this conversation didn't get any deeper. 'Run along now. Have you got any homework to do?'

I ran along. I didn't want to continue the conversation as by now both of us were very embarrassed.

I belonged to a girls' choir where there was of course a boys' choir. I was 12 years old when I was walked home from Evensong by Peter who was shorter than me. That was not right, the boyfriend had to be taller than the girl. We talked over the garden gate for ages but this relationship owing to his size was not going to continue. I knew Peter from Binstead School where I used to chase him around the playground just before I left. I did not know why I liked chasing him. I didn't catch him as I was not sure what to do if I did.

I was 14 years old when I experience my first kiss. I was with a friend Mary and we were having an awkward conversation with some boys from Kingarth School which was a private school set up in Binstead near the beach. The pupils were mostly foreign. I was first kissed by a Greek boy whose name was Dimetri Dimetrious. We were at the top of the muddy lane which led down to Binstead Beach.

'I'll kiss Jo, if my friend François can kiss Mary,' said Dimetri. A deal was struck and I was kissed. It was such a thrill!

We parted and I never saw him again. It was my first kiss but not for Mary who was obviously more experienced. She couldn't understand my joy.

'It was only a peck on the cheek. I don't know why you are making such a fuss,' she said.

She was a year younger. I felt like a late developer.

I learnt about relationships with men as I went along. I was shy. I would not go up to a boy and strike up a conversation. I might say 'Hello' but that was all. I learnt that if I wore black or dark coloured clothes I disappeared into the back ground at a dance. I started to wear brighter and lighter colours and I got asked to dance. It never occurred to me that the boys opposite were going through the same anxieties about asking a girl to dance.

I would rather walk home than ask a boy for a lift on his scooter. They had to ask me. That was the way life worked.

On our television set hired from Radio Rentals in Ryde I watch the pop programme called "Oh Boy". My affections turned quickly from the America actor Robert Horton to the pop singer Cliff Richard. I collected his records and cut out pictures of him to put on my bedroom wall. I adored him. This adoration lasted about four years. I made him a Valentine card which I got Mummy to put in the mail at the post office in Ryde. I heard nothing of course as he must have had thousands and being a Valentine I did not add my name.

I read in the New Musical Express which came out every Friday that he was going to do a tour with the Shadows and was coming to Portsmouth Guildhall. Mummy wouldn't let me go alone unless I had Carolyn with me. She didn't really want to go but I persuaded her to come with threats of 'I will make your life miserable if you don't.' I hadn't planned on how I would carry out this misery and I don't think she took it too seriously either.

Mummy bought the tickets for the first show starting at 5.30 in the evening. This finished in time for us to get a bus to the ferry to get home. The trip to Portsmouth started early in the afternoon so that we could be outside the stage door when the tour bus arrived. I was hoping to see him, Cliff Richard, the guy I was in love with. He didn't travel on the bus as he was obviously too famous and I never did discover how he got into the theatre without being seen. I raced around the building from the front entrance to the stage door. Carolyn chased after me.

'Mummy told me to keep an eye on you,' she gasped. 'Can't you slow down and stay in one place.'

'No I might miss him,' I shouted at her. 'Come on!'

The fans collected autographs of anyone who went in or out of the stage door. I often didn't know who they were but felt that they might be famous in the future.

I had made a rosette with a picture of Cliff in the middle and wore it on my coat. This had a paper frill around the edge and was made of crepe paper, card and glue. We sat in the fourth row from the front on the left hand side. I was in the aisle seat. He had sung two songs and was half way through his act when I took off my homemade rosette and rushed the stage. A large security man stopped me. I looked at Cliff and he beckoned me forward. I gave him my rosette. He took it touching my middle finger! He nodded his thanks as he was singing at the time. I turned and sat down again.

Carolyn was in tears with embarrassment! 'How could you do that?' she snarled. 'How could you embarrass me like that?' I took no notice and continued to scream with all the other girls in the theatre.

I dropped Cliff when the Beatles turned up. They were with the American singer, Chubby Checker and had come to Portsmouth Guildhall. Again we went early to try to get autographs and I was at the stage door when the tour bus arrived. Towards the back of the bus was Paul McCartney. He was my favourite and he was taking autograph books through the small window. I saw him sign my book and pass it to a tall man standing outside the bus who in turn passed it to me. I had Paul McCartney's autograph and I had seen him sign it! He had touched my book!

An officious looking man said that the Beatles would sign more autographs if we would like to give him the books and he would take them in. I was not going to be parted from my Paul

McCartney signature so I handed him an envelope. Just before the show was to start the stage door was opened and these books and my envelope were returned duly signed. I had all their autographs.

Not yet that famous, the "Beatles" were the second act to Chubby Checker who had come over for the tour from America. They finished the first half of the show. Carolyn was pleased that we were in the fourth row but in the middle hemmed in by other fans, so I couldn't escape and rush the stage.

As they grew more famous we discovered that the "Beatles" played at The Cavern Club in Liverpool. Photos of this appeared in the newspapers. The Cavern club was in a basement: the ceilings were low and made of bricks and were curved. A new club opened up in Ryde and although a great deal smaller had the same type of ceiling. This was called the Diamond Club and consisted of four interlocked small rooms. This was our "Cavern Club". We loved it. There was a bar which sold soft drinks and crisps in one corner of the first room from the entrance and on Saturday evenings a local band played in the opposite corner. The noise was excruciating. People stood motionless as dancing was impossible; there were far too many people packed in unable to move at all.

There was a toilet. Just the one. There was always a thin layer of water across the floor as there was a leak. It was barely used.

The club was in Church Lane opposite the Mead Tennis courts. The entrance was low down and everyone had to stoop as they stepped down into the club. No-one ever called this The Diamond Club: its members called it "The Hole." It had the right atmosphere.

Right from the start there was opposition to its existence. An elderly local councilor couldn't understand why the "young people" were not satisfied with the designated Youth Centre at the top of the town. This was a large cold hall with bright lights and lots of space. The 'Hole' was dark and had very little space. Owing to entrance it was secretive. Being a shy teenager it suited me. I wasn't in the light. I couldn't see the boy's facial expressions and they couldn't see mine.

'Are you coming?' said my friend Sarah one day during school lunch hour. 'I'm going down The 'Ole.'

'Yeah! You bet!' I replied. I didn't bother with my packed lunch. We ran down the High Street and went to "the Hole".

The local paper reported the councilor: 'This nickname, size of the venue and type of person who goes there does not give this a good reputation.'

The paper did not give any description of the "the type of person" he was referring to. I didn't consider myself any bad type of person. There was no alcohol but thinking back there must have been some drugs although I didn't see them or was offered any.

'Girls,' said Reverend Mother one morning at assembly, 'I wish to talk about The Diamond Club. It is not a place where you should go. If I find any girl going to the Diamond Club they will be expelled from this school!'

At lunch time that day "The 'Ole" was full of Convent girls dressed in brown and gold uniforms. No-one was caught or expelled. The club, fortunately for the Convent and the nuns, was closed soon after by the Council.

We were furious, when they had closed our club. Like the protest marches we had seen on the television, one was organised. The news spread by word of mouth and approximately 300 teenagers gathered at the pier and marched through the town shouting 'We want the 'Ole'. Apart from being reported in the County Press nothing further happened and we all found other venues to meet.

The next time the Beatles came to Portsmouth Guildhall they were incredibly famous and I could not get tickets at all.

With Carolyn we travelled up to London to see the New Musical Express awards show at the Wembley Arena. We took ciné film of this but they were so far away without sound you couldn't differentiate which group was playing.

"The Rolling Stones" for some reason or another came to the Ryde Pavillion. This grubby seaside theatre had a very small stage. They stayed at the Castle opposite the theatre. I went to the show with a friend, Sophia, who was a bit quieter than me and who certainly would not rush the stage. Before the show I was around the back with Sophia and a member of a supporting band was outside having a cigarette. It had a strange smell.

We got talking. He was a guitarist and singer of this other band in the show.

He offered me a roll up cigarette. 'Would you like one,' he said. I knew nothing about drugs but this roll up cigarette without a tip was not one I was used to. 'No thank you,' I said putting Convent nose high in the air. 'I don't smoke those.'

He didn't reply and continued to puff on his roll up with droopy eyelids. 'How could he be ready for the show if he was so tired?' I thought.

Whereas I could almost date when my teenage years began the finish is more blurred. Carolyn had gone to work in London and my plan was to join her. I was determined not to spend my life chasing boys at local dances on the Isle of Wight.

18 WHISPERS

I stood outside the kitchen door one day in October 1962 and heard Mummy and Carolyn talking quietly in whispers. Carolyn had had a letter from the college telling her that she was to attend a meeting about the possibility of there being a nuclear war and a bomb being dropped on England. I was 15 at the time and no letter was given to me at school.

'I don't really know what I am supposed to do if a bomb did drop,' Carolyn said, 'I mean where should we put a shelter in this house?'

'I don't know,' Mummy said, 'We will find out at the meeting I suppose. I got a letter at work. I am to go to one too.'

'Just how dangerous is it if a bomb fell on London?' Carolyn went on. 'We are a long way away. They are not likely to drop a bomb on the Isle of Wight are they?'

'Let's pray we don't ever find out and they all come to their senses in time to stop this.'

As I entered the room they stopped talking. I knew that there were problems between America and Russia. The Berlin Wall had been erected in August 1962 and in the paper I had seen a picture of an East German soldier jumping over barbed wire to escape from the East. I had read with horror how the East German guards had let a boy die. He had been shot and was stuck on the wire and they left him there.

Now on the television news I had seen ships containing armaments heading for Cuba, but I didn't understand its true significance.

Carolyn and Mummy were careful not to talk about the dangers in front of me and spoke a lot in whispers. Everyone seemed to be on edge and too frightened to talk about it. I overheard Mummy telling Carolyn, 'I think that the middle bedroom would be best place for the shelter.'

I knew about the atom bombs that were dropped on Japan and how that eventually stopped the Second World War, but I couldn't imagine the scale of devastation that this bomb would create. 'Would London be like Hiroshima? How long would we have to stay in that shelter Mummy?' I asked.

'Sweetheart I just don't know,' she replied. 'We have got to trust that President Kennedy will be able to talk to the Russian leader Mr. Khrushchev and stop this madness.'

'Why are they threatening us?' I asked.

'They are threatening the USA and we are friends with America. The Russians have put nuclear warheads aimed at America on Cuba. Cuba is an island close to America and they are sending more.'

'Why would they want to do that?'

'I don't know,' she answered honestly. 'I just don't know.'

Fortunately for everyone the ships turned around and went back towards Russia. An agreement was reached and the world it seemed breathed a sigh of relief.

President Kennedy was one of Mummy's heroes as he had averted this major disaster.

'Thank God for President Kennedy. Thank God he was able to be patient and take the right action. He has stopped what would have been World War III.'

News reports were never hidden from us but Mother explained them in simple terms. The truth was always told but in a gentle way.

It was with shock when we found Mummy crying in her chair in the sitting room. We had walked home from choir practice on Friday 22nd of November 1963.

'They have killed the President,' Mummy said through her tears as she watched the news unfold on the television.

'What are you talking about?' Carolyn asked.

'Someone has shot President Kennedy and he is dead.'

'Oh Mummy,' I said. 'That's awful, how sad.'

'He did such a lot of good. Why did they kill him?' Mummy went on.

Her cheeks were wet with tears. We joined her and sat silently listening to the news unfold.

'Did you have a good choir practice?' Mummy said trying to change the subject.

'Oh Mummy this is just dreadful,' I said. Carolyn went over and comforted here.

I didn't cry. I sat shocked that someone could do this. It was so upsetting that the event that had happened on the other side of the world had affected my mother so much. This was one of the times in my life when I realised that the world was bigger than the small area in which I lived.

I cried when I saw the picture in the newspaper of President Kennedy's three year old son standing and saluting his coffin at his funeral.

Although she shielded me from the prospect of a nuclear war Mother never shielded us from the horrors that had occurred. I was six when one morning at breakfast we were talking about how Jesus was born a Jew.

'Jews have been victimized throughout history,' Mummy explained. 'I mean that they have been hated for a long time.'

'In the last war Hitler the German leader didn't like Jews. He persecuted them so much that he organised a system where Jews from all over Europe were sent to concentration camps. There they were gassed and their bodies were burned.' Her voice was quiet.

My immediate thought was for our safety.

'He can't get us, can he?' I said 'We are not Jews, we go to church and we live on the Isle of Wight.'

'No darling you are right. Hitler is dead and the war is over'.

That had been enough for me to understand. Nothing more was said and we ate the rest of our breakfast in silence.

Mother cared for all people and was a great socialist at heart although she told me she always voted for the Conservative candidate at general elections. She was incensed at the injustice that occurred when the Titanic was sinking.

It was Mummy's birthday and we were eating lunch. 'I was born on the 23rd of March 1912 just a month before the Titanic sank.' she told us.

'Surely you don't remember it?' Carolyn joked.

'No, no! I was only a month old! My mother was very shocked over this and she told me that tragically there were not enough lifeboats and they were allocated to the rich people in the first class cabins. There were none left for those people who were travelling in steerage.'

'Steerage, what's steerage?' I asked thinking of the steering wheel in our car.

'Steerage means the cheaper sleeping areas down in the lower part of the ship,' she told us. 'The further down in the ship you have your sleeping arrangements, the less you pay for the journey.'

There was silence as she dished up more stew.

'Dreadful, it was just dreadful,' she continued. 'There should have been more lifeboats; enough for everybody. The poor were treated so badly!'

We had a newspaper every day. On the Saturday 16th of August 1952 when I was five I spotted a picture of half a house with a rag doll stuck on a beam. There was water running underneath. Mummy saw me looking at the picture.

'Why is that dolly stuck up there?' I asked her.

'Because a great flood washed away the house and the dolly got left behind,' she explained. 'I expect some little girl is missing that dolly, don't you think?'

'Why didn't she take it with her?' I asked innocently.

Mummy sat down and pulled me on to her knee. 'A lot of water made a small stream into a big river and it rushed through the town and knocked some houses down.'

'How big was the water?' I said trying to understand what was a lot of water. 'Was it big water like from our sea in Binstead?'

'No darling our sea is where it is meant to be. This water came from the rain in the hills around the town and it poured down into the river they already had and made it much bigger. The river was wider than the road outside. That little girl probably had to leave her dolly behind because she left with her mummy very quickly.'

We sat for a minute while I looked at all the sad pictures of Lynmouth. There were houses with the outside wall missing and all the decorations seen and some of the furniture left.

'All right my darling?' she asked. I got down from her lap. 'I'll go and get on in the kitchen.' I was fascinated and stayed there staring at these pictures.

It was February 1958, Carolyn was reading the paper and called out, 'There's been an air crash in Munich.' I was ten years old.

We all leant over the paper and Mummy read out. 'A BEA plane caught fire shortly after take-off yesterday afternoon. There were 38 passengers and six crew.'

She paused as she read on in silence. She gasped, 'Some footballers have been killed.'

We didn't follow any football team nor did we watch matches on the TV. Football to me was a game that boys played at break time.

'What was the name of the team?' I asked.

'Manchester United and the young players all aged around 24 were nicknamed the "Busby Babes". Oh how awful. They were so young.'

Mother cried for the Manchester United Team.

The television was still new to us and we watched everything. We were thrilled to see on the ITV News in June 1959 a news report from the Isle of Wight!

'A new revolutionary method of travel has been developed on the Isle of Wight. It is called a Hovercraft,' the television newsreader said. 'The SR-N1 was shown to the public and press. It is capable of carrying four men at a speed of 28 miles per hour. This was developed by Saunders–Roe on the Isle of Wight.' Carolyn and I were thrilled.

'Mum!! The Isle of Wight is at the top of the ITV news!' I shouted to Mum in the kitchen.

'Look Mum that must be Cowes,' Carolyn said. 'Is that the road near to the chain ferry?'

'Could quite well be,' Mum said.

'What is a Hovercraft?' I asked.

'Shut up! If you listen they will tell us,' Carolyn snapped.

I watched and saw this flat saucer shaped vessel with a round turret on top glide from the land and into the sea. When it hit the water there was a heavy spray which almost hid the craft.

'It rides on a cushion of air,' Carolyn informed me.

'Oh,' I replied not really understanding. I was more interested that Cowes Isle of Wight had made the top of the ITV News.

We made the television news again on the 20th May, 1961.

'Carolyn! Jo! Look at this, said Mum as she was going up to bed. 'There is a large fire. The sky is red over Ryde'.

Carolyn ran up the stairs and looked out of the dormer window on the landing. Above the trees the sky was red.

'It must be an enormous fire for us to see it from Binstead,' said Carolyn.

'That's funny, I didn't hear the fire siren go off.'

'No neither did I,' Carolyn remarked.

I got out of my comfy bed and went upstairs. 'What's all the fuss about?' I asked. Carolyn, Mummy and I stood looking at the red sky.

'Listen, there is another fire engine going down Binstead Hill.' Mum said.

We listened and heard the bell ringing as it raced through.

'The fire must be big if they have called for the Newport Fire Brigade as well. I wonder what it is?' Mum remarked.

We stood quietly. Nothing was happening.

'It must be a big building. Pack and Culliford is a big building. I wonder if I shall have a job working there tomorrow. A fire this size must have destroyed a lot.'

Bored looking at the trees in the dark with the red fire behind, I went back to bed.

'There is not a lot to look at is there?' Mum said. Carolyn and Mum followed soon after.

Mum took her usual bus to work the next morning. There was no school as it was Saturday.

'The bus turned the corner from Garfield Road into the High Street,' Mum told us later. 'My heart was in my mouth. Pack and Culliford was covered in black soot. As we got closer it became clear that it was the Theatre Royal nearby. My job was safe. The shop was still there.'

I cycled into Ryde and went to my friend, Liane's flat. Together we went up St. Thomas's Street to look at the damage. There was no wall on the Lind Street side.

'You should have seen it last night,' Liane told me. 'I had just gone to bed when Mum woke me up.'

'There's a big fire up the road,' she said. 'Get dressed, we'll go and have a look.' As soon as we walked out into St. Thomas's Street, we could see that it was the Theatre Royal. It was well ablaze. There were flames shooting high out of the building. We walked from our flat and up St. Thomas's Street. There were no barriers so we could get quite near to it. There were large pieces of burning material floating in the air.'

'I bet that was the material from the seats.' I suggested.

'The fire brigade were also spraying water on Pack and Culliford,' Liane went on. In case the shop also caught fire.

'Good job too,' I said. 'Otherwise our Mums would not have a job this morning.'

We turned to look at the ruin and walked closer.

'I wonder if that wall went down in one go,' Liane said.

Also missing was the wall that was behind the screen. We could see the whole of the inside of the building. There were no seats or decorations left. All had been burnt.

'Look!' said Liane, 'there are the three projectors on the top floor.' The fire had not taken the front of the building. The foyer and stairs to the different floors could be seen. Just then a man walked across the top floor.

'I hope the floor is solid and he doesn't fall,' I said.

'How sad the projectors look,' I said. 'There will be no more films shown from them.'

The television report included a film of the fire and they also showed a poster announcing the next week's features which was, "Too Hot to Handle" staring Jayne Mansfield.

In 1953 we had no television to watch for the Coronation. We listened to that on the radio but we watched Sir Winston Churchill's funeral on Saturday 30th of January, 1965.

'He was such a leader,' Mum said, 'when he said "We will fight them on the beaches we will fight them in the hedge rows, we will never surrender." I vowed I would do just that. We have a lot to thank him for.'

'Auntie Vonnie learnt how to shoot you know. She told me "If anyone threatened Roma my daughter or Bonnie my dog I would shoot them and kill them." England was alone. We had just seen our boys come home from Dunkirk having left all our equipment and guns behind. All the little ships went. Some came from the Isle of Wight and we rescued thousands of men who were stranded on the beach in France. England was on its own then; the whole of Europe was under Nazi occupation. Every day we were aware that the Nazis might invade but when Churchill spoke to the whole country, we listened and we were behind him.'

We watched the service and then the trip down the Thames on a barge.

'Look Mum. Look at the cranes, they are all bowing,' I said.

Mum was crying at this point and Carolyn and I were quiet.

---oOo---

When I had my family it was Mummy and I who would talk in whispers in her cottage in Wootton.

She used to get up very early to read her "Daily Word" booklet that was sent to her every month from America. After she had finished the page for that day, she used to sit quietly and doze.

I too am an early riser and came downstairs.

'Shall I make us a cup of tea?' I said to Mum.

'What a good idea. Yes please. Here take my cup I have already had one this morning.'

Quietly I went to the kitchen, desperately trying to be silent enough not to wake the children. I took an extra cup for myself and made tea for two in a tea pot. I returned with the two cups. The cottage was very small and we would gossip for ages, sometimes having to stifle laughter. We used to reminisce and then put the worlds to right. All said in whispers.

Mum was very old and in a nursing home when in New York, USA the Twin Towers were attacked in September 2001. Her mind was deteriorating and she spent most of her last days on this earth sleeping. This event had shocked the whole world and I longed to ring my Mum and chat but knew that was impossible. She died a month later.

19 THE COLLEGE AND LEAVING HOME

'Being a wife and mother is a very honourable calling!' Sister Regis said after having told me that I was not clever enough to have a career. 'Your only value is life is to be a good wife and mother. Find yourself a husband, get married, have children and bring them up well,' she continued.

Sister Regis gave me this advice just prior to my taking my 'O' levels. I loved children and the prospect of being a mother thrilled me. My mother was good at the job and I decided I would equally be so.

This statement made me worry about the forth-coming exams. 'They are expecting me to fail,' I thought.

'Mummy I don't think I am going to do very well in these exams!' I told her. 'I should be studying now and I can't. I don't know what to look at.'

Mother had the answer. 'Have an early night before each exam. You can't do any more now. You have worked well this past year. What will be will be.'

During that last year at school I had done everything I was told, but nothing more. However, owing to the constant nagging by the nuns I felt that I had not done enough.

'If you are tired when you sit the exam, you certainly won't do well! Have an early night. Get up refreshed and do your best. Don't worry about the future, you are still my Jo and I love you.' She kissed me and I went to bed.

The week of the exams passed very quickly. There were a few problems but on the whole I was able to complete each paper. I wrote absolute gibberish in my English essay,' I told Mum. 'I said that my life was planned out and that I couldn't change it. Mum, that was nonsense! I didn't believe it at all.'

'I am pretty sure that it's the English language they will be looking at darling,' Mother replied, 'not your beliefs.'

'I was able to write loads in the English Literature paper. The questions on "Northanger Abbey" were alright, and the "Twelfth Night" questions were fine. It was all about Sir Toby Belch. I liked him so there was lots to say. The only problem was the poetry. I wrote rubbish.'

During the practical cookery text in the Domestic Science exam, the examiner came over to me and asked, 'How much did you pay for meat?'

'Mum, I don't think I gave the right answer.'

'Why?'

'Because I told her I didn't know and that my Mummy bought it.'

The Art exam went without a hitch. There were three sections, still life, a view from a window and a pencil drawing of a plant. I knew the plant that we had to draw before the exam as my friend Sophia who had changed schools and was in Hazlemere did that part of the exam a day before us. She wrote and told me what is was. The postal system was very reliable so I was able to practise drawing a piece of ivy. I don't think it helped much.

The French exam was awful. I wasn't ready for that.

In August the exam results were sent to my home and addressed to Mum. I was working at the Wimpy bar in Ryde and Mummy came in. 'Well done, you have passed four out of the five you took.' I had done well!

Women's pay in the 1960s was less than the amount paid to men. I accepted this. There were certain jobs which were done by men and it never struck me that I should become a builder, engineer, carpenter, bus driver or a vicar. They were jobs for men. Women were home makers. We cooked, cleaned and brought up children. We were secretaries who worked for male bosses. We were shop girls who sold dresses to ladies. Men who sold suits to men received more pay. I never thought this unfair: it was just how it was. I would never have been a suffragette two generations before.

A place was found for me at the Isle of Wight Technical College. There were two basic courses for girls. You could either study house management which included cooking, or you could go and learn how to work in an office. There were four levels for the office work courses, Secretarial A and B and Commercial A and B. I was not the cream of the crop as I was in Secretarial B.

Any momentum I had gained during that last year in the Convent was lost. I had a lovely time at College. Mummy was making more money because there were no school fees and I got a free bus pass. I made new friends and my social life blossomed.

The place to be was the 69 club at the York Hotel in Ryde on a Saturday nights. I lied about my age to get in.

'How old are you?' said the lady selling membership.

Knowing I looked older than I was I said, 'I'm 17!' I felt that that wasn't too much of a fib, as I was 16 at the time.

The Island band called the Cherokees played all the Beatles songs just as well, or so we thought as the real ones. I bought a gin and orange and made it last all night. The dance finished after the last bus had left and I walked home from Ryde to Binstead. When I arrived at Leys Mother was always in bed.

'Did you have a good time?' she called out. 'Yes thanks, Mum.' I went into the kitchen and in the centre of the table was a glass of water, a tin of Andrews Liver Salts and a spoon. There was nothing else on the table at all.

'Thanks Mum,' I called out to let her know I had found it.

At College I couldn't get any pleasure out of Pitman's shorthand. It seemed that everyone else understood before me and I couldn't keep up.

The typing class room had specially designed typewriter desks lined up in rows similar to a typing pool we were told. When we arrived there were no typewriters to be seen. Each desk had a typewriter hidden in it under a large wooden top. This was lifted to reveal a machine set lower than the top of the desk.

In front of me was an Imperial Typewriter with a "QUERTY" keyboard.

After an explanation of how to load the paper Mrs. Gardener instructed us on how to find the home keys.

'Rest your fingers of these starting with your little fingers on the A and the semicolon.' she said, 'Hit each key hard with your fingers,' continued Mrs. Gardener.

We attempted to print out some letters. 'Keep your hands on the home keys. Your fingers work independently.' 'Use your right thumb to hit the space bar at the bottom.'

We practised typing a,s,d,f, space, semicolon, l,k,j, space" again and again.

'Keep your wrist high, with the same pressure hit each key individually,' Mrs. Gardener instructed.

'The silver bar on the left is to return the carriage to start the next line and moves the paper up. Use the first finger of your left hand.'

The blue, spiral bound typewriting text book stood on the desk supported by a treasury tag attached to the front cover and fitted to the back

'Look at the book!' Mrs. Gardener shouted above the noise 'Not keys girls!'

'Why do I have to look at the book,' I thought. 'I know what to type.'

Eventually the classroom was filled with the uniform and rhythmic sound of the tap, tap, tap of the keys.

We were taught how to set out a letter, reports and minutes of meetings.

We had other lessons all connected with being a good office worker. Book keeping was difficult for me as I had been thrown out of Maths at the Convent in the second year when I was 12. This left me with a fear of numbers.

Mr. Gloster taught us French. I had failed my 'O' level in French at school and I was desperate to pass it. Mrs. Felgate at the Convent was an excellent teacher. She gave out praise. I asked Mummy if I could take extra lessons with her. She agreed and I travelled to her house in Seaview. I decided to take two exams under different educational boards. One was to be taken at the Convent and the other at the College.

However at the beginning of May of the final term at the College Mr. Gloster announced to the class who would go on to take the French 'O' level. The names were read out and mine was not there.

'Why is my name not there Mr. Gloster?' I piped up without putting my hand up to speak.

'Because you are not good enough,' he replied.

'But I am having extra lessons from Mrs. Felgate.'

'No you are not good enough,' he repeated.

'Well!' I said, 'I'm going to see Mr. Cargeige about this.' He was the head of the Secretarial and Commercial courses.

I stood up scraping my chair on the floor. My friend Mandy gasped loudly. The rest of the class were silent and all looking at me. I marched smartly to the door and left the classroom, shutting the door behind me. I walked across the corridor and knocked on his Mr. Cargeige's door.

'Come in,' he said.

Without waiting for him to speak I said, 'Mr. Gloster won't let me take 'O' level French, and I am having extra lessons from Mrs Felgate. I want to take this exam.' I was so angry that I spoke loudly and forcefully.

He didn't argue. 'OK Miss Drawbridge,' he said quietly, 'I'll make a note of that. Now would you return to the classroom please?' I quietly went back to the class with a successful smile on my face.

I passed my French 'O' level at the College, but failed the exam I retook at the Convent. It was a low pass but that didn't matter I had five 'O' levels that I could put down on any application form for a job.

My typing speed was quite slow, and my shorthand was passed at the basic level.

During lunch one day a fellow student Gloria told me that she had been an au pair in France.

'I used to look after two children and go to school and improve my French,' she said.

That appealed to me. I could look after children which was what I really wanted to do. I truly didn't want to sit in an office and type.

After discussing this with Mother, we agreed that I would go to London where my sister was and look into this at a later date.

I continued with my all important social life going to 69 club every Saturday at the York. One night I got a lift home with Robbie on the back of his scooter.

There were two groups of teenagers in the 1960s. There were the "Mods" who rode scooters and wore American style Parkers. These baggy coats were similar to those worn by American Service Men. The girls based their fashion on the Mary Quant style. She had a shop called Bazaar in the Kings Road. Girls dressed like their mothers in the 1950s. Mary Quant taught us to dress differently. We dressed in shift dresses, some were pinafore style with which we wore a blouse done up at the neck with a ribbon tied into neat bow. Girls had asymmetrical hair styles short at the back and longer at the sides. I was a Mod and so was Robbie.

The "Rockers" wore tight Levi jeans and leather jackets. Mandy my friend from College was a "Rocker".

'How do you get your jeans so tight fitting?' I asked her. 'Do you buy them that tight?'

'No,' she said. 'I bought the jeans and then I filled the bath with hot water and sat in it until they had shrunk to my size. Then I hung them out to dry. There was a problem with that though.'

'Oh what's that?'

'It's getting them on. I peeled them off when they were wet and as they dried they shrunk a bit more. I struggled as I pulled them up my legs, one at a time, then I had to lie down on the floor to do up the zip. My jeans were so tight I had to get a coat hanger, hook it into the zip and pull with both hands.'

'Aren't they uncomfortable?'

'Yeah a bit to start with, but they feel great. They soften the more I wear them.'

In my Mod outfit of a shift dress I rode on the back of my Mod friend Robbie's Lambretta. He dropped me off at the top of Binstead Hill, kissed me goodnight, and then drove off down the hill on his way back to St. Helens. I heard a bang as I walked down Church Road. When I arrived home I found Mummy standing at an open window. 'I'm so glad to see you, there's been a crash!' she said.

The next day I discovered through a friend that the crash had involved my "lift". Robbie and his Lambretta had been hit by a car and he was in hospital.

Isle of Wight College Commercial section photo take July, 1965. The author is standing in the middle of the back row.

I went to see him in Ryde Hospital where he was lying flat on his back. He had concussion. Helmets were not worn then; they were not fashionable. This started a relationship. I would travel to St. Helens on the bus to go and see him. His scooter had been written off so there was no lift home for me. It was buses all the way.

This relationship lasted for four months, until I found Mummy crying one day.

'Robbie is not right for you darling!' she said. 'You are too strong for him, you would make each other unhappy. You have made plans to go to London. Finish it'.

I knew she was right. I wasn't in love with him but he was a Mod and so was I. He didn't have a scooter any more but mixed with those who did. So I finished with him without a further thought. He was devastated and he repeatedly called at the house and cried on Mummy's shoulder. She eventually persuaded him that I was not the girl for him and after a loud altercation between Robbie and me, he left my life.

I finished at the Isle of Wight College in July, 1966. Just as I was all set to go to London I met Simon at a dance at the Manor House in Lake. He was tall and in the army Signal Corps. He had a car! It belonged to his father but it meant that I had got transport home. His father was the manager of the Wimpy Bar where I had worked as a waitress. This was one of the first fast food restaurants. A wimpy cost 3/- (three shillings) and a coffee was 6d (six pence). I was taught how to carry more than two plates. I got a bit ambitious with this new skill and managed to pile on 11 plates of "Wimpys" on my arms. As I started off I dropped the lot.

I had left being a Wimpy waitress when I fell hook line and sinker for Simon. He wasn't the most good looking but he was mature and confident. We dated for the rest of his leave and then he returned to Germany. His next planned army leave was in January 1966. I was so in love that I dreaded the long six month wait until I was to see him again.

I left the Island and went to work in Bedford Square at the London Masters Building Association until I could arrange to be an au pair in France. My salary was a £9.19s.6d a week paid weekly and handed to me in a little brown paper envelope. Out of that I paid for my place in the YWCA Youth Hostel, my lunches and my trips back to the island. A ticket from Waterloo to Ryde was 42 shillings (£2.2s.0d) return. That translates into a mere £2.10p in today's money.

I started that job in August 1965 and left it in November to go to Paris.

20 SAD DAYS

Christmas 1966 was a normal celebration. Carolyn and I returned home from London and Daddy was home having just finished a job. We went to Midnight Mass, we opened presents in the morning and ate Christmas dinner which was as delicious as always. In the afternoon we opened Christmas tree presents which Mummy had organised and watched a film on TV together. We watched John Betjeman's film about the Holy Land at 6.15 then at 8.55 as we tucked into cheese and biscuits with our drinks we watched a film with Doris Day and Frank Sinatra called "Young at Heart".

'I wish they could have shown a Fred Astaire and Ginger Rogers film,' Mum said. 'I just loved the dancing.'

On Boxing Day we ate leftovers capon, ham and sausages with potato salad and tomatoes for dinner. There was some bread sauce left which was shared out equally.

'I think I like cold bread sauce better than when it is hot!' Carolyn announced.

Charles Bryan Drawbridge my Father sitting on Brading Down with Willie Pickle in 1956.

We had not finished the Christmas pudding the day before so Mother cut this into four equal slices, covered them with brandy and set alight again. She made fresh custard.

Daddy took a week off before going back to work on the Sunday 1st January. Carrying his suitcase in one hand and his heavy tool case in the other he walked up the road. Mother waved him goodbye at the gate.

'He forgot to turn around and wave again at the bend in the road,' she said quietly.

'He just forgot, that's all,' Carolyn replied.

I was in the common room of YWCA Hostel in Acton West London on Saturday morning the 7th January 1967. I was working on a black dress I was making for a party at Carolyn's flat.

'Jocelyn Drawbridge! Jocelyn Drawbridge!' Elizabeth called out over the balcony near the public phones. 'There is a phone call for you.'

I went to the phone. It was Carolyn. 'I have had a phone call from Mummy and she wants us to go home!' she said.

'Why?' I replied.

'Because Mummy said so.'

'Why?'

'Because Mummy wants us to.'

'Why?' I repeated

'Mummy told me not to tell you!'

'That is ridiculous! Why?'

There was silence and a pause 'Daddy's ill,' she said.

Daddy with his cine camera taken in the garden of 11 Church Road during the summer of 1966.

'I'll go and pack.'

'Come here first and we will travel together.' Carolyn instructed.

I rushed to my room and got my suitcase out and started packing. Elizabeth came into my room, 'What's the matter?'

'My Dad is ill!' I said and then the reality hit me. 'Oh God don't let him die before I get there,' I sobbed.

As soon as I got to Carolyn's flat she told me the truth.

'Daddy has already died.'

I was shocked and strangely didn't cry.

'What have we got to do?'

'We are going home to be with Mummy. She has things to sort out and we have to help.'

We sat silently on the train from Waterloo. We had a giggle when I returned from the loo and announced. 'The toilet is all sloppy, there's water in the bottom.' We looked at each other and felt guilty that we were laughing when Daddy had just died.

We were happy to see Auntie Ruth at the end of the pier.

'I thought you would like a lift home,' she said.

The following day it was arranged that I would spend the day with Auntie Ruth and Carolyn would go with Mummy up to Amersham, where Daddy had died.

'Because he died away from home I have to formally identify his body,' Mum said.

'Will I have to look at the body?' Carolyn asked.

'No, no not if you don't want to.'

Auntie Ruth dropped Mummy and Carolyn at the pier head and took me to her house in Wootton. I was still and quiet. I didn't want to talk. Ruth's friend Basil was there too and I just sat still and watched the television.

'There's a Cary Grant film this afternoon. Would you like to watch that?'

'Yes thank you, that would be nice.'

'It's called "I was an American War Bride".'

'Thank you,' I said.

I got gripped by the film. I loved Cary Grant and in this film he was playing a French man who had married an American service woman. He was involved in a lot of misunderstandings, but in the end he managed to get on the ship chartered for war brides dressed in women's clothes and wearing wig made of the tail of a horse.'

When the film finished I sobbed silently.

Auntie Ruth collected Mummy and Carolyn from the pier and drove us all home. I felt better once the three of us were together.

'There has to be a post mortem to determine the cause of death.' Mum explained. 'They think it must have been a massive heart attack. He didn't suffer. He just fell asleep and didn't wake up again. There was no pain on his face when I kissed him. He was just so cold.'

'The policeman who took me in was so nice,' she told me. 'When I asked if I could kiss him he said I could and politely turned away.'

My tears started to fall again. 'Darling he's not there, his body is just a shell. The bit that was Daddy, the Daddy we loved, has gone to heaven.'

The funeral was fixed for the following Friday. 'They don't expect any problems with the post mortem and have allowed us to book the church and crematorium,' Mum explained. 'The funeral director will arrange for the coffin to be brought to the church where it will be in the chancel ready for the service.'

Mum said, 'We will have to work out what we will give our guests after the service.' I had never been to a funeral before. I didn't know what happened at all.

'I know let's make another Christmas cake, without the icing of course as I don't think that would be appropriate. But your recipe Jo, the one you got from school, is so delicious I'm sure everyone will like it.' The three of us focused on getting the ingredients and putting this cake together. It took our minds away from just being sad.

We went to the church on the Thursday evening to receive the coffin. I held on to Mummy's hand and squeezed so tightly.

On the day of the funeral I discovered that unbeknown to me, Mum had been to the doctor and got a bottle of medicine to help us through the service. 'I don't want that!' I objected. I was overruled and was given a spoonful of this foul tasting liquid.

The funeral service went well and then we followed the hearse to the new crematorium at the bottom of Lushington Hill.

As the coffin disappeared Mummy whispered to me again. 'Remember he is not there. The bit that was Daddy is in heaven.'

We returned to the house for tea and all the guests took a slice of my cake and liked it.

Daddy's sister, her husband and daddy's brother came to the funeral.

'Thank you Betty,' said Daddy's sister, 'thank you for making him happy. He loved you so dearly.'

Mummy's cousin, Clare Woodward, came and was a great support. She stayed on after the funeral.

'Now girls,' Mum said the day after, 'we brought you up to be independent. You must go back to London. I do not need any looking after.'

'But won't you be lonely?' I asked.

'No not at all! Well I shall miss you but Daddy would not want you to mooch around on the Island looking after me when I don't need looking after. Clare is staying with me for a week. You are your father's daughters and you must do what he did. Be independent. Despite his deafness that is what he did. You must get on with your lives and look after yourselves.'

Determined to be the person Dad and Mum would be proud of I did just that. We continued to work and live in London.

Carolyn and I travelled back on Sunday night as usual. "Songs of Praise" was on the television when we left. Mummy and Clare waved to us at the gate and we turned around to at the bend in the road. 'Bye,' we called out, 'see you at the weekend.' We walked up to the bus. Everything was normal.

Carolyn and I often came down to the Island for weekend breaks and brought her presents. Once I had found a serving dish that matched her set.

'You don't have to buy me presents,' Mum said 'but I do think it is lovely. It's just lovely.' She was smiling; I liked that.

---oOo---

My sister Carolyn was buried in the St. Edmund's churchyard as it had been her wish. As her coffin was lowered into the filthy yellow clay, I remembered Mum's words. 'Carolyn is not there, the bit that was Carolyn has gone to heaven.'

It was March 2009, I had just gone to bed when the phone rang. It was Clare-Louise my niece, Carolyn's and David's daughter.

'This is not to worry you but Mum is in St. Mary's. She has pancreatitis,' she said.

'What on earth is that?' I asked.

'An inflammation of the pancreas which lies next to the gall bladder and she has gall stones. One of these has logged itself at the exit and caused the problem.'

'Oh my goodness, what does it mean?' I asked.

'It's not fatal,' Clare reassured me, 'but the pain is so bad that they have put her into an induced coma and she is now in the Intensive care ward.'

'I must come and see her,' I said.

'No rush, she is unconscious at the moment. She won't know you are there.'

'OK I'll come at the first opportunity.'

That was the Sunday before Easter. As we travelled down on the Wednesday I thought of nothing else but my sister, my friend and confidante. We had grown out of rowing like we did when we were children and had become closer especially after Mummy had died. We went straight to St. Mary's Hospital.

Carolyn Mary Bennison, my sister taken at the stable door of the cottage in 2008.

After speaking on an intercom at the side of the door marked Intensive Care, I entered a corridor and was ushered to the waiting room. Clare Louise explained the procedure of going in to see her. I was given a plastic apron to wear and a nurse came and instructed us when we could go in.

Carolyn looked totally lifeless lying back in a semi recumbent position. There were tubes connected to her everywhere and monitors which were regularly checked by the nurses.

'It is so difficult,' I said to Clare. 'I don't know what to do or say.'

'I was told that she may be able to hear us.'

'I don't know what to say.' At that point Clare and I cuddled, both of us crying.

On the journey back to London I told Robert of my shock at seeing her. 'She didn't look anything like they do on the television soaps. All her muscles were relaxed and had no shape at all.'

During the following weeks Clare rang me with updates. 'I'm afraid there is nothing to report. Everything is much the same.'

'She has not got any worse then?' I said optimistically.

'No everything is the same and yes we need to be positive.'

Easter came and went and we spent the break in our flat in the Strand that we had bought for holidays and weekends on the Isle of Wight.

We returned to London and the telephone updates continued.

My birthday was highlighted when I was given a book that Carolyn had chosen before she became ill.

'It was one of the last things she did,' Clare assured me as I was given the present. Later that week Clare phoned the good news. 'They are going to remove some of the life support hoping to bring her round.'

She didn't respond. 'They are sending her for a scan as she is not reacting as she should,' Clare said in her latest bulletin to me.

With that news I relaxed and was deeply asleep when the phone rang at 11 o'clock. 'So sorry Auntie Jo,' Clare said, 'the scan has revealed that Mum has had a stroke.'

I was silent.

'The stroke has occurred in the central cortex of the brain and she is unlikely to regain consciousness.'

I found making any comment difficult. There were no positive pleasantries I could make to ease the situation. My sister was dying.

Early next morning, we packed up and went directly to the flat on the Island. Clare was strong and was able to hold everything together. When it was decided that she should be allowed to pass away Clare took everything in hand. The Archdeacon of the Isle of Wight gave Carolyn the last rites.

'The service was surprisingly peaceful and reassuring,' David, her husband said.

It was decided that the following day the doctors were to remove the life support.

We were at the flat, David, Clare her sister Katie, Mandy, my daughter, Robert and I were altogether when Clare broke down. 'I don't want her to be alone,' she sobbed.

'I'll be with you,' my daughter, Mandy, said.

'She will be lonely in that cold horrid room.'

Mandy and Clare cuddled each other. 'I'll be with you, don't worry, I'll be there.'

Robert and I were to remain with David and Katie to cook a meal at the flat, while the cousins Clare and Mandy left for the hospital. 'Try and keep everything as normal as possible for Katie and Pa,' Clare instructed me.

At the hospital Clare and Mandy sat with Carolyn while they removed each of the tubes. They chatted to her and sang hymns.

'She took about 20 minutes to die,' Mandy told me afterwards. 'Her breathing got shallower and shallower and then it just stopped.'

'She's gone,' said the nurse. They kissed her and left the room. They returned to the flat and we ate supper. We were all very quiet.

'This is lovely Auntie Jo,' said Clare, 'This pork roast is one of Mum's favourites.'

'Yes I know. I'm sure she is with us now.'

The funeral took place on Friday 8th May, 2009 at St. Edmund's Church, Wootton where Robert and I had married in 1969. This tiny Norman Church which dated back to the 12th Century, and one of two Anglican churches in Wootton was packed. Carolyn was Church Warden to both St. Edmund's and the other church, St. Mark's.

Carolyn and David had decided a while ago that she would like a Requiem Mass. Apart from the locals there was a minibus full of friends from Holy Cross Greenford church where she had been church warden too.

I was surprised and amazed at the enormity of her popularity. People go to funerals out of loyalties or to support surviving relatives. All those people had come for my sister Carolyn.

Clare stood up and read her eulogy. She started with the phrase, 'What have I lost?'

It made me question what I had lost. I was the last of that family of four who had such fun and adventures when we were young.

There was a reception for the entire congregation at St. Mark's. Mandy had covered a display board with pictures of Carolyn's life. I was greeted with hugs and kisses from lots of people some of whom I didn't know. I was surprised when a young man came up to me, put his arms around me and squeezed me tight. I was expecting him to say something about Carolyn instead he said. 'I'm glad I have caught up with you.' He stopped squeezing me and I stood back and looked at him. 'Jo you changed my life!' I recognised him as Neil who was son of Clare's landlady in Acton.

'I did what?' I said.

'Do you remember giving me a talking to when I was about to fail my ASA Teachers Exam through laziness.'

'Yes I do!' I said, 'you had not completed your Log Book and it was needed for you to complete the course.'

'You gave me a second chance,' he went on. 'I stayed up all night, finished the lesson plans and questions and never looked back. I would never have got as far as I have without that telling off.'

'What are you doing now?' I asked.

'I'm working in Eastern Europe as the director of a group of Health Clubs in Poland.'

'Compliments come in strange forms,' I thought. Carolyn in one of our last phone chats had said 'I'm really proud of you Jo, you have done so well in your studies and work.'

'Don't be daft,' I replied. 'You have done well also.'

We all managed to hold it together. After the guests had gone we retired to the cottage, sat and had a cup of tea. Millie then aged six, Mandy's daughter and Carolyn's great niece, was drawing. She drew a picture of a rainbow using every colour in the box. She then started to write. 'How do you spell Auntie Carolyn?' Katie answered her and helped her, stating each letter slowly enough so she could write them.

'How do you spell 'gone'?' the room fell silent as we looked towards Millie and her drawing.

'How do you spell 'heaven'?' Katie spelt the next word.

'There!' she said and handed her the picture of the rainbow on which Katie read out 'Today Auntie Carolyn has gone to heaven.'

'Can I have another chocolate biscuit please?' said Millie and she took one and stuffed it in her mouth.

The group were reduced to silent tears.

Carolyn and I were so different, and yet we were the same. We both had determination to see projects through to the end. We both worked hard when we had found what interested us. She was a successful Church Warden and ran Holy Cross Church in Greenford with a rod of iron. She took those skills of being Church Warden to the two Anglican churches in Wootton Bridge when she and David retired to the Isle of Wight.

When we were young, we played together well but the next moment we rowed like cat and dog. We stopped these silly squabbles once we had left home and didn't live together.

She was outspoken. She didn't hold back saying what she thought. Not long after the funeral I met Sue at the Health Club after an Aquafit session. We spoke about her saying just what she thought. She told me of an incident at church, 'Holy Cross Greenford used to put on a pantomime every year. Carolyn's job was the prompt. One rehearsal had not gone very well. Carolyn had her work cut out for her that day. I was playing the Fairy Godmother in Cinderella. Carolyn had to keep reminding us all of our lines.

The director was Tom and he was not happy. 'We haven't got that many rehearsals left before we open, he said tactfully. 'We will meet again on Thursday and hope it goes better.'

Sue continued telling me the story. 'Carolyn poked her head out from around the curtain and shouted at the group. 'And you will know all your lines by Thursday!'

'Oh Sue,' I said 'how rude. What did you all do?'

'We learnt our lines by Thursday.'

She was bossy and so can I be in certain circumstances.

As children we both loved the sea and in the summer we spent hours in the water. We picked each other up marvelling at the weightlessness. We "danced" in the sea, we sat on the bottom, we floated and wallowed chatting all the time.

In sunny weather we played in the garden. Tennis was a favourite; we used our imagination to create stories which we would act out.

We cycled together, played in the garden and the woods.

'What had I lost?' I thought, 'I had lost the last of my family and my friend.'

21 ROBERT

'Oh by the way Jo,' Susan called from the other end of the corridor between the bedrooms, 'you are not going up with Bob. You are coming up with us instead. He is driving up with his friend from the Section house and his girlfriend.'

'Oh thanks,' I said somewhat disappointed. Bob had asked me out to go to the Hovel.

The Hovel was a Methodist run disco in King's Cross which ran every Friday night. I lived in the YWCA in Acton and needed a lift to get there.

I sat dejected on the bed. 'I can't be bothered.' I thought, 'I won't go.' I pondered for a while. It was Friday night and I was doing nothing that evening. The rest of the girls were going so I decided. 'I'll go!'

I had met Bob at the Youth Hostel when he had called with his mate. They were both policeman from the local police station in Acton. They had obviously called with some pretence knowing that the whole building was full of unattached girls. The following day I was playing tennis in the park opposite when he walked by and called us.

Robert and the author on Beachy Head during the summer of 1968

'There's thingy and whatsit,' I said to Lynda my Canadian friend. We walked over and spoke to them.

'Would you like to come to the Hovel next Friday night?' he asked me

'Yes, I'd love to,' I replied.

'I'll pick you up at 7.00 from the hostel.'

On Friday I was sure he had asked me out on a date and now I was going up with the others.

I did not change my clothes. I was wearing my crimson crepe blouse with a short plaid skirt. 'That'll do,' I thought. 'Bob is obviously not interested so I don't really care.' I was upset and insulted. My hair needed a wash and I could have done with a bath. I didn't do either. I repaired my makeup went downstairs and piled in the car with the others. They didn't seem to notice my disappointment at all.

The dance was busy. The hall was packed. I bought a drink. Being a Methodist run dance there was no alcohol. I sat with the others and watched the dancing.

Bob approached me and said, 'Would you like to dance?'

'No thank you,' I said immediately and I turned away. 'Blooming cheek!' I thought, 'He has insulted me and now he is expecting me to dance with him.'

The music stopped and he approached me again. 'Go on, please come and have a dance.'

I thought for a minute and as no one else was asking me I casually replied, 'Well alright then.'

The record was "Delilah" sung by Tom Jones. This fast piece invited us to move around the floor like a Viennese Waltz.

We spun around and around. I laughed and that was it. I stayed dancing with him all night.

He was hot and getting hotter as his turquoise blue shirt with a white collar changed to a darker colour with his sweat. I didn't like the shirt and his shoes were a bit old fashioned but he did make me smile.

We went home together in his car, parked up and talked until the early hours. We were totally at ease in each other's company. I had a late key that night which allowed me to let myself in after the deadline of 11.00 pm.

'Would you like to meet up tomorrow night?' he asked.

'Don't you mean today. It is three o'clock in the morning.'

He laughed. 'I am swimming backstroke for the youth club at 6.30 in Isleworth Baths and after that we can go to a Stock Car Racing meet in Wimbledon. Is that alright with you?'

'Yep sounds good.' I hadn't a clue what Stock Car Racing was but thought it was worth it to go out with him again.

'I'll pick you up at 5.00.'

He was very prompt and he took me to Isleworth Baths and directed me to the gallery of the pool to watch the race. Bob came in last. That finished, we drove in his Morris Countryman to Wimbledon.

There is a distinct smell that goes with Stock Car Racing which I noticed. As we approached the turn-stile the aroma hit me.

I sniffed the air and made a face.

'That's the smell of burning rubber from the tyres and hot oil. Lovely isn't it?' he enthused.

'Yes I suppose so,' I lied.

I was totally inappropriately dressed for the evening, wearing a skirt, blouse, high heeled shoes and a coat.

The cars lined up on the track, the flag was waved and off they went around the stadium. I did not understand what I was looking at.

Half way through the race I asked 'Who's winning?'

'He is.' Bob said pointing to a car. I was none the wiser.

'Which one?'

'Number 306, George Polly! Look there he goes!'

I was still none the wiser.

'Look he is driving the purple Hot Rod in the body of a Ford Anglia.'

I stared at this car. Robert kept his eye on the race.

'But they are going round and round. How do you know who is in the lead?'

'Because he is at the front,' still staring at the race Robert was getting exasperated.

'But that car is in front of him.'

'Yes but he is last!'

I did not understand at all but I was with Bob and I enjoyed his company. As I didn't have a late key that night I had to be back indoors before 11.00. We raced back to the hostel and agreed he would pick me up for a quiet drink on Sunday evening.

We went out every night after that. When he was late "turn", from 2.00 pm to 10.00 pm, I met him after work at 10.00 pm. When he was on night duty I met him early before he went to work at 10.00 pm and when he was on early turn we went to the pictures. The local cinema let Policemen in free. After the film had finished we went to the local fish and chip shop and got a free portion of chips.

'I went out with Bob last night. We went to a show and then had a meal,' I told my friends at breakfast.

In the summer of 1968 whilst living at the hostel I stupidly said one meal time. 'Oh how I long to get out of this hostel and share a flat with someone.'

My big mouth had finally got me into trouble. I didn't really want to leave but I couldn't go back on what I had said. I agreed to leave the hostel and join a group of girls in a flat. This was an expensive venture. The two bedroomed fully furnished flat was situated on the A4 and not convenient at all for me to get to work.

After about five weeks Bob was changing at the flat ready for work. He was doing his tie up in front of the mirror when he said, 'Do you want to marry me?'

This was it! I should be hearing bells and violins.

I gulped and said, 'Yes.'

He finished doing up his tie and said nothing.

'Hang on a minute,' I piped up, 'Do you want to marry me?'

'I haven't made up my mind yet!' was his reply.

He kissed me goodbye and went to work. He had another girl friend at the time. He obviously had not seen her for a while but she was there in the background. I made the biggest gamble I have made in my life and told him.

'It's either her or me,' I said. 'You must finish with her or I will finish with you.'

He wrote her a letter and broke off their relationship. We did not mention it again.

Six weeks after we had met was my 21st Birthday. Mother had planned a family party for me at her cottage on the Isle of Wight. Bob was unable to come as he was working on the Saturday but was able to come on the Sunday.

He arrived early at the house and I opened the door.

'You didn't bring me a present! It is my birthday and you are my boyfriend.'

'I wanted to get you an engagement ring,' he said.

'Don't be ridiculous. Everyone will laugh. I have only known you for six weeks.'

We agreed to get engaged at Christmas, planning to marry on the 17th May 1969. I was now embarking on my career as a wife and mother. I vowed I would be a good one.

We were engaged. Mum's friend Ruth, who had been so helpful and kind when Daddy died two years previously, invited Robert and me to come and have coffee with her. This was an uncomfortable experience. She grilled Robert.

During their next meeting Ruth announced to Mum, 'I don't think Jo has chosen well. He is not good enough for her! She can do better.'

Mother saw red! She mustered all the politeness she could. 'He is a very nice young man. He has a good career in the police force and they have a flat to live in.'

Ruth was dumbfounded; Mother had never answered her back.

'But they have no money put by!'

'Jo is still working and he has a good wage. I fail to see what it had to do with you.'

Mother left the lunch early. A few days later Ruth came to apologise and left a little turquoise broach as a gift to me.

I knew nothing of the row until I received the gift.

The wedding was to be simple and without fuss. I chose a Simplicity paper pattern to make my own wedding dress and those of bridesmaids. I planned to have three: Bob's sisters Christine and Elaine and my friend, Mandy's daughter, Angela, who was just three years old.

In the absence of my late father, I asked Mum to ask my godfather Uncle Percy to give me away. This he agreed to happily.

'It would be an honour to represent Bryan,' he said. During the cup of tea that followed he requested that his two granddaughters, Samantha and Alexandra could also be bridesmaids.

'I'm sure that will be O.K.', Mum replied on my behalf. 'Their mother was my bridesmaid in 1943.'

I now had five bridesmaids. I chose a white satin striped cotton for my dress and a turquoise blue for the bridesmaids from John Lewis in Oxford Street. The total cost of the material, paper patterns, zips and thread was £30.7s 6d.

Sitting at my sewing machine at the hostel I made my dress, and three dresses of the bridesmaids. My cousin, Elizabeth, made the dresses for her daughters Samantha and Alexandra.

Mum found a headdress and veil from Pack and Cullifords. I wore this in the way Princess Margaret wore hers, at the back behind the bun on top of her head. Mum arranged for the reception to take place at the Sloop Inn in Wootton, conveniently close to the cottage. The reception buffet came from a local caterers and cost four shilling and nine pence a head.

We travelled down to the Island and met the vicar. I had only been in the church a couple of times when I went to a service with Mum. Robert had not. We walked in and looked around.

'It's Norman,' said a voice behind me. 'Good afternoon, I'm Reverend Rayner.'

We introduced ourselves and continued to walk down the aisle of this tiny church between the fixed pews either side. It seemed to me that the chancel was as long as the aisle. There was a side chapel in an extension on the left.

'The door way you have just walked through is Norman and dates from when the church was built in the 11th century,' he continued 'The area in which you are standing is the original and once had a dirt floor, the chancel and the chantry chapel on the left dates from the 13th Century.'

I tried to appear interested as we looked around, but my thoughts were on marrying Robert not on the building.

We sat in the front pew of the church under the pulpit. The Reverend Rayner sat opposite. I had been a member of Holy Cross Church Choir and knew the wedding service inside out. Bob did not.

I can remember little of Reverend Rayner's long sermon type talk except being angry at his repeated insistence that we understood and respected the sanctity of marriage. 'That was what I planned to do,' I thought. 'He obviously doesn't know me at all.'

'What hymns would you like?' he asked us.

'Praise my soul the King of Heaven,' I said quickly. 'It is my mother favourite and she had it at her wedding in 1943.'

'And the second one?' he asked

We both paused as we hadn't discussed that at all.

'It's Whitsun!' the rector jumped in. 'You should choose one that is appropriate for this time of year.'

We were confused. 'Yes OK,' I said

'Yes that would be OK,' Robert joined in.

I cannot recall what that hymn was, but I can remember that it was not popular as the volume of singing from our friends in the congregation decreased as they struggled through the verses, not knowing it at all.

Bob's relations from Kent came down in a hired coach which dropped them off in Southsea where they took the new-fangled Hovercraft to the Island. This was the first time they had been on such a machine. A further coach took them to the church.

Other items on the shopping list of getting married were the cars and the photographer. The cars were chosen for their price, just five pounds. They were old London taxis. Mum paid for the photographer and we bought the prints.

My wedding was not all about the day I got married. It was about the life I was to lead as Robert's wife.

Money was short for us. We had borrowed £200 from the bank and this helped us furnish our allocated police flat but there was none left for a honeymoon. We stayed on the Island.

Just married Mr. & Mrs. Cooper posed in front of the Norman door of St. Edmunds Church Wootton.

We had a list of wedding gifts and received a lovely collection of household items. Everything given was used: nothing was wasted. We had had nothing to start with.

Our flat was furnished with second-hand items; a carpet, a three piece suite, a year old Cannon gas cooker with a foldaway grill and a very old second hand small fridge. My mother-in-law gave us a drop leaf table which I put in the kitchen. Much to her irritation I covered this with bright blue sticky backed Fablon. With the £200 we bought a red circular dining table and four chairs, a pine Welsh style dresser and a bed.

'Get a good bed,' Mother said to me when we were alone. 'It will have a lot of use.' I giggled and covered my face with embarrassment. I don't think mother realised the double entendre she had made.

We started our married life together in our police flat in Pitshanger Lane in Ealing and travelled down to the Island to see Mum in Wootton whenever Bob had a weekend free.

Robert drove a Morris Countryman car. His policeman's wage only allowed him to buy this cheap car. It constantly broke down but he had a friend in the business. Geoff was a mechanic who worked in Acton. Together they took this Countryman to bits, repaired it and put it back together again. However, unfortunately there was always a nut left over that had no place to go, or a missing bolt that had to be replaced as it had been lost.

After the latest repair of a new gear box we went for a drive. The MOT was not as strict in those days and the indicator lights had only recently been put on the list of items to be checked. The indicator system was broken on Bob's car.

'That'll be OK because I can wind down the window and do a hand signal which is legal.'

All was well until he discovered that he couldn't open the window with one hand: he had to use two.

'That'll be OK,' he assured me, 'You can hold on to the steering wheel steadily for me whilst I open to window with two hands to indicate.' All went well and after he had indicated he shut the window and returned both hands to the wheel.

The car was running well until the gears kept slipping out so Bob had to hold on to the gear stick as he drove.

'What is going to happen when you have to indicate?' I asked.

'That'll be OK,' he said, 'you hold the gear stick firmly with one hand and the steering wheel with the other whilst I open the window and indicate.'

So I held the gear stick and the steering wheel while he wound down the windows with both hands and indicated.

'There is no knob on the gear stick!' I said.

'I know I couldn't find it when we had finished putting the gear box in, I'll have to get a new one from the scrap yard.'

'And I thought this was a new gear box. The gears shouldn't slip out like that!' My technical knowledge about cars was very weak. 'Should they?'

'No but this is a reconditioned gear box. Geoff was able to get this at a very reasonable price!'

The Countryman's life was to come to an end when the reconditioned gear box failed. One of our trips to the island coincided with a visit with Carolyn. We travelled back together. Robert was holding the gear stick in his hand throughout. Carolyn was in the back and we were overtaking a car just outside Guildford when the fourth gear went and the car slowed down. The car we were overtaking overtook us on the inside.

'What's happening?' I said. 'Why are you slowing down?'

'I'm not. The car is!' he replied.

Tentatively he drove on using the third gear.

'Carolyn, I'll take you to Richmond. 'You can get a train home from there,' Bob said. 'I don't think the gear box is going to last much longer.'

'OK!' she replied.

Shortly after that was agreed the third gear failed and we struggled to Richmond in second gear, dropped Carolyn off at the station and then he drove me back to the flat.

The Countryman was taken back to Geoff who decided that Bob should get a new car.

'I have got a mate who is selling his Morris Minor,' Geoff enthused, 'and at a very good price.'

We had the Morris Minor for a while until it had to go for its MOT in October 1969. This test was much stricter that it had been. Bob took it to the MOT centre and it failed as it needed four new tyres.

Bob took the car to Geoff.

Without checking it further Geoff assured him 'I know it is mechanically sound. Get four new tyres! It's fine!'

With four new tyres Bob confidently took it back for the MOT. It failed again. Neither the previous tester nor Geoff had looked at the bottom of the car, it was so rusted that it was not safe.

I worked for Honeywell in Brentford and I heard that Daniel who also worked there had a Morris Traveller which needed new tyres. A price was agreed to buy the new tyres from our car. He came to the flat where we had parked the Morris Minor.

Daniel jacked it up ready to take off the front offside wheel. He turned his back to pick up a spanner when suddenly there was a loud crunch as the jack went through the floor. The car ended up down on its wheels on the tarmac; the jack had disappeared completely through the floor of the car. With planks of wood Bob and Daniel together managed to get the new tyres off, replacing them with Daniel's old ones. The car stayed in the car park to be removed by a Scrap Merchant taking it away to his yard.

With two wages coming in and no rent to pay on the tied flat we were able to get a more upmarket car and we were free from breakdowns for a many years.

We stayed at the flat in Pitshanger Lane for 18 months. I was left some money in Clare Woodward's will in 1971 and immediately invested this into a house in Greenford. 'She always gave us lovely Christmas and Birthday presents!' I said to Bob at her funeral, 'and now the best present ever.'

In February 1972 we moved to Greenford and stayed there until 2013 when we moved back to the Isle of Wight.

POSTSCRIPT

In 2013 I came home. Bob and I retired from our jobs and moved back to my Island.

'I married a London policeman in 1969. He came from Sevenoaks in Kent and we made our home close to his work in London.' I tell people when they ask me why I chose to retire to the Isle of Wight. 'Now he is retired he has come home with me.'

I am the last of the four Drawbridges that lived at 11 Church Road, Binstead and who spent the first quarter of her life here in this pretty place.

There have been many changes to the area but they have not dulled the memories. I drive down Church Road and pass number 11. The fields that surrounded it are all gone and are replaced by houses. The woods I played in are now securely fenced off which prevents my access to view where I played "Kick the Can".

'But you are too old for that sort of game now Nan,' Millie my granddaughter reminds me.

'Sadly, yes, I am,' I reply, longing to play the game again.

Holy Cross Church is nearly the same as it was. The church porch is unchanged, the climbing rose bush that is visible in Mum and Dad's wedding picture and was always there during my childhood is still alive on the right side. Despite the fire in 1969 which destroyed the roof of the nave, the whole building remains as lovely as ever. However, there are some scorch marks on the pews where the burning rafters fell. The new roof rafters which used to be black are now pale brown and beautiful. The craftsmen who rebuilt it have made it a work of art. I have re-joined choir and look down from the gallery at the pew where Mum and Dad used to sit on the right hand side in the middle. The large oil painting that was on the wall between the first and second windows was burnt in the fire. A few of the stained glass windows were lost and have been replaced by magnificent new ones.

There is no evidence of the small holly and ivy fire that Mum put out in the middle south window long ago during the Christmas Nine Lessons and Carols Service in 1955. I am the only witness to that event.

The font where Carolyn and I were christened has been moved to the east end of the north aisle. The iron gates to the chancel are gone as are the two boys' choir stalls which seated eight. There is now only a women's choir. The altar has been moved away from the wall giving enough space for the minister to stand and walk behind whilst delivering the service. A kitchen and a toilet have been added.

Some of the old upright tomb stones have been relocated to close beside the outer wall. 'It was necessary to move them out of the way of the builders who were repairing the church roof,' Hillary, still a choir member and now one of the Lay Readers told me. However the flat ones we climbed on are still in place.

In Partlands Avenue, Ryde nothing remains to hint that there was a Parents National Teachers Union (PNEU) school. The building in which the school met had started out as a large Victorian family home. With the school gone, it was changed into flats.

Binstead School in Arnold Road has been converted into three dwellings. The front door and the steps, down which I was pushed, are visible. The playground where I played, chased the boys and the May Day celebrations took place now has three houses built on it. Some of the original surrounding wall remains. There is a new modern Binstead School, where the records for the previous school are stored. The head teacher was kind enough to let me view them and I found my name amongst other pupils who entered the school at the same time. I was also given access to the diary which recorded very briefly events that occurred. There were references to the architect calling. I surmised that this was about the building of new modern toilets to replace the long bank of antiquated privies.

St. Therese Presentation Convent next to the Catholic Church in High Street Ryde is still standing and from the High Street looks very much like it did in the 1960s. However, when viewed from the back in Warwick Street, the building is shown to be in a sad and derelict condition. The paintwork is peeling and the windows are either smashed or boarded up. The playground where I excelled at hitting the ball in a game of "Rounders" is now used as a private car park for residents.

There is a public pay and display car park at the bottom of the Mead Tennis Club in Church Lane, Ryde where we went in the summer term to play tennis. Opposite the entrance to the Diamond Club, better known to us as "The Hole", is bricked up. The hockey pitch in Players Lane now is part of Ryde Academy High School.

The long path leading to Binstead Beach still has the large cobbles set in the earth which can trip you up. The smell of the stagnant water at the end of the path just before you reach the beach is still there but the entrance to the beach is different. Wooden steps have been erected as the path where the strange naked man cut us off that day has disappeared. Binstead beach, once a lovely playground is now devoid of any sand in the area where we used to sit. I discover as I paddle that the blue slipper clay that squeezed between my toes in the 1950s is still there. The tree we used to climb is gone as the sea continues to wash away the foreshore.

'This is due,' a local man walking his dog tells me, 'to the large Fishbourne to Portsmouth car ferries. They had to dredge a deeper channel because the boats are so much bigger.'

'What has happened to reed beds which stretched out there and created a peninsula?' I ask.

'A rumour has it that the Oil Refinery at Fawley near Southampton dumped poisonous waste into the Solent and that killed the vegetation.'

I sigh, 'There's not much left that reminds me of the fun we had on the beach.' I look down and pick up one of the many flat stones. 'My Dad taught me to skim stones across the surface of the water.' The tide was far enough in for me to try. I held the stone in my right hand gripping it with my thumb and first finger. Holding it flat I throw it across the water. 'Look two bounces!'

'If you want to find the sand it's at Appley,' the dog walker continues. 'There is a west to east drift in the tide and the sand has ended up in Ryde mainly at Appley.'

'That's right. Years ago when the tide was in it came right up to the wall in front of the huts. Now the sand covers a large area, and there must be 25 metres of sand before you get to the water when the tide is in.'

'You're right there!' he continues, 'you can now almost step down from the walkway to the sand. In the 1950s there was a long drop and you could see more of the wall.'

'And there are now only three steps in front of Appley Tower,' I continue, 'there used to be 12 or 13.'

The weather also is eating away at the coasts along the Military Road. The lovely beaches are now used extensively by surfers throughout the year. Every winter more of the cliffs fall into the sea and the road has had to be moved further inland. Families still crowd these beaches in the summer months to enjoy the flat sands and rock pools.

The author with her mother and sister, Carolyn, walk along the beach at Appley in 1951. The sea is coming in and the wall, unlike today, is more exposed.

When returning home from Newport to Ryde we often take the Downs Road. 'Shall we go over the top?' asks Robert, my husband.

'Oh yes, of course,' I reply – I never say 'no'.

We take the Sandown Road, pass by Arreton and then turn into the Downs Road at the 'Hare and Hounds'. We look to our right and see the whole of the south of the Island. We continue down the hill and up again where we follow the road to Ryde. At the top just after the turning to Brading we look to the left and see the north of the Island, the Solent and Portsmouth.

'Look how beautiful it is today,' Robert says.

Printed in Great Britain
by Amazon